"十三五"江苏省高等学校重点教材（编号2017-1-047）

An Introduction to Chinese and Western Culture

中西文化概况

（修订版）

主　编◎孔　文　颜榴红
编　者◎邱　菲　王小燕　Dave Hufton

本书配套资源

南京大学出版社

前　言

　　目前国际交流日益频繁,了解本国及英语国家的文化背景、风土民情及社会习俗等,不仅是学好语言、成功交际的关键,更能提升自身文化修养与内涵。不同民族在其不同的生态环境下创造了自己特有的文化,而母语文化与目的语文化之间的差异往往会导致语用失误,从而影响交际。外语学习到了一定的阶段,其主要障碍已不在语言本身,而在于学习者对目的语和母语文化知识的了解程度,以及在此基础上形成的对两种文化差异的思辨。成功的交际很大程度上取决于了解彼此文化背景的程度。跨文化交际不是同一种文化之间的交际,也不是文化融入,必须同时强调母语文化与目的语文化素质的培养,不能只重视外族文化,而忽视或放弃自己的文化根基。为此,我们为广大英语学习者编写了这本《中西文化概况》。

　　本教材自 2014 年 10 月由南京大学出版社出版和发行以来,得到全国高校从事中西方文化教学的同行教师认可,受到广大学生的喜爱。2016 年 8 月重印,2018 年 1 月荣获 2017年江苏省高等学校重点规划教材(修订教材)建设立项。这一系列成绩的取得既是对我们以往努力的肯定,令我们备受鼓舞,也督促我们修订教材时更加严格要求自己,精益求精。

　　本教材分别对英美文化和中国文化进行了较为全面、系统、精炼的介绍,主要具有以下特点:

　　1. 结构明晰:本教材共有十章,每章一个主题,分别介绍英国、美国和中国文化。每个章节后附有词汇表,以方便学习者自学;课外阅读部分主要利用网络资源,向学习者推荐加拿大、澳大利亚和新西兰国家的相应主题文化;小组任务部分则针对每一章的主题文化设计了相应问题,旨在帮助学习者培养其思考问题和解决问题的能力。

　　2. 选材时效性、趣味性强:本教材所选材料内容新颖,图文并茂,增加了教材的形象性、活泼性和趣味性。

　　3. 语言难易适中:本教材尽量选用常用词汇,个别较难词汇列在每一章的词汇表中。英文注解部分可以帮助学习者更深入地了解相关专有名词的文化内涵,充分体现了语言学习和文化学习的相互渗透。

　　4. 课堂教学与自主学习相结合:本教材主课文部分可供教师根据学生水平和具体课时

选用进行课堂教学;课外阅读部分可用于培养学习者自主探寻获取信息的能力;小组任务既涉及对所学内容的思考,又超越了书本内容,旨在帮助学习者培养自主构建知识和探索创新的能力。

在本次修订过程中,为使教材内容更加充实、新颖,语言更加流畅和通俗易懂。本教材补充和完善了以下内容:

1. 由原来九章增加到十章,增加了第四章哲学。

2. 更新章节部分内容。譬如,更新了历史内容,添加了英国脱欧,特雷莎·梅当选首相,特朗普当选美国总统,以"中国梦"为目标,"一带一路"建设等。

3. 对中国文学和民间艺术方面内容进行了拓展。譬如,添加了近年来中国当代作家作品,丰富了雕刻、剪刻、织绣、表演、装饰陈设等方面的中国民间艺术内容。

4. 对原教材语言重新进行了审校。

本教材不仅可以作为高等院校中英文化教材,也适用于广大涉外工作人员、英语教师和英语学习者更好地了解中英文化。

本教材编者在编写过程中参考了众多现有的国内外出版的教材、报纸、杂志,借鉴了大量的网络文本和图片资源,在此表示由衷的感谢。

衷心感谢英国的 Dave Hufton 博士,他不仅是位教育家,更是一名哲学家,而且对中国文化也颇有研究。他为本教材的每个章节精心设计了小组任务,这些任务引人深思,极具挑战性,为每个章节起到了画龙点睛的作用。

由于中西文化涉及内容多,覆盖领域广,加之编者水平有限,书中难免有不足疏漏之处,敬请广大读者和专家批评指正。本教材在编写过程中得到常州大学和周有光语言文化学院领导的大力支持,得到南京大学出版社有关编辑的帮助,在此表示衷心的感谢。

编 者

2019 年 6 月

Contents

Chapter 1   Geography

Section A   Geography of the United Kingdom

1. Physical Geography

The United Kingdom of Great Britain and Northern Ireland, commonly known as the United Kingdom (or the U.K.), or simply Britain, is a sovereign state located off the northwestern coast of continental Europe. It includes Scotland, England, Wales and Northern Ireland (not actually on the island of Great Britain). The total area of the U.K. is approximately 245,000 km^2 with a population of about 60 million people (2009 estimate). The U.K. lies between the North Atlantic and the North Sea, and comes within 35 km of the northwest coast of France, from which it is separated by the English Channel. The Channel Tunnel bordered beneath the English Channel, now links the U.K. with France.

Geographical Location of the U.K.

▶ England

England is in the southern part of Great Britain and is divided into nine governmental regions. It is sometimes, wrongly, used in reference to the whole United Kingdom, the entire island of Great Britain, or indeed the British Isles. This is not only incorrect but can cause offence to people from other parts of the U.K.

The south of England is mostly low-lying land, with hills and agricultural land and the north of England is mostly covered in moorlands and mountains. England covers over 50,000 square miles (130, 439 km^2)

England

and is the largest of the countries comprising the island of Britain, covering about two-thirds of the island. No place in England is more than 75 miles (120 km) from the sea.

The landscape is determined mainly by different types of rocks underlying it. In the south, chalk has produced the gently rolling hills of the Downs[1], while hard granite is the basis for the mountains of the north and the high moorlands in the southwest. Much of the land in England is flat (low-lying)—less than 1,000 m above the sea level, forming meadowlands and pastures and less than 10 percent of the area is covered by wood-

The River Thames

lands. Farmers raise animals or grow crops in the fields. The landscape of England is more rugged in the north and the west. The highest elevations are in Cumbria and the Lake District in the west. The southwest is a long peninsula with bleak moorlands and rocky outcrop. In the southeast, a horseshoe-shaped ring of chalk downs surrounds the formerly wooded area of the Weald[2]. The southeast corner has dramatic chalk cliffs bordering the English Channel. England's best known river is the River Thames which flows through southern England. It is the longest river in England and the second longest in the U.K., next to River Severn. England has a long coastline of 3,200 km. In the south and west, the coastline can be rocky with steep cliffs. The east coast is often flat and low-lying with beaches and mud flats.

▶ Scotland

Scotland is a mountainous country in the north of Great Britain and shares a land border to the south with England and is bounded by the North Sea on the east and the Atlantic Ocean on the west. Its capital city is Edinburgh. Scotland has some 790 islands. It is famous for its fresh water lochs—there are over 600 square miles of them. One of the most famous is Loch Ness where a mysterious monster is said to lurk in the depths of the water. It is also famous for its clans, kilts, medieval castles, as well as poetry and songs of Robert Burns. Theatre lovers from around the world come to Edinburgh for its famous theatre festivals.

Scotland

Scotland's terrain is divided into three regions: the Highlands, the Central Lowlands, and the Southern Uplands. The Highlands cover more than one-half of Scotland and include the Grampian Mountains. The range's highest peak, Ben Nevis (1,343 m/4,406 ft), is also the highest in Great Britain. Scotland's population is concentrated in the Central Lowlands, which include the cities of Glasgow and Edinburgh. The Southern Uplands primarily consist of a moorland plateau with valleys and mountainous outcroppings. The River Clyde is the principal navigational river.

▶ Wales

Wales is situated on the western side of central southern Great Britain. It is a mountainous land, bordered by England to the east, the Bristol Channel to the south, St George's Channel in the west, and the Irish Sea to the north. It is about 274 km from north to south and at least 97 km wide, with a total area of 20,779 km^2.

Wales

Wales has a varied geography with sharp contrasts. In the south, flat coastal plains give way to valleys, then to ranges of hills and mountains in mid and north Wales. There are many national parks and areas with outstanding natural beauty. 80 percent of the land is dedicated to agriculture, ranging from crops to livestock. The largest mountains in the north are part of the Snowdonia range, with the largest mountain being Snowdon at 1,085 m. There are over 1,300 km of coastline ranging from long flat sandy beaches to towering cliffs.

▶ Northern Ireland

Northern Ireland is an integral part of the U.K.. It is situated in the northeastern portion of the island of Ireland. Northern Ireland is also known as Ulster, because it consists of six of the nine counties that were parts of the former province of Ulster: Antrim, Armagh, Down, Fermanagh, Londonderry, and Tyrone. Northern Ireland measures about 85 miles (135 km) north and south, and about 110 miles (175 km) east and west.

Northern Ireland

Northern Ireland's landforms were influenced greatly by Ice Age glaciers. The terrain consists of rounded hills and low mountains separated by broad valleys. Only in a few areas do deep, steep-sided valleys cut the land. Principal mountain ranges include the Mourne Mountains in the southeast and the Sperrin Mountains in the northwest. Slieve Donard, in the Mournes, is the country's highest peak, reaching 2,796 ft (852 m) above the sea level, where the mountains extend to the sea, the coasts are marked by cliffs and steep slopes.

2. Climate

Regional climates in the U.K. are influenced by the Atlantic Ocean and latitude. Northern Ireland, Wales and western parts of England and Scotland, being closest to the Atlantic Ocean, are generally the mildest, wettest and windiest regions of the U.K., and temperature ranges here are seldom extreme. Eastern areas are drier, cooler, less windy and also experience the greatest daily and seasonal temperature variations. Northern areas are generally cooler, wetter and have slightly larger temperature ranges than southern areas. Though the U.K. is mostly under the influence of the maritime tropical air mass from the southwest, different regions are more susceptible than others when different air masses affect the country: Northern Ireland and the west of Scotland are the most exposed to the maritime polar air mass which brings cool moist air; the east of Scotland and northeast England are more exposed to the continental polar air mass which brings cold dry air; the south and southeast of England are more exposed to the continental tropical air mass which brings warm dry air (and consequently the warmest summer temperatures most of the time); and Wales and the southwest of England are the most exposed to the maritime tropical air mass which brings warm moist air. If the air masses are strong enough in their respective areas during the summer, there can sometimes be a huge difference in temperature between the far north of Scotland (including the Islands) and southeast of England—usually around 10 – 15℃ (50 – 59℉) but can be as much as 20℃ (68℉) or more. An example of this could be that in the height of summer the Northern Isles could have temperatures around 15℃ (59℉) and areas around London could reach 30℃ (86℉). However, the temperature varies with the seasons, seldom drops below −11℃ (12℉) or rises above 35℃ (95℉).

Section B   Geography of the United States of America

The United States of America or the U.S.A. is a country in the Northern Hemisphere, Western Hemisphere, and the Eastern Hemisphere. It consists of forty-eight contiguous states in North America, Alaska, a peninsula which forms the most northwestern part of North America, and Hawaii, an archipelago in the Pacific Ocean. There are several U.S. territories in the Pacific and Caribbean. The term "United States", when used in the geographical sense, means the continental U.S., Alaska, Hawaii, Puerto Rico, Guam, and the Virgin Islands of the U.S.. The country shares land borders with Canada and Mexico and maritime (water) borders with Russia, Cuba, and the Bahamas in addition to Canada and Mexico.

1. Physical Geography

The United States of America may be divided into seven broad physiographic divisions from east to west: the Atlantic Plain, the Appalachian Highlands, the Interior Plains, the Interior Highlands, the Rocky Mountain System, the Intermountain Region, and the Pacific Mountain System.

▶ The Atlantic Plain

The Atlantic Plain is a rather flat stretch of land that borders the Atlantic Ocean (including the Gulf of Mexico). It is approximately 2,200 miles long, stretching from Cape Cod, through the southeast U. S. and through Mexico, ending with the Yucatan Peninsula. The western border of the coastal plain is easily defined by a long series of mountain ranges, including the Appalachian Mountains and the Great Smoky Mountains. The eastern border isn't well defined since most of the plain is at or

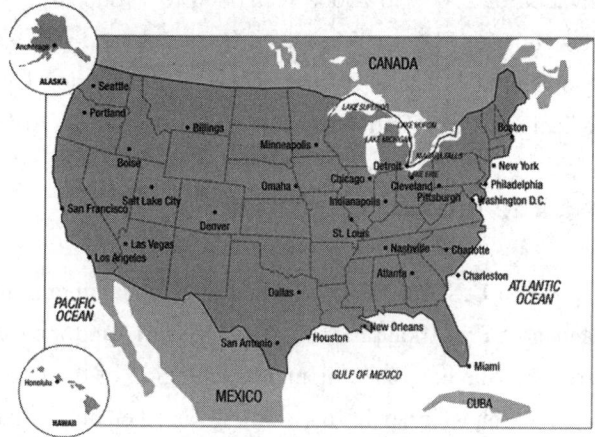

Geographical Location of the U.S.

below the sea level. Some define the east border to be the coastline. Currently, the coastal plain is very wet, including many rivers, marshes and swamplands. It is primarily used for agriculture.

▶ The Appalachian Highlands

Appalachian Highlands, an upland area of eastern North America, chiefly in the U.S., extends from eastern Canada to central Alabama. The entire system is almost 2,000 miles (3,200 km) long, and up to 300 miles (480 km) wide. The region's higher and rougher parts form the so-called Appalachian Mountains.

The Appalachians first formed roughly 480 million years ago during the Ordovician Period, and once reached elevations similar to those of the Alps and the Rocky Mountains before they were eroded. The Appalachian chain is a barrier to east-west travel as it forms a series of alternating ridgelines and valleys oriented in opposition to any road running east-west. The scenic beauty of mountains, streams, forests and the region's historic sites make the Appalachians a popular vacation area.

▶ The Interior Plains

The Interior Plains, the largest physical region in the U.S., are located west of the Appalachian Highlands, east of the Rocky Mountains, and north of the Gulf Coastal Plain. The region's greatest dimensions are about 1,200 miles (1,900 km) east-west and 1,300 miles (2,100 km) north-south. Thick beds of sedimentary rocks underlie this vast area of plains. North of the Missouri and Ohio rivers are deep glacial deposits.

At about the 100th meridian, the Interior Plains divide into the Great Plains, to the west, and the Central Lowlands, to the east. Both sections have vast stretches of flat land and of gently rolling land. A major difference between the two areas is elevation—the Great Plains lie at an elevation of 2,000 to 6,000 feet (600 to 1,800 m), and the Central Lowlands are much lower. The Interior Plains are bordered by two upland regions—the Superior Uplands on the north, and the Central Uplands on the south. The Superior Uplands are in Minnesota, Wisconsin, and Michigan. The Central Uplands are in Missouri, Arkansas, and Oklahoma.

● The Interior Highlands

The U.S. Interior Highlands is a mountainous region spanning eastern Oklahoma, western and northern Arkansas, southern Missouri, and the extreme southeast corner of Kansas. The area refers to the combined mountainous region of the Ozarks and Ouachita Mountains, which form a distinct physiographic division. It is the only major highland region between the Rocky Mountains and the Appalachian Mountains in the U.S..

The region is occupied by the Ozark mountain forests, an ecoregion of temperate broadleaf and mixed forests. Parts of the area are covered by three national forests: the Ouachita National Forest in Oklahoma and Arkansas, the Ozark-St. Francis National Forest in Arkansas, and the Mark Twain National Forest in Missouri.

● The Rocky Mountain System

The Rocky Mountain Range actually represents a series of more than 100 separate mountain ranges, rather than one uninterrupted mountain chain. These ranges stretch through New Mexico, Idaho, Montana, Wyoming, Utah and Colorado, and also extend into British Columbia and Alberta, Canada. The entire series of mountain ranges measure approximately 3,000 miles. Mount Elbert near Leadville, Colorado, has an elevation of 14,433 feet, making it the tallest peak in the mountain range. The popular Pikes Peak, the second most visited peak in the world, is the 31st highest, rising 14,110 feet above the sea level.

Mount Elbert in July

Because of the vast expanse covered by the Rocky Mountain Range, it holds several national parks. Rocky Mountain National Park, Yellowstone National Park, Grand Teton National Park, Glacier National Park and the Royal Gorge Park, all give guests the opportunity to explore the Rockies. It also serves as the habitat to 66 mammal species, including the rare lynx and wolverine.

● The Intermountain (Intermontane) Region

The Intermountain Region or the Intermountain West is located between the Rocky Mountains on the east and the Cascade Range and Sierra Nevada on the west. It covers the state of Utah and the neighboring parts of Arizona, Nevada, Colorado, western Wyoming, eastern Idaho, and a small portion of southwestern Montana.

Its wetlands, rivers, and lakes provide habitats for many birds. The Intermountain Region is a home to a massive 1.6 million breeding ducks and over 100,000 over-wintering ducks, geese, and swans. It is thinly populated because people don't have the proper necessities to live there along with the proper food supply. This is a good thing because the land is left alone for the animals to enjoy, and it leaves the environment in a beautiful state.

● The Pacific Mountain System

Between the Intermountain Region and the Pacific Ocean is the Pacific Mountain System, the series of mountain ranges that stretch along the West Coast of North America from Alaska south to Northern and Central Mexico. It runs for some 4,500 miles (7,250 km) in the U.S. and extends northward into Canada for another 1,000 miles (1,600 km). This province includes the active and sometimes dead or extinct volcanoes of the Cascade Range and the young, steep mountains of the Pacific Border and the Sierra Nevada.

The Cascade Range is a backpacker's paradise. Hikers can experience a striking ecological transition across the range, from temperate rain forests on the western, windward slopes to open pine savanna and shrub steppes on the eastern. The Sierra Nevada is a 400-mile-long mountain range of singular beauty. While the Sierra high country has its share of rugged topography, including sawtoothed volcanic ridges and some mighty river gorges, much of it offers the backpacker remarkably gentle terrain of undulating granite highlands, as well as some of the most moderate mountain weather.

2. Climate

The climate in U.S. varies across different parts of the country. Generally, the western and southern parts of U.S. have warmer weather as compared with the eastern and northern parts. The eastern and northern parts of U.S. experience chilly winters with heavy snowfalls but the summers are pleasant. The western and southern parts have extremely hot summers and comparatively tolerable winters.

The U.S. can be divided into six climate regions (Northwest Pacific, Mid/South Pacific, Midwest, Northeast, Southeast, Southwest), excluding Alaska, Hawaii and outlying territories.

The climate varies considerably among different regions.

Northwest Pacific (*Includes states like Oregon and Washington to the crest of the Cascade Mountains*)

This is perhaps the wettest part of the country. There are scattered rain showers all year round. Temperatures are mild averaging around 40 ℉ (32.2 ℃). The summer months are pleasantly warmer and never too hot. You can see fogs along the coast during the warmer weather but the fog is less dense during mid-day.

Mid/South Pacific Rockies (*Includes states like California, Idaho, Montana, Wyoming, Colorado, Utah and Nevada*)

These states have generally dry and delightful summers. California has excellent weather all the year round, with the northern part of the state somewhat cooler (quiet chilly in the winter but seldom freezing). There are few places in California that experience snow, and the state is known for its nice weather. Most of the cities have tolerable winters. The winter months in the other states like Montana, Idaho and Wyoming can be very cold, with temperatures dropping well below 0 ℉ (-17.8℃). Colorado, Utah and Nevada are known for their excellent skiing.

Midwest (*Includes states like Dakotas, Kansas, Illinois, Iowa, Minnesota, Wisconsin, Michigan, and Indiana*)

This region is moderately dry. Precipitation occurs mainly in late spring and early summer. Summers are pleasant but winter time can be harsh, with lots of snow and heavy chilly winds. Extremes within the Midwest can drop down to -50℉ (-45.6℃).

Northeast (*Includes states like Ohio, Pennsylvania, Washington D.C., and Maryland*).

This entire area is moderately rainy. In winter, the region experiences heavy snow and freezing rain. Summers are usually pleasant, sunny and warm. The fall is especially beautiful in wooded areas.

Southeast (*Includes states like portions of Arkansas and Louisiana, Kentucky, West Virginia, Virginia*)

Like the Northeast, this entire area experiences moderate rains fairly and evenly throughout the year. The spring, summer and fall seasons are all very pleasant. Some snow and freezing rain fall in winter, but for the most parts, the winters are quite mild and short lived. Southern Florida, like California, usually has excellent weather all the year round.

Southwest (*Includes states like Arizona, New Mexico, Texas, Oklahoma and western portions of Arkansas and Louisiana*)

This is the hottest and high rainfall region of the U.S.. You must be prepared to face heavy rains accompanied with thunder storms, dangerous lightening and occasional tornadoes. The winters are generally short but some freezing rains do occur. The spring and fall seasons are quite long and temperatures are generally excellent. The summers are very hot with temperatures approaching and exceeding 100℉ (37.8℃) on many days.

Section C　Geography of China

Located in the east on the Asian continent on the western shore of the Pacific Ocean, the People's Republic of China (PRC) is the world's most populous country, with a population of over 1.35 billion. Covering approximately 9.6 million km^2, China is the world's second largest country by land area, and the third largest country in total area behind Russia and Canada, and very similar to the U.S..

1. Physical Geography

China has been officially and conveniently divided into 5 homogeneous physical macro-regions: namely Eastern China (subdivided into the northeast plain, north plain, and southern hills), the Xinqiang-Mongolian uplands, and the Tibetan highlands.

▶ Eastern China

Northeast Plain

Northeast plain is also called Manchurian Plain or Sungliao Plain, heart of the central lowland of northeastern China. It has a surface area of about 135,000 square miles (350,000 km^2), all of which lies below 1,000 feet (300 m) above the sea level. The plain, largely the product of erosion from the surrounding highlands, is mostly undulating, with fertile black soils. It is bordered on the west by the Da Hinggan Range, on the north by the Xiao Hinggan Range, and on the east by the Changbai ranges, but on the south it is open to the Gulf of Liaodong. It is drained by the Sungari River [3] and its tributary, the Nen River, in the north and by the Liao River in the south. It connects via a narrow strip of coastal plain with the great alluvial North China Plain to the southwest.

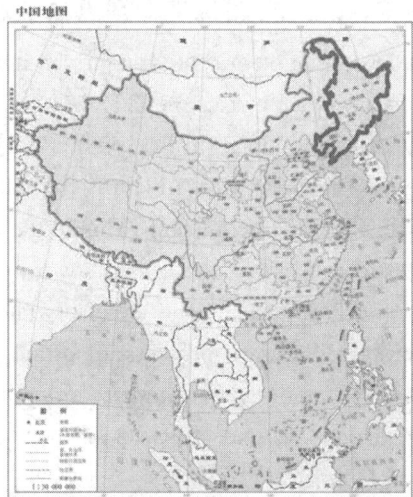

Northeast Plain

　　The Northeast Plain is China's major soybean-growing area, and it also produces corn (maize), rice, wheat, sorghum, sugar beets, and flax. After 1949, large state farms were established and land reclamation projects begun. It is also an important base of heavy industry with an extensive system of railways, and it is rich in natural resources (iron ore, coal, and oil).

The major industrial cities on the plain are Harbin, Shenyang, and Changchun. The Sanjiang Plain at the confluence of the Sungari, Amur[4], and Ussuri[5] rivers in the far northeast is generally considered to be part of the Northeast Plain.

North Plain

North plain, also called Yellow Plain or Huang-Huai-Hai Plain, is a large alluvial plain of northern China, built up along the shore of the Yellow Sea by deposits of the Yellow River and the Huaihai, and a few other minor rivers of northern China. Covering an area of about 158,000 square miles (409,500 km^2), most of which is below 160 feet (50 metres) above the sea level, it is one of the most densely populated areas in the world; since earliest times, it has been a major focus of Chinese (Han) culture. The plain is bordered on the north by the Yan Mountains, on the west by the Taihang Mountains and the Henan highlands, and on the southwest by the Tongbai and Dabie mountains. To the south it merges into the Yangtze Plain. From northeast to southeast it fronts the Bo Hai, the hills of Shandong Peninsula, and the Yellow Sea. Most of the rivers flow across the plain on elevated beds that are above the surrounding areas. Beijing, the national capital, is located on the northwest

The Taihang Mountains
in North Plain

The Penglai Pavilion
in Shandong Peninsula

edge of the plain, and Tianjin, an important industrial city and commercial port, is situated near the northeast coast. The Grand Canal, beginning at Beijing, crosses the eastern part of the plain and then continues to the south and southeast to Suzhou and Hangzhou.

The North China Plain is the gift of the Yellow River and the other streams which flow out from northwestern China. This fertile plain is a region of wide diversification in crops. One-quarter to one-half of the land is sown to winter wheat in October, the amount being greater in the south. Barley and beans are also winter crops. Kaoliang (Sorghum) is the leading spring-planted crop. Millet is slightly less important, although locally it may exceed kaoliang. Cotton and hemp are scattered widely. Summer cropping consists of corn, millet, soybean, sweet potatoes, peanuts, and sesame. Tobacco is also locally important.

South (Hills)

East of the Tibetan Plateau, deeply folded mountains fan out toward the Sichuan Basin, which is ringed by mountains in 1,000 – 3,000 m elevations. The floor of the basin has an average elevation of 500 m and is home to one of the most densely farmed and populated regions of China. The Sichuan Basin is capped in the north by the eastward continuation of the Kunlun range, the Qinling and Dabashan. The Qinling and Dabashan ranges form a major north-south division across China Proper, the traditional core area of China. Southeast of the Tibetan Plateau and south of the Sichuan Basin is the Yunnan-Guizhou Plateau, which occupies much of southwest China. This plateau, with an average elevation of 2,000 m, is known for limestone karst landscape.

The core of South China is the fertile Yangtze Plain—often divided into middle and lower parts. About 70 percent of the Yangtze Plain is cultivated. Rice is the major crop and it has long been the primary commercial grain; the other main crop is winter wheat. The majority of South China's population is located on or near it; it contains nearly all of the region's major manufacturing centers; and it is the most prosperous part of South China, producing more wealth than the rest of the region combined.

▶ The Xinjiang-Mongolian Uplands

The Xinjiang-Mongolian Uplands occupy the vast desert areas of northwestern China. Northwest of the Tibetan Plateau, between the northern slope of Kunlun and southern slope of Tian Shan, is the vast Tarim Basin of Xinjiang. The Tarim Basin, the largest in China, measures 1,500 km from east to west and 600 km from north to south at its widest parts. Average elevation in the basin is 1,000 m. To east, the basin descends into the Hami-Turpan Depression of eastern Xinjiang, where the dried lake bed of Lake Ayding at −154 m below the sea level, is the lowest surface point in China and the third lowest in the world. With temperatures that have reached 49.6 ℃, the lake bed ranks as the hottest place in China. North of Tian Shan is Xinjiang's second great basin, the Jungar. The Jungar Basin is enclosed to the north by the Altay Mountains which separates Xinjiang from Russia and Mongolia.

Northeast of the Tibetan Plateau, the Altun Shan-Qilian Mountains range branches off the Kunlun and creates a parallel mountain range running east-west. In between in northern Qinghai is the Qaidam Basin, with elevation of 2,600 − 3,000 m and numerous brackish and salt lakes. North of the Qilian is Hexi Corridor of Gansu, a natural passage between Xinjiang and China Proper that was part of the ancient Silk Road and traversed by modern highway and rail lines to Xinjiang. Further north, the Inner Mongolian Plateau, between 900 − 1,500 m in elevation, arcs north up the spine of China and becomes the Da Hinggan Range of Northeast China.

Between the Qinling and the Inner Mongolian Plateau is Loess Plateau, the largest of its kind in the world, covering 650,000 km^2 in Shaanxi, parts of Gansu and Shanxi provinces, and some of Ningxia-Hui Autonomous Region. The plateau is 1,000 − 1,500 m in elevation and is filled with loess, a yellowish loose soil that travels easily in the wind. Eroded loess silt gives the Yellow River its color and name. The Loess Plateau is bound to the east by the Luliang Mountain of Shanxi, which has a narrow basin running north to south along the Fen River. Further east is the Taihang Mountains of Hebei, the dominant topographical feature of North China. Important products in this area are cotton, tomatoes, oat and so forth. In the more arid grasslands, herding of goats or sheep is a traditional method of subsistence.

▶ The Tibetan Highlands

Mount Everest

This region lies in southwestern China, with an area approximately 2 million km² and an average elevation, 4,000 - 5,000 m. It consists of a vast plateau bordered by towering mountains, the Himalaya on the south, the Pamirs on the west, and the Kunlun on the north. The world's highest mountain, Mount Everest, rises 29,028 feet (8,848 metres) above the sea level in the Himalaya in southern Tibet. Two of the world's longest rivers, the Yellow River and the Yangtze River, begin in the highlands and flow eastward across China to the sea.

The northern and central parts of the Tibetan Highlands (known locally as Chang Tang) consist of flat or rolling plains (elevation 4,600 - 5,200 m) alternating with relatively short mountain ranges. The ranges have broad, flat watersheds, gentle slopes only slightly affected by erosional processes, and numerous bodies of rock fragments. Despite its enormous altitude, Chang Tang has the appearance of a region with middle-mountain topography; only individual peaks that rise above the snow line have glaciers and alpine characteristics. In the outlying areas of the Tibetan Highlands, especially the areas adjacent to the Tansiie Shan and the Himalayas, the elevation of the plains decreases to 3,500 m, and the plains frequently assume the form of intermontane basins. The slopes of the peripheral ranges are precipitous and strongly dissected, the river valleys (especially in the east) forming deep gorges.

The most important crop in Tibet is barley. Meat dishes are likely to be yak, goat, or mutton, often dried, or cooked into a spicy stew with potatoes. Mustard seed is cultivated in Tibet, and therefore features heavily in its cuisine. Yak yogurt, butter and cheese are frequently eaten, and well-prepared yogurt is considered something of a prestige item. Butter tea is very popular to drink. The beauty of Tibet's soaring Himalayas, the warmth of its nomadic and deeply devout people, and the mysteries of its ancient Buddhist monasteries attract tourists all over the world.

The Buddhist Monastery—
the Potala Palace

2. Climate

China's climate is extremely diverse. Since the country covers such a vast geographical area that stretches across 35 degrees of latitude, China's climate ranges from being sub-tropical in the south to sub-arctic in the north. Variations in land elevation also contribute to the extreme climatic differences.

Northeast China is known for its hot, dry summers and long, cold winters. In central China, the summers are hot and humid, with heavy rainfall during the late summer months. The climate on the Yunnan-Guizhou High Plateau is generally mild, with warm summers and cool winters and with very little rainfall. Southern China's climate, around Hong Kong and Guangdong province, is considered to be sub-tropical. Rainfall is evenly distributed throughout the year. Summers are long, hot and humid while the winters are short with cooler temperatures. On the Tibet Qinghai Plateau, summer is short and moderately warm while winters can get very cold at higher altitudes.

In general, the areas north of the Yangtze River have extremely cold winters but somewhat milder summers. The central area around the Yangtze River Valley has long hot summers with heavy precipitation from monsoons and typhoons. Monsoons are the winds that bring rain from the south in summer and snowstorms from the north in winter. Monsoons have been the source of massive flooding along the Yangtze for years. Typhoons typically hit the southeast coast between July and September.

Notes

1. **the Downs**: The Downs are a roadstead or area of sea in the southern North Sea near the English Channel off the east Kent coast, between the North and the South Foreland in southern England.

2. **the Weald**: The Weald is the name given to an area in South East England situated between the parallel chalk escarpments of the North and the South Downs. The Weald was once a vast forest covering this area. The name, Old English in origin, signifies woodland, which still applies today: scattered farms and villages betray the Weald's past, often in their names.

3. **the Sungari River**: The Sungari River (the Songhua River) is a river in Northeast China, and is the largest tributary of the Heilong River (Amur), flowing about 1,434 km from Changbai Mountains through Jilin and Heilongjiang provinces.

4. **the Amur River**: The Amur River or Heilong Jiang is the world's tenth longest river, forming the border between the Russian Far East and Northeastern China (Inner Manchuria). The largest fish species in the Amur is the kaluga, attaining a length as great as 5.6 metres.

5. **the Ussuri River**: The Ussuri River or Wusuli River runs in Khabarovsk and Primorsky Krais, Russia, and in the southeast of Northeast China. It is approximately 897 km long. The Ussuri River drains to the Ussuri basin, which covers 193,000 km^2. Its waters come from rain (60%), snow (30 − 35%) and subterranean springs.

Glossary

sovereign [ˈsɔvrin] *adj.* 有主权的

moorland [ˈmuələnd] *n.* 高沼地；广袤的荒野

chalk [tʃɔːk] *n.* (地质)白垩地层；石灰石

meadowland [ˈmedəulænd] *n.* 草地；牧场

pasture [ˈpɑːstʃə] *n.* 草地；山坡；牧场

rug [rʌg] *vt.* 用厚毯包裹

peninsular [piˈninsjulə] *adj.* 半岛的

outcrop [ˈautkrɔp] *n.* (岩层等的)露头

loch [lɔk] *n.* 湖；内河，内湾

lurk [ləːk] *vi.* 潜伏；埋伏；潜藏

kilt [kilt] *n.* (苏格兰高地男子穿的)褶叠短裙(通常用格子呢制作)

terrain [təˈrein] *n.* 地形，地面，地域，地带

Ulster[ˈʌlstə] *n.* 阿尔斯特(原为爱尔兰一地区)

archipelago[ˌɑːkiˈpeligəu] *n.* (*pl.* archipelagoes, archipelagos) 多岛海区；群岛，列岛

physiographic [ˈfiziːəuˈgræfik] *adj.* 地文学的,地形学的

sedimentary [sediˈmentəri] *adj.* 沉积的

deposit [diˈpɔzit] *n.* 沉积物；矿藏，矿床

lynx [liŋks] *n.* (*pl.* lynx, lynxes)猞猁狲，山猫

wolverine [ˈwulvəriːn] *n.* 狼獾，豹熊

savanna [səˈvænə] *n.* (美国东南部)无树平原

topography [təˈpɔgrəfi] *n.* 地形，地势，地貌

sawtooth [ˈsɔːtuːθ] *n.* 锯齿

gorge [gɔːdʒ] *n.* 峡，峡谷

undulate [ˈʌndjuleit] *vi.* (水面，风中的麦田等)波动，(土地等)起伏

homogeneous [ˌhɔməuˈdʒiːnjəs] *adj.* 同种的，同类的，相似的

tributary [ˈtribjutəri] *n.* 支流

alluvial [əˈluːvjəl] *adj.* 冲积的

sorghum [ˈsɔːgəm] *n.* 蜀黍，高粱

beet [biːt] *n.* 甜菜 [*pl.*] [美]亚麻捆

flax [flæks] *n.* 亚麻；亚麻纱，亚麻纤维

reclamation [ˌrekləˈmeiʃən] *n.* 开垦

confluence [ˈkɔnfluəns] *n.* 合流；汇流(处)

hemp [hemp] *n.* 大麻(纤维)

limestone [ˈlaimstəun] *n.* 石灰石

karst [kɑːst] *n.* 水蚀石灰岩地区

brackish [ˈbrækiʃ] *adj.* 含盐的；碱化的

loess ['ləuis] *n.* 黄土

subsistence [sʌb'sistəns] *n.* 生存，生计；给养

alpine ['ælpain] *adj.* 高山(性)的

peripheral [pə'rifərəl] *adj.* 周界的；边缘的

precipitous [pri'sipitəs] *adj.* 险峻的，陡峭的

mustard ['mʌstəd] *n.* 芥；芥末；芥菜酱

yak [jæk] *n.* 牦牛(主要产于中国西藏)

yogurt ['jəugət] *n.* 酸奶；酸乳酪

nomadic [nəu'mædik] *adj.* 游牧的；流浪的

devout [di'vaut] *adj.* 热诚的，虔诚的

monsoon [mɔn'suːn] *n.* 季(节)风

Further Reading

1) **Geography of Canada**

http://en.wikipedia.org/wiki/Geography_of_Canada

http://faculty.marianopolis.edu/c.belanger/QuebecHistory/encyclopedia/GeogofCan.htm

2) **Geography of Australia**

http://en.wikipedia.org/wiki/Geography_of_Australia

3) **Geography of New Zealand**

http://en.wikipedia.org/wiki/Geography_of_New_Zealand

http://www.tourism.net.nz/new-zealand/about-new-zealand/geography.html

Group Tasks

Accounts of the physical features of one country or another are accounts of place and time. It is another branch of geography to map human responses to the terrain and this brings out the relationship that people have with the land, which may vary hugely. It is a vast subject; however, it might be interesting to consider how geography affects the intellectual inclinations and distribution of the population.

In groups of 3 to 5, consider the geography of China, the U.K. and the U.S. and research the major intellectual centers of each country. See if you can draw any links between the geography of the countries and the distribution of their centers of learning. Why, for instance did London become the U.K.'s capital city: why Washington, or Beijing? Think about the two world renowned centers of learning in the U.K., Oxford and Cambridge, for instance, or the "Ivy League" Universities of the U.S., Princeton, Harvard etc., or Beijing, Qufu and Nanjing as examples.

Can we establish if and how geography influences the routes through which these (or other) centers communicated with other national and international centers? Can we say how, why and when they rose and fell relative to neighbors and competitors?

Of course, this could be a vast subject, encompassing the history of civilizations, politics as well as geography, but limit your research and discussions to consideration of how physical and political geography affects the development of networks of academics, merchants and diplomats, for this will also be a map of how communication developed in the three countries and it will form a useful and interesting base upon which to reflect on the "facts" you have been given and to deepen your awareness of the interconnectedness of all the subjects in this book.

Consider sketching the main features of your discussions onto a wall chart and annotate your drawings; then share your process and findings with at least two other groups to see how others interpret the task and what they conclude.

Chapter 2   History

Section A   History of the United Kingdom

British history is not as long as some ancient civilizations, but its cultural impact is widespread and deep in many countries throughout the world.

1. Origin of the British Nation

Before the great Ice Age, Great Britain was joined to the continent of Europe. When the Ice Age ended in 7,000 B.C., English Channel and the North Sea formed, and Britain was isolated from the European continent and became an island. Early British history was a history of invasion. Up to Norman Conquest, the British island was invaded by migratory tribes off and on who were living along the southern and eastern coastlines. These invaders came to Britain, settled here, and created early British civilization.

▶ Iberians and the Celtic Invasion

The first known settlers by now were Iberians who came from Iberian Peninsula in Mediterranean in around 2,500 B.C.. Although they were called Iberians, they consisted of different peoples. The Iberians lived in Britain during the Stone and Bronze Ages. They began the early agriculture and used some original tools made of stone. At the same time, the Iberians built the mysterious and great prehistoric monument—Stonehenge, which stands on the vast Salisbury

Stonehenge

plains, and it still remains a secret that how the original settlers built and what it used to do.

From 700 B.C. to 300 B.C., Celtic tribes from territory that is now Germany and the Netherlands came to Britain and drove the Iberians to the highlands of Wales, Northwest England and Scotland. Compared with the prior settlers, the Celts were better at ironwork and art. They brought their own language and government style with them and imposed them on the settlers in the south. Their government style was based on the basic extended families or clans which gradually formed tribes. They already had a set of standards of protection and punishment, which showed justice among the extended families to some degree. They continued to develop agriculture slowly, and began to hunt and fish although at the same time they still used herding, weaving, and metalwork left by Iberians. Together with the later Germanic tribes, Celtic civilization laid the foundation for modern British history and culture.

▶ Roman Invasion

In addition to the Iberians and Celtic invasions, Roman was the third one that invaded Britain. In contrast to the previous invaders, Roman conquerors preferred to assimilate Britain rather than colonize it.

In 55 B.C., the Roman leaders Julius Caesar started the first invasion to Britain; however, it failed because of the bad weather. Just one year later, in 54 B.C., he launched a second attack on Britain. It was a military success, while it did not lead to Roman occupation. It was not until 43 A.D. that Roman took complete control over the Britain land. At that time, Claudius was the Roman Emperor. Nevertheless, the Roman legionnaires were also confronted with severe occupation. For the next hundred years, wars and civil unrest diverted the Roman leaders from further invasion. The Roman left Britain in 410 A.D., because their own country was going to collapse and soldiers needed to protect their own homeland. In the process of Roman invasion of Britain, Britain went through a temporary civilization.

▶ The Invasion of Anglo-Saxons

After the Romans had retreated, the Anglo-Saxons began to invade England. They came from what is now called Scandinavia and Germany. The Anglo-Saxons killed some Celts and pushed the other Celts into the mountains or overseas to Ireland. They established a dominant culture, a common religion and a common form of government.

During this period, the king who was selected as the leader did not have all the power to make the decisions; many decisions were made by twelve of the most respected men within each village. Few of the decisions had been written down; those which hadn't been written down were called Common Law. There is a strong oral literary tradition and Beowulf is a famous epic which survives today.

About the religion the Anglo-Saxons were converted from Pre-Christian to Christianity. Two Irish missionaries, St. Patrick and St. Augustine, brought the Christianity into England and Ireland. Those two versions of Christianity were not the same. One stressed the government of churches by the Roman Pope and the other had self-governed churches. The Anglo-Saxon kings gave the land to bishops and monasteries and forced people to give the tax to Roman Catholic Church.

During the 600 – 800 years, the Heparchy[1] (Kent, Sussex, Wessex, Essex, Northumbria, East Anglia and Mercia) was established because of the fight between the powerful tribes.

▶ The Invasion of Vikings

At the end of 8th century, the Vikings from Norway, Sweden and Denmark invaded the Great Britain. These marauders came with their keeled boats through the Danube River and the Mediterranean. Ireland, Scotland and Northern England were attacked by the marauders from Norway and Sweden, the southeastern England was invaded by the people from Denmark. Later the Vikings established small kingdoms in these places.

Later these small kingdoms were united by Alfred the Great (849 – 899) who was the king of Wessex. He was the first one in the history of Britain who called himself as the king of England, and he had many achievements. He defeated Danish attempts to expand "the Danelaw"[2], and regained land, including London; he built a navy

Alfred the Great

and established strong garrisons for protection; he also founded the first public schools for the sons of noblemen and magistrates; meanwhile he began the Chronicle. His son Edward the Elder and his grandson Athelstan were the first true kings of England.

2. The Founding of the Nation

▶ The Norman Conquest

The most important historical episode in British history is the Norman Conquest. The Norman conquest of England began in September 1066 with the invasion of England by William, Duke of Normandy. He became known as the Conqueror after his victory at the Battle of

William the Conqueror

Hastings in October 1066, who defeated the king Harold II of England. On December 25, 1066, William was crowned William I at Westminster Abbey in London. By early 1071, William had secured control of most of England, although rebellions and resistance continued to approximately 1088.

The Norman Conquest largely removed the native ruling class by replacing it with a foreign, French-speaking monarchy, aristocracy, and clerical hierarchy, which brought about a transformation of the English language and the culture of England in a new era—Norman England.

After the Norman invasion, people in Britain spoke three major languages. The clergy

spoke and wrote Latin, the language of Roman; the rulers, military leaders and leaders spoke French; and the common people spoke a variety of German dialects, known as old English.

The Consolidation and Development of Monarchy

During the rule of William's next two successors, strong and centralized government continued in a feudalized society. Henry II was the king of England and Normandy, and at his time, almost 2/3 Frances were under his rule. Henry II made great contribution to the laws at that time, because he introduced the jury system to British law, and he was called the founding father of the British common law. Besides, the birth of the parliament gave more powers and rights to the common people, and the basis of the political system was established. From 1343, it was divided into two chambers: the upper house (the House of Lords), and the lower house (the House of Commons). The essential spirit was freedom and democracy.

Henry II

Henry II's younger son John was succeeded to throne after his elder son, and at his time, the king's power was growing. In 1204, John lost Normandy and most of his French possessions. Then on June 15, 1216, John was forced to accept the famous document the Great Charter [3] which limited the power of king and included sixty-three clauses. Although the Great Charter had been long popularly regarded as the foundation of English liberties, it was a statement of the feudal and legal relationships between the Crown and the barons, protected the freedom of the Church and the rights of citizens, and limited the power of the king. Its two general principles were that the king was subjected to the law and the king should observe the law.

Edward I was King of England from 1272 to 1307, and he was an effective ruler, because he expanded power in England. During his reign, the power of royal courts increased while that of the baronial courts deceased.

In a word, the three kings Henry II, King John and Edward directly or indirectly contributed to the development of British politics from Monarchy to constitutional Monarchy.

The Decline of Feudalism

During the Feudal society, there were several wars. The most famous two were the Hundred Years' War and the Wars of the Roses.

The Hundred Years' War was a series of wars between France and England from 1337 to 1453. Although it was called the Hundred Years' War, in fact, it lasted about 116 years. The war had its roots in a dynastic disagreement dating back to the time of William the Conqueror. As the rulers of Normandy and other lands on the continent, the English kings owed feudal homage to the king of France. In 1337, Edward III of England refused to pay homage to Philip VI of France, leading to the French king claiming confiscation of Edward's lands in Aquitaine, and the war broke out. The attempt by Talbot to retake Gascony, was crushed by Jean Bureau and his cannon at the Battle of Castillon in 1453, which was considered the last battle of the Hundred Years' War. The Hundred Years' War had a significant impact on the English society. It promoted the concept of English nationalism and the development of the textile industry. In addition, the war raised the social position of the bourgeois class. All these factors contributed to the decline of feudalism in Britain.

During the Hundred Years' War, Britain was affected by the Black Death. The bubonic plague broke out firstly, which killed many English. Hence, the number of English population decreased seriously, leading to crops rotted in the field; farm land not cultivated; and food prices rose. The inflation of prices caused hardship to the workers, and many people crowded into the cities. The labor shortage continued and was mostly responsible for the decrease of feudalism and increase of centralized monarchy. The Black Plague, war, famine, and death had ravaged the countries. People began searching for an explanation, and the current church could offer none. The Hundred Years' War was a part of a series of events that shifted people's thinking and paved the way for the period of Reformation that would follow.

The Wars of the Roses were a series of wars for the throne of the England between supporters of two rival branches of the royal House of Plantagenet: the House of Lancaster (with red roses as their symbol) and the House of York (with white roses as their symbol). Both houses battled for power, wealth and ultimately the throne, and it lasted thirty years from 1455 to 1485. At last, the House of

The Wars of the Roses

Lancaster won and their leader Henry Tutor became the King Henry VII. Henry VII united the two houses together by marrying Elizabeth, a daughter of Yorkist Edward IV, and made a new symbol, the Tudor rose, which also meant the end of the Wars of the Roses. After the unity, the economy developed quickly, and the agriculture began to change from the feudal agriculture to the capitalist agriculture, which made the industry and manufacture in England develop very quickly.

3. Transition to the Modern Age

▶ The Tudor Monarchy

The Tudor family ruled England from 1485 to 1603. Under the Tudors, England became a national state with an efficient centralized government, and started changing from a medieval to modern country.

▶ The New Monarchy

Henry Ⅶ was the first monarch of the Tudor Monarch. By careful diplomacy, Henry Ⅶ gave England peace at home and abroad, which enabled him to build up England's navy and foreign trade. One of the main concerns of Henry Ⅶ during his reign was the re-accumulation of the funds in the royal treasury. Through his strict monetary strategy, he was able to leave a considerable amount of money in the Treasury for his son and successor, Henry Ⅷ.

▶ Religious Reformation

Henry Ⅷ

Henry Ⅷ was responsible for the religious reform of the church. The reform began as a struggle for a divorce and ended in freedom from the Papacy. Henry Ⅷ wanted to divorce Catherine of Aragon but the Pope refused. Henry's reform was to get rid of the English Church's connection with the Pope, and to make an independent Church of England. He dissolved all the England's monasteries and nunneries because they were more loyal to the Pope than to their kings. The laws such as the Act of Succession of 1534 and the Act of Supremacy of 1535 made his reform possible. He established the Church of England as the national church of the country, and he made himself the supreme head of the Church of England. Henry Ⅷ's reform stressed the power of the monarch and strengthened his position; his attack on the Pope's power encouraged many critics of abuses of the Catholic Church and helped England move away from Catholicism towards Protestantism.

Henry Ⅷ's son Edward Ⅵ carried out drastic religious change. His switch to Protestant theology and his drastic reform had been called "The Reformation" in English history.

After the death of Edward Ⅵ in 1553, his elder sister Mary Tudor became the Queen. Mary, like her mother Catherine, was a devout Catholic. She married Philip Ⅱ of Spain and reestablished Catholicism and brought the Church back under the power of Rome. Mary persecuted and burnt many Protestants for their insistence on Protestant views, so she was given the nickname "Bloody Mary".

Mary ruled for only a few years and in 1558 she died. Her ostensibly Protestant sister, Elizabeth Ⅰ, became Queen. Elizabeth's religious reform was a compromise of views. She broke Mary's ties with Rome and restored her father's independent Church of England, i.e. keeping to Catholic doctrines and practices but to be free of the

Mary Tudor

Papal control. Her religious settlement was unacceptable to both the extreme Protestants known as Puritans and to ardent Catholics. For nearly 30 years, Elizabeth I successfully played off against each other, the two great Catholic powers, France and Spain, and prevented England from getting involved in any major European conflicts. Through her marriage alliances which were never materialized, Elizabeth I managed to maintain a friendly relationship with France, so England was able to face the danger from Spain.

Elizabeth I

The English Renaissance

The English Renaissance was a cultural and artistic movement in England dating from the late 15th and early 16th centuries to the early 17th century. Like most of northern Europe, England saw little of these developments until more than a century later. Renaissance style and ideas were slow in penetrating England, and the Elizabeth era in the second half of the 16th century is usually regarded as the height of the English Renaissance. Renaissance represented the transition in Europe from the Middle Ages to Modern era.

William Shakespeare

Though Renaissance came to England much later than to the rest of Europe, yet once it did, it was to produce such towering figures as William Shakespeare, Edmund Spenser, Sir Thomas More, Francis Bacon, and to produce a variety of glorious works in world literary heritage. In different countries, Renaissance found varied emphases. The impact on Italy and France was mainly felt in fine arts and science, and in Germany it was religion. Despite all these features, however, the English Renaissance was largely literary, achieving its finest expression in what is known as Elizabethan Drama.

The Civil Wars and Their Consequences

Because of the absolute rule of Charles, the confrontation between Charles I and the parliament developed into the civil war. The war began on August 22, 1642 and ended in 1651. Charles I was condemned to death. The English Civil War is also called the Puritan Revolution. It has been seen as a conflict between the parliament and the King, and a conflict between economic interests of the Crown and that of the urban middle class. The latter class coincided with their religious (Puritan) ideology while the former correspondingly allied with Anglican religious belief. The English Civil War not only overthrew feudal system in England but also shook the foundation of the feudal rules in Europe.

▶ The Restoration

When Oliver Cromwell died in 1658 and was succeeded by his son, Richard, the regime began to collapse. One of Cromwell's generals, George Monck, occupied London and arranged for new parliamentary elections. The Parliament that was elected in 1660 resolved the crisis by asking the late King's son to return from his exile in France as King Charles II. It was called the Restoration.

▶ The Glorious Revolution of 1688

In 1685 Charles II died and was succeeded by his brother James II. James was brought up in exile in Europe, and he was a Catholic. He hoped to rule without giving up his personal religious views, but England was no more tolerant of a Catholic king in 1688. Therefore, the English politicians rejected James II, and appealed to a Protestant king, William of Orange, to invade and take the English throne. William landed in England in 1688. The takeover was relatively smooth, with no bloodshed, nor any execution of the king. This was known as the Glorious Revolution, because it was bloodless and successful. In the following year, Parliament passed the Bill of Rights, which limited the power of the monarch and guaranteed the authority of Parliament. Parliament succeeded in removing a ruling monarch they didn't like and establishing a system known as constitutional monarchy.

4. The Rise and Fall of the British Empire

▶ The Industrial Revolution

The Industrial Revolution may be defined as the application of power-driven machinery to manufacturing. In the 18th century, all of Western Europe began to industrialize rapidly, and in England the process was most highly accelerated. England's head start may be attributed to a number of simultaneous factors or favorable conditions which no other country could match, including stable government, economic freedom, available capital, and mobile labor.

The basic ground for Industrial Revolution was prepared by the Glorious Revolution which ensured the political stability in the country and paved the way for the rapid growth of capitalism in England. The laissez faire policy[4] and domestic tariff-free commerce not only encouraged the development of production but also helped the expansion of markets, domestic and foreign. The capitalists accomplished their "primitive accumulation of capital" through plunder and exploitation during the period between 1688 and the mid 18th century. At home, this was mainly done by the large scale Enclosure Movement. Many small landowners were deprived of their property, and the new class of "landless laborers" had to seek paid employment from large landowners or to find work in the rapidly growing industrial areas. Abroad, from the colonies in America and India, Britain acquired enormous wealth with which to develop its industries. The colonies provided Britain with necessary raw materials and a large market for its industrial products. Such a continuous increase of colonial wealth and trade provided a constantly rising market for British goods. It was this demand for ever-increasing quantities of goods that forced men to use their wits on the mass production of commodities and it was the basic cause of the Industrial Revolution.

The First Industrial Revolution began in the textile industry and was marked by a series of inventions. They were the Spinning Jenny, the water frame, the power loom and the steam engine. These inventions completed the mechanization of the textile industry and prepared the way for a new system of production: large scale industry.

The Spinning Jenny

With these developments came a need for a cheap means of transportation. To meet it, entrepreneurs invested in digging canals to ship goods to market. In 1814, the steam locomotive was invented. The first railway was completed in 1825. By 1850, Great Britain had established a railroad system encompassing over 10,000 kilometers of track. Meanwhile, it had also built a large merchant fleet, which carried British-manufactured goods to all parts of the world.

By the middle of the 19th century, the Industrial Revolution was accomplished in Great Britain. The Industrial Revolution brought about dramatic changes in nearly every aspect of British society, including economy, politics, social structures and institutions. Its industrial productivity increased dramatically. As a result, British goods almost achieved a monopoly position in the world market and Britain became the "workshop of the world" by 1830. The country also underwent a process of mass urbanization, and many new cities sprang up, such as Manchester, Leeds, Birmingham and Sheffield. The Industrial Revolution also created changes in the class structure. The capitalist class replaced the old nobility as the most important force in the country, while the industrial working class, the proletariat, worked and lived in an appalling condition.

◉ The Formation of the Empire

The foundation of the empire was already laid in the time of Queen Elizabeth Ⅰ. But the empire came into being during the Industrial Revolution in the 18th and 19th centuries.

By the time Queen Victoria ascended the throne in 1837, Britain had been an empire known as the First British Empire. It included the colonies in Canada, Australia, New Zealand, India and many small states in the West Indies. These early colonies were usually started by individual business people for the purpose of trade.

The Victorian Age witnessed the establishment of the Second British Empire. Queen Victoria ruled from 1837 to her death in 1901, the longest reign of any monarch in British history. During Victoria's reign, especially from the 1870s, the British government adopted a very aggressive foreign policy known as New Imperialism. In order to plunder available resources, the government sent British fleet anywhere in the world to dominate the local people. British aggression against China was also in line with this pattern. The British government waged the Opium War against China and forced the Qing government to sign the Treaty of Nanking in 1842. By the end of the

Queen Victoria

19th century, the British Empire included a quarter of the global population and nearly a quarter of the world's landmass. It became the largest empire in human history, "an empire on which the sun never set".

▶ Britain in the Two World Wars

By the beginning of the 20th century, the world had entered the period of imperialism. Britain's dominance was challenged by other countries, because they had also established their large manufacturing industries, and they were also in need of foreign markets and raw materials. A conflict of interests and colonial rivalry divided Europe into two camps: "the Central Powers", including Germany, Austria-Hungary, Ottoman Empire and Bulgaria; "the Allied Powers", including the British Empire, France, the Russian Empire, Italy and the U.S.. World War I from 1914 to 1918 was primarily between two European Power blocs. Ultimately, more than 32 countries were involved, 28 of which supported the Allied Powers. The War ended with the victory of the Allies. During the war, the Britain lost much. Apart from the loss of manpower, there had been considerable disruption in economy and society. Though victorious, Britain came out of the war with a huge national debt, and its business was slack. By 1931 Britain entered the Great Depression, which made its position in the capitalist world further weakened.

With the rise of the Nazi Party in Germany, Hitler and Nazism showed off their aggressive momentum in Europe. The German troops invaded Poland on September 1, 1939. Chamberlain, the Prime Minister, found his policy of appeasement of German aggression was no longer tenable, and was forced to declare war on Germany on September 3, 1939. The next year Chamberlain resigned and Winston Churchill became the Prime Minister. The whole nation was mobilized and industries were centered on war production. In 1940, the Germany Air Force attacked the airfields in southeastern England, and it destroyed many cities. It was the most critical period of the war for Britain. But the fighter air planes of the Royal Air

Winston Churchill

Force wore down the German strength, and at last the Germans were forced to abandon their plans of invasion. In 1941 the pressure was somewhat alleviated for England. The Nazi invasion of the Soviet Union gave new hope to Britain. The Japanese attack on Pearl Harbor brought the U.S. into the war. A Grand Alliance was formed. With the unified efforts of Anti-Nazi forces, Germany surrendered unconditionally on May 7, 1945, and Japan was forced to surrender unconditionally in August. World War Ⅱ was over. Great Britain had triumphed over all her enemies, but at great costs—much bloodshed and heavy loss of wealth.

◑ The Fall of the Empire

One of the most far-reaching consequences of the wars was that it hastened the end of Britain's empire. Most of the colonies had joined in the war and contributed to the victory. They were tempered by the war and consequently a large independence movement swept the world soon after the war. The process of decolonization in Africa and Asia accelerated during the late 1950s, after which, of Britain's Asian possessions, only Hong Kong (returned to China in 1997) was still under British control. The British Empire faded away, to be replaced by the Commonwealth of Nations, a loosely organized community of former British colonies.

5. Britain since World War Ⅱ

After World War Ⅱ, the Labor Party under Clement Attlee came into power and created a comprehensive welfare state, with the establishment of the National Health Service, entitling free healthcare to all British citizens and other reforms included the introduction of old-age pensions, free education at all levels, sickness benefits and unemployment benefits, most of which was covered by the newly introduced national insurance, paid by all workers. The Bank of England, railways, heavy industry, coal mining and public utilities were all nationalized.

The Conservatives returned to power in 1951, accepting most of Labor's postwar reforms and presiding over 13 years of economic stability. Labor returned to power under Harold Wilson in 1964 and oversaw a series of social reforms including the decriminalization of homosexuality and abortion, the relaxing of divorce laws and the banning of capital punishment. Edward Heath returned the Conservatives to power from 1970 to 1974 and oversaw the decimalization of British currency, the ascension of Britain to the European Economic Community and the height of the Troubles in Northern Ireland. In the wake of the oil crisis and a miner's strike, Heath introduced the three-day working week to conserve power.

Margaret Thatcher

Labor made a return to power in 1974 but a series of strikes carried out by trade unions over the winter of 1978/1979 (known as the Winter of Discontent) paralyzed the country and as Labor lost its majority in parliament, a general election was called in 1979 which took Margaret Thatcher to power and began 18 years of Conservative government. Thatcher initially pursued monetary policies and went on to privatize many of Britain's nationalized companies such as BT Group, British Gas plc, British Airways and British Steel. The controversial Community Charge (poll tax), used to fund local government attributed to Thatcher being ousted from her own party and replaced as Prime Minister by John Major in 1990.

Major replaced the Poll Tax with the council tax and oversaw British involvement in the Gulf War. Despite a recession, Major led the Conservatives to a Surprising victory in 1992. The event of Black Wednesday in 1992, party disunity over the European Union and several scandals involving Conservative politicians led to Labor under Tony Blair winning a landslide election victory in 1997. Blair led Britain into the controversial Iraq War, which contributed to his eventual resignation in 2007, when he was succeeded by his Chancellor Gordon Brown. A global recession in the late 2000s led to Labor being defeated in the 2010 election and replaced by a Conservative-Liberal Democrat coalition, headed by David Cameron, which has pursued a large series of public spending cuts to help reduce Britain's budget deficit. Cameron committed his government to

David Cameron

Britain's continuing role in Afghanistan and stated that he hopes to remove British troops from the region by 2015.

On September 18, 2014, a referendum was held in Scotland on whether to leave the U.K. and become an independent country. The referendum resulted in Scotland voting by 55% to 45% to remain part of the U.K..

On February 20, 2016, David Cameron announced that a referendum on the UK's membership of the EU (European Union) would be held on June 23, 2016. The result of the referendum was in favor of the country leaving the EU with 51.9% of voters wanting to leave. After the result was declared, Cameron announced that he would resign by October. In the event, he stood down on July 13, with Theresa May becoming Prime Minister.

Theresa May

On July 12, 2018, the British government published a long-awaited white paper on Brexit (Britain exiting from the EU), seeking to create a free trade area with the EU. Secretary of State for Exiting the European Union, Dominic Raab told the House of Commons that leaving the EU may involve both challenges and opportunities and the country may rise to the challenges and grasp the opportunities.

Section B   History of the United States of America

1. Pre-Colonial America

Archeologists believe that the present-day U. S. was first populated by people migrating from Asia via the Bering Land Bridge sometime between 50,000 and 11,000 years ago. These people became the indigenous people who inhabited the Americas prior to the arrival of European explorers in the 1,400s and who are now called Native Americans.

One recorded European exploration of the Americas was by Christopher Columbus in 1492, sailing on behalf of the King and the Queen of Spain. He sailed west in search of a new sea route to India. However, he failed to reach India but reached a group of islands which now are called Bahamas. He mistook these islands for part of India and called the people there Indians. Another important figure in the process of the discovery of the New World was Amerigo Verspucci. He was not the discoverer of the new continent, but it was he who first confirmed the fact that a new continent rather than Asia had been discovered. Therefore, the newly-found continent was later named after him and became known as America. After a period of exploration by various European countries, Dutch, Spanish, English, French, Swedish, and Portuguese settlements were established.

2. America in the Colonial Era

European colonists arrived at the New World after 1600. In 1607, the Virginia Company of London established the Jamestown Settlement on the James River, and it was the first successful English colony in North America. In 1620, a group of Puritans, who were later called the Pilgrim Fathers, sailed for Virginia on a ship called the Mayflower. They had been persecuted in Britain, because they refused to abide by the rules of the Church of England, and they went to the New World in search of reli-

The Mayflower

gious freedom. They finally landed in what is now Plymouth, Massachusetts. By 1679 they had set up four New England colonies. Spain controlled a large part of what is now the central and western U.S.. In 1682, French explorer, Sieur de La Salle, discovered the Ohio and Mississippi valleys, and claimed the entire territory as far south as the Gulf of Mexico. By the 1770s, 13

British colonies contained 2.5 million people. They were prosperous and growing rapidly, and had developed their own autonomous political and legal systems.

3. Formation of the United States

Soon afterwards, the contradiction between Britain and her 13 colonies became acute. Britain imposed new taxes partly in order to defray the cost of fighting in the Seven Years' War[5], and expected Americans to lodge British soldiers in their homes. The colonists resented the taxes and resisted the quartering of soldiers. Some colonies such as Massachusetts began to make preparations for war with Britain.

The Boston Tea Party in 1773 was often seen as the event which started the American Revolution. The first continental congress was held in Philadelphia in September, 1774. The Battles of Lexington and Concord in April, 1775, were the first military engagements of the American Revolutionary War. The battles marked the outbreak of open armed conflict between Britain and its 13 colonies in the mainland of British North America. On July 4, 1776, the Second Continental Congress meeting in Philadelphia declared the independence of the U.S. in a remarkable document, the Declaration of Independence, primarily authored by Thomas Jefferson.

Finally the U.S. won its independence from Britain with the help of France in the American War of Independence, and the Declaration of Independence rejected British authority in favor of self-determination. During and after the war, the 13 states were united under a weak federal government established by the Articles of Confederation[6]. The structure of the government was profoundly changed on March 4, 1789, when the states replaced the Articles of Confederation with the U.S. Constitution. The new govern-

The Declaration of Independence

ment reflected a radical break from the normative governmental structures of the time, favoring representative, elective government, rather than the existing monarchial structures common within the western traditions of the time.

4. Westward Expansion

Westward expansion is the history of U.S. territorial acquisitions. In 1783, the Treaty of Paris with Britain defined the original borders of the U.S.. The Louisiana Purchase, in 1803, gave western farmers use of the important Mississippi River waterway, removed the French presence from the western border of the U.S., and provided U.S. settlers with vast potential of expansion.

The Monroe Doctrine in 1823, proclaimed that European powers should no longer colonize or interfere in the Americas, but it was later extended to justify U.S. imperialism in the Western Hemisphere, and it was an important symbol of American expansionism. In 1830, Congress passed the Indian Removal Act, which authorized the president to negotiate treaties that exchanged Indian tribal lands in the eastern states for lands west of the Mississippi River.

Westward Expansion

In the 1840s, western expansion proceeded at a rapid pace. Promises of wide-open spaces and inexpensive land with rich soil enticed many people in the east to pack up their possessions and head west. The 1840s became a decade of rapid territorial acquisition and expansion. Americans streamed into Texas, settled there, formed an independent republic, and asked that Texas become part of the U.S., but Mexico refused to accept the annexation of Texas, which led to Mexican-US War (1846 – 1848). California, New Mexico and adjacent areas were ceded to the U.S. under the 1848 Treaty of Cuadalupe Hidalgo.

Through the westward expansion, the U.S. expanded from the Atlantic Coast to the Pacific Coast, and it became one of the most powerful nations in the 20th century. However, this expansion also resulted in great suffering, destruction, and cultural loss to the Native Americans.

5. Civil War Era

The Civil War was from 1861 to 1865. Abraham Lincoln was elected president, the South seceded to form the Confederate States of America, and the Civil War followed, with the ultimate defeat of the South.

The Civil War began when Confederate Army opened fire upon Fort Sumter. They fired because Fort Sumter was in a confederate state. After four years of bloody combat that left over 600,000 soldiers dead and destroyed much of the South's infrastructure, the Confederacy collapsed, slavery was abolished, and the difficult reconstruction process of restoring national unity and guaranteeing rights to the freed slaves began. In the Reconstruction era (1863 – 1877), the U.S. ended slavery and extended legal and voting rights to the Freedmen.

6. America Before and During World War Ⅰ

After its civil war, America experienced an accelerated rate of industrialization, mainly in the northern states. Machinery steadily replaced the use of hand labor; railway extended from coast to coast; ships were built. Transportation and communications were greatly improved to meet the needs of an industrial society. By 1894, America had become the world leading industrial country.

The U.S. began its rise to international power in this period with substantial population and industrial growth domestically, and a number of military ventures abroad. The US-Spanish War was the first imperialist war for redividing the world, and it marked a new stage in which the U.S. transformed into an imperialist power.

At the outbreak of World War I in 1914, the U.S. pursued a policy of non-intervention. As the war went on, Germany announced that submarines were to be used to sink all ships, including neutral ones, going to Britain, which would greatly harm the American trade. Besides, the Germans attempted to interest Mexico in going to war as Germany's ally against the U.S., and Britain intercepted the message and presented it to the U.S. embassy in Britain. After the sinking of several U.S. merchant ships by submarines and the publication of the Zimmerman telegram[7], the U.S. declared war against Germany on 6 April 1917. In 1918, Wilson implemented a set of propositions titled the Fourteen Points to ensure peace, but they were denied at the 1919 Paris Peace Conference. Isolationist sentiment following the war also blocked the U.S. from participating in the League of Nations, an important part of the Treaty of Versailles.

7. America Before and During World War II

Between World War I and World War II, there were two decades—the 1920s and 1930s. The 1920s was noted for the so-called prosperity, while the 1930s was characterized by the Great Depression and the New Deal. During most of the 1920s, the U.S. enjoyed a period of unbalanced prosperity, and the boom was fueled by an inflated stock market, which later led to the Great Depression. The first outward sign of the depression was the collapse of the stock market in October 1929, followed by the closing of thousands of plants and banks. Franklin Roosevelt's New Deal program had some initial remedial effect, but it failed to produce recovery and solve the problem of unemployment. The crisis continued to deepen until a change was brought about by the outbreak of World War II.

The U.S. didn't enter World War II until after the rest of the active allied countries had done so, and its first contribution to the war was simultaneously to cut off the oil and raw material supplies needed by Japan to maintain its offensive in China.

On December 7, 1941, the Japanese attacked Pearl Harbor killing over 2,000 people and damaging or destroying eight battleships, greatly harming the Pacific fleet. The following day, Roosevelt successfully urged a joint session of Congress to declare war against Japan. After that, Germany and Italy declared war against the U.S., and America had to fight on two fronts: Europe and the Pacific. The U.S. did play an important role in the war against fascists. On the other hand, however, it is necessary to point out that the U.S. entered the war mainly for its own benefits, which reveals the nature of imperialism.

8. Cold War Era

During World War Ⅱ, the U.S. and the Soviet Union fought together as allies against the Axis powers. However, the relationship between the two nations was tense. Americans had long been wary of Soviet communism. For their part, the Soviets resented the Americans' decades-long refusal to treat the USSR (Union of Soviet Socialist Republics) as a legitimate part of the international community as well as their delayed entry into World War Ⅱ. After the war, these grievances ripened into an overwhelming sense of mutual distrust and enmity. In a hostile atmosphere, the U.S. and the Soviet Union emerged as opposing superpowers and began the Cold War, confronting one another indirectly in the arms race and space race.

A new policy, the Cold War policy, went into effect by the spring of 1947 when Truman Doctrine came forth. This was a plan to give money and military aid to countries threatened by communism. A major event in the Cold War was the Berlin Airlift[8]. After World War Ⅱ, the U.S. and its allies divided Germany into two parts: West Germany, controlled by the U.S. and East Germany, supported by the Soviet Union. Then there rose the Berlin crisis.

After World War Ⅱ, the cold war became the basis of the American foreign policy. It fully revealed the ambition of the U.S. to gain the world domination. In East and Southern Asia, the U.S. tried hard to control as many regions as possible through military and economic aggression to achieve this goal.

From 1953 to 1961, General Eisenhower was in presidency. The Eisenhower Doctrine contained the points of instant and massive retaliation, avoidance of getting involved in frustrating wars of containment. Crisis in Korea, and Vietnam prompted the use of this doctrine, but with little success. In Africa, the U.S. took the advantage of the weakening old colonial powers and the national liberation struggles for independence in those countries to intervene in their affairs by means of economic aid. The American relation with the Latin American countries was deteriorating, and the Latin American countries were getting more disenchanted with the U.S..

On January 20th, 1969, Richard Nixon took the oath of office as president. He gave priority to foreign affairs and significantly redirected U.S. policies. Nixon continued to bomb on a large scale many cities in North Vietnam and in April 1970, he cast American troops into Cambodia, escalating the aggressive war. A negotiated peace settlement finally came in January 1973 through a long time bargaining. Two months later, the last American left Vietnam and the long-lasting Vietnam War ended. The Vietnam War was a

The Vietnam War

long-time suffering for the U.S.. The war started under Eisenhower and was continued by Kennedy and Johnson. The war greatly weakened the U.S. imperialism and sharpened the country's internal contradictions. Relations between East and West also improved when Richard Nixon was president. Besides, it is President Nixon who moved toward improving relations with China, and the "ping-pong diplomacy" helped normalize the relations between the two countries.

A major change in the Cold War took place in 1985, when Mikhail Gorbachev became leader of the Soviet Union. He met four times with President Ronald Reagan, and he withdrew Soviet forces from Afghanistan, and signed an agreement with the U.S. to destroy all middle-distance and short-distance nuclear missiles. The Cold War ended when the Soviet Union dissolved in 1991.

Ronald Reagan (Right) and Gorbachev (Left)

9. The U.S. after the Cold War

After the fall of the Soviet Union, the U.S. emerged as the world's sole remaining super-power and continued to involve itself in military action overseas. Following the election of Bill Clinton in 1992, the 1990s saw one of the longest periods of economic expansion.

As the 21st century began, international conflicts centered on the Middle East and were heightened significantly following the September 11 attacks and the War on Terrorism that was subsequently declared. On September 11, 2001, the U.S. was struck by a terrorist attack when 19 al-Qaeda hijackers commandeered four airliners and intentionally crashed into both twin towers of the World Trade Center and into the Pentagon, killing nearly 3,000 people, mostly civilians. On October 7, 2001, the U.S. and NATO then invaded Afghanistan to oust the Taliban regime, which had provided safe haven to al-Qaeda and its leader Osama bin Laden.

In 2003, the U.S. launched an invasion of Iraq, which led to the collapse of the Iraqi government and the eventual capture of Iraqi dictator Saddam Hussein.

In December 2007, the U.S. entered the longest post-World War II recession, Major problems included the housing market crisis, subprime mortgage crisis, soaring oil prices, automotive industry crisis, rising unemployment, and the worst financial crisis.

In 2008, the unpopularity of President Bush and the Iraq war, along with the 2008 financial crisis, led to the election of Barack Obama, the first African American President of the U.S.. As president, Obama officially ended combat operations in Iraq on August 31, 2010. At the same time, Obama increased American involvement in Afghanistan, starting a surge strategy using an additional 30,000 troops. In May 2011, after nearly a decade's hiding, the founder and leader of Al Qaeda Osama bin Laden

Barack Obama

was killed in Pakistan in a raid conducted by U.S. naval special forces under President Obama's direct orders. In 2012, President Obama was reelected in November with the help of a similar voter coalition as in 2008.

Section C   History of China

China is a country with a long and rich history and ancient civilization. Anthropologists have uncovered the remains of China's earliest discovered anthropoid, "Yuanmou Man", who lived in Yunnan Province approximately 1.7 million years ago. "Peking Man", who lived in Zhoukoudian, to the southwest of modern Peking, 400,000 − 500,000 years ago, could walk upright, make and use simple tools, and knew how to make fire. The Neolithic Age started in China about 10,000 years ago, and relics from this period can be found all over the country. Artificially grown rice and millet as well as farming tools have been found in the remains of Hemudu in Yuyao, Zhejiang Province, and Banpo, near Xi'an City, shaanxi Province, respectively. These relics date back some 6,000 − 7,000 years.

1. Ancient times (from antiquity to 1840 A.D.)

The history of China can date back to as early as 4000 B.C.. Chinese civilization began with the legendary sage-emperors Huang Di and Yan Di in the area of the Yellow River Basin. After centuries, the two tribes gradually merged into one by the time of the Xia Dynasty. Chinese people, usually regard themselves as "the descendants of Yan and Huang".

▷ The Xia Dynasty (2070 B.C. − 1600 B.C.)

Chinese generally tell the history from Xia Dynasty, which was founded in 2070 B.C.. The center of its activities was the western section of modern Henan Province and the southern section of modern Shanxi Province, and its sphere of influence reached the northern and southern areas of the Yellow River. With the Xia Dynasty, China entered slave society. People were agrarian, and they were familiar with the phenomena of seasonal changes and arranged their farm activities according to the alterations of the seasons.

▷ The Shang Dynasty (1600 B.C. − 1046 B.C.)

The Shang Dynasty controlled the central part of China, extending over much of modern Henan, Hubei, Shangdong, Anhui, Shanxi, and Hebei provinces. The Shang enjoyed the most advanced bronze civilization in

Oracle

the world, and the development of a writing system can be witnessed on the oracles like tortoise shell or animal bones, and these writings were the beginning of the written Chinese language.

▶ The Zhou Dynasty (1046 B.C. - 221 B.C.)

The Zhou Dynasty reigned for the longest period of all Chinese dynasties. The Zhou Dynasty fell into several sub-periods: the Western Zhou (1046 B.C. - 770 B.C.), the Eastern Zhou which was further divided into the Spring and Autumn Period (770 B.C. - 476 B.C.) and the Warring States Period (475 B.C. - 221 B.C.). The Zhou Dynasty was a turning point in Chinese history for it evolved into feudal system, and witnessed the territorial expansion, economic prosperity and cultural flourishing. During this period, philosophy and other branches of scholarship were unprecedentedly thriving, with the rise of Confucianism, Daoism and the development of Chinese philosophy. Famous philosophers, Laozi, Confucius, Mencius, Mozi, Zhuangzi, Han Feizi, Xunzi, Sunzi, etc., made huge impact on Chinese culture. The Spring and Autumn and Warring States periods are famous for the cultural prosperity with "Hundred Schools of Thought". During this era, many poets voiced their opinions of criticism and emotions, many of which were preserved in "the Book of Songs", the first important work of literature in Chinese history.

▶ The Qin Dynasty (221 B.C. - 207 B.C.)

Ying Zheng, a man of great talent and bold vision, established the first centralized, unified, multi-ethnic feudal state in Chinese history—the Qin Dynasty, and called himself Shi Huang Di (the first Emperor), historically known as Qin Shi Huang. During his reign, he standardized the written script, currencies, weights and measures; many constructive public projects were undertaken; roads and irrigation canals were built throughout the country. On the other hand, he executed many of his opponents and burned the books written before the Qin Dynasty to wipe

The Great Wall

out ideas which conflicted with the Emperor. He had worked on his enormous mausoleum started early in his reign. The terracotta warriors of the "underground army" guarding the mausoleum, unearthed in 1974, amazed the world. The 8,000 vivid, life-size pottery figures, horses and chariots have been called "the eighth wonder of the world". The Qin Dynasty was well-known for beginning the construction of the Great Wall which was later augmented and enhanced during the Ming Dynasty. The Qin Dynasty marks the beginning of a more than 2,000 years long history of a centralized state with an emperor being the head of a state and a comparatively uniformed culture.

◗ The Han Dynasty (206 B.C. – 220 A.D.)

At the end of the Qin Dynasty, Liu Bang, a peasant leader, overthrew the Qin regime in cooperation with Xiang Yu. A few years later, Liu Bang defeated Xiang Yu and established the Han Dynasty. The Han Dynasty fell into three periods: Western Han (206 B.C. – 8 A.D.), Wang Mang's Xin Dynasty (8 A.D. – 23 A.D.), and Eastern Han (25 A.D. – 220 A.D.). During Emperor Wudi's reign, the most prosperous period of the Han Dynasty, the territory of the empire was expanded from the Central Plain to the Western Regions (present-day Xinjiang and Central Asia). Emperor Wudi dispatched Zhang Qian twice as his envoy to the Western Regions, and in the process a trade route was forged known as "the Silk Road" from Chang'an (today's Xi'an, Shanxi Province), through Xinjiang and Central Asia, and on to the east coast of the Mediterranean Sea. As contacts between the East and West increased, Buddhism spread to China in the first century.

In Han Dynasty, science and technology made remarkable achievements. Paper, the compass, and the seismograph were invented, steel was manufactured, and advances in medicine, astronomy, and cartography were also noteworthy in history. The Han regime existed for a total of 426 years and its agriculture, handicrafts and commerce were well developed.

◗ Three Kingdoms (220 – 265), Jin (265 – 420), Southern and Northern Dynasty (420 – 589)

The collapse of the Han Dynasty was followed by the Three Kingdoms Period of Wei, Shu and Wu. Continuous wars among the three states developed various wise political and military thoughts, and produced talented persons, such as Zhuge Liang, Cao Cao, etc., who demonstrated their special ability not only in military and political affairs but also in literature.

The Three Kingdoms was followed by the Western Jin with Luoyang as its capital city, and Eastern Jin with Jiankang (Nanjing) as its capital city. The Jin Dynasty did not last long with a lot of confrontations and conflicts.

After the Jin Dynasty, the Southern and Northern Dynasty appeared, and it was an age of civil war and political disunity. On the other hand, it was an era of the quick and wide spread of Buddhism, and the flourishing in poetry, music, calligraphy, painting with representatives like the great calligrapher Wang Xizhi and the outstanding painter Gu Kaizhi. It also enjoyed the great advancement in technology. For instance, Zu Chongzhi introduced the approximation to π which is correct to 7 decimal places, and made unique contribution to mathematics.

The Sui Dynasty (581 - 618)

China was reunified by the Sui Dynasty founded by Emperor Sui Wendi. The Sui Dynasty was short-lived, lasting for 38 years. However, the social economy in this period underwent rapid recovery and development; the system of "Three Departments and Six Ministries" was set up to strengthen the central authorities; the privilege of the noble families was abolished; the Imperial Examination System for the selection and appointment of civil servants was adopted, which was later used for over 1,300 years. Besides, the Sui Dynasty witnessed various reforms and achievements such as the construction of engineering feats like the Grand Canal from Beijing to Hangzhou and Zhaozhou Bridge. Confucianism began to regain popularity, and Buddhism was further spread and encouraged throughout the empire to reunite the people of different regions.

The Tang Dynasty (618 - 907)

Li Yuan founded the Tang Dynasty with its capital at Chang'an. Li Shimin, or Emperor Taizong, the son of Li Yuan, was one of the greatest emperors in Chinese history. He adopted a series of policies known as the Zhenguan reign period reforms, pushing the prosperity of China's feudal society to its peak. The boundaries of China were extended to Siberia in the North, Korea peninsula in the east, Vietnam in the south, and west in Aral Sea in mid-Asia. At that time, China ranked among the most advanced countries in the world.

During the Tang Dynasty, Buddhism flourished and gradually became localized as an important part of Chinese traditional culture. A Buddhist monk Xuan Zang traveled from Chang'an through Gansu, Xinjiang and central Asia to India for the furtherance of Buddhist classics. It was also the golden age of literature and art, which produced the most brilliant poetry of the country. The best-known poets in the Tang Dynasty were Li Bai, Du Fu and Bai Juyi.

Emperor Taizong

The "An Lushan and Shi Siming Rebellion" brought about the political disturbance and weakened the empire, and began to push the mighty Tang Dynasty to an end. After the Tang Dynasty, there came the Five Dynasty and Ten Kindoms (907 - 960).

The Song Dynasty (960 - 1279)

Zhao Kuangyin, General of the Later Zhou Dynasty, rose in mutiny and founded the Song Dynasty. It was divided into two phases: Northern Song and Southern Song. During the Song Dynasty, agriculture, handicraft industry, shipbuilding industry and commerce flourished, and science and technology made impressive advancements. There was a great development in calligraphy, painting, sculpture and weaving art; achievements in porcelain manufacture surpassed all previous dynasties; gunpowder were widely used for military purposes; the compass was employed for navigation; and the invention of movable printing by Bi Sheng was a great revolution in printing history. Song poetry was a new and popular literary form, and there were many famous poets at that time, such as Su Shi, Xin Qiji, Li Qingzhao, etc.. Shen Kuo's "Dream Pool Essays" covers many fields like astronomy, physics, chemistry, geology, medicine and so on. The Song Dynasty was considered to be another period of prime time in Chinese history after the glorious Tang Dynasty.

▶ The Yuan Dynasty (1271 – 1368)

In 1206, Genghis Khan unified all the tribes in Mongolia. Later, his grandson Kublai Khan founded the Yuan Dynasty in 1271 and made Dadu (Beijing) the capital. Due to the reunification, the economy, science and culture were boosted, and contacts and communications with foreign nations were also increased. For instance, Marco Polo's trip to China aroused the interest and awe of the world. A new kind of literature form Yuan Drama emerged, and the most influential

Genghis Khan

works are Wang Shifu's *Romance of the Western Chamber* and Guan Hanqing's *Dou E Yuan*. The Yuan Drama was one of the greatest Chinese literary heritages.

▶ The Ming Dynasty (1368 – 1644)

In 1368, Zhu Yuanzhang, a peasant uprising leader, founded the Ming Dynasty in Nanjing. In 1421, his son Zhu Di officially made Beijing the capital. In 1644, the Ming Dynasty was overthrown by the peasant armies led by Li Zicheng. In Ming Dynasty, many enormous constructive projects were undertaken, such as the restoration of the Grand Canal and the Great Wall, and the establishment of the Forbidden City in Beijing. With the growth of shipbuilding industry and the navigation technology, a eunuch named Zheng He led a fleet of many ships to make seven far-ranging voyages. Passing the Southeast Asian countries,

Zheng He

the Indian Ocean, Persian Gulf and Maldives Islands, Zheng He explored as far as Somalia and Kenya on the eastern coast of Africa. These were the largest-scale and longest voyages in the world before the age of Columbus. The literature in Ming Dynasty was also noticeable. There were many classic fictional novels, such as *The Romance of the Three Kingdoms*, *Water Margin*, *Pilgrim to the West*, and *The Golden Lotus*. Besides, *The Peony Pavilion* written by the famous playwright Tang Xianzu was one of the most famous plays in Chinese history.

▶ The Qing Dynasty（1644 - 1911）

In the late Ming Dynasty, the Manchus in northern China grew in strength and invaded the central plain for three generations in succession. Finally the Qing Dynasty was founded. The two most famous emperors of this period were Emperor Kang Xi and Emperor Qian Long, and the Qing Dynasty reached its peak during their reigns, which was known as the "times of prosperity"（Kang Qian Sheng Shi）. Its territory was extensive; economy and commerce developed; culture of various forms thrived. However, the late years of the Qing Dynasty began to decline with the massive social strife, economic stagnation, and western penetration and invasion. After the Opium War, the Qing court was confronted with crisis both at home and abroad.

2. Modern Period（1840 - 1919）

The Revolution of 1911

The Opium Wars lasted from 1840 to 1842 and 1856 to 1860 respectively. From then on, China was reduced to a semi-colonial and semi-feudal country. After the Opium Wars, the Qing court succumbed to the west invaders, and humiliatingly signed the unequal treaties, which brought about the tragic consequences for the development of China. To oppose feudal oppression and foreign aggression, the Chinese people waged heroic struggles. The Revolution of 1911, a bourgeois-democratic revolution led by Sun Yat-sen, ended the rule of the Qing Dynasty. The revolution was of great significance in modern Chinese history. The monarchical system that had been in place in China for more than 2,000 years was discarded with the founding of the provisional government of the Republic of China. But the fruits of victory were soon compromised by concessions on the part of the Chinese bourgeoisie, and the country entered a period of domination by the Northern Warlords headed by Yuan Shih-kai.

3. New Democratic Revolution Period（1919 - 1949）

Under the influence of the October Revolution in Russia, China's May 4th Movement broke out. It was an anti-imperialism and anti-feudalism movement, and it brought out a drastic change in Chinese society. In 1921, the Communist Party of China（CPC）was founded. In 1924, Sun Yat-sen worked together with the CPC to organize workers and peasants for the Northern Expedition. After Sun Yat-sen passed away, Chiang Kai-shek founded the Kuomintang regime in Nanjing, and in 1927 Chiang began to relentlessly chase the CPC armies and leaders from their bases in southern and eastern China. In 1934, the CPC forces were compelled to start the tough Long March across China's most desolate terrain to the northwest, where they established a guerrilla base at Yan'an in shaanxi Province. During the Long March, the communists reorganized under a new leader, Mao Zedong. In July 1937, Japan launched the all-out aggression against China. In August 1945, Chinese people won the victory of the War of Resistance against Japan. From June 1946, the Kuomintang launched an all-round attack on the Liberated Areas led by the CPC, and an unprecedented large-scale civil war started. Three years later, the CPC overthrew the rule of the Kuomintang and won a great victory in the new democratic revolution in 1949.

4. Contemporary Period (1949 -)

The Grand Ceremony Inaugurating
the People's Republic of China

On October 1st, 1949, a grand ceremony inaugurating the People's Republic of China was witnessed by 3,000,000 people in Beijing Tian'anmen Square. Chairman Mao Zedong solemnly proclaimed the formal establishment of the People's Republic of China. The early days of New China were a period of economic recovery. While developing production, China gradually established socialist public ownership of the means of production.

The Cultural Revolution lasted for 10 years from 1966 to 1976. During this period, the new China underwent disastrous experiences in every area. This "revolution" did not come to a close until the CPC smashed the Jiang Qing clique in October 1976. A new era of development unfolded in Chinese history.

In 1977, the CPC reinstated Deng Xiaoping in all the party and government posts he had been dismissed from during "the Culture Revolution". Deng Xiaoping took up a policy slogan "the Four Modernizations", originally invented by Premier Zhou Enlai. The party's task would be to set China on the right path in four areas: agriculture, industry, science and technology, and national defense. The Third Plenary Session of the CPC 11th Central Committee held at the end of 1978 represented a great turning point of profound significance in the history of New China. In 1979, China instituted a guiding policy of "reform and opening to the outside world" under Deng Xiaoping's leadership, and the focus was shifted to modernization. Great changes have come about in China from then on. As part of the encouragement of entrepreneurship, Deng Xiaoping designated four areas on China's coast as Special Economic Zones, which would be particularly attractive to foreign investors. He indicated that the economic policies of reform were not going to be abandoned, and the massive growth rates that the Chinese economy has posted ever since have justified his decision. In the first decade of the 21st century, annual growth has run at a historically unprecedented rate of about 10%. The situation in the country is the best ever, and the people are enjoying more material benefits than ever before.

In 1989, Jiang Zeming, taking office as the General Secretary of the Central Committee of the CPC, President of the People's Republic of China and Chairman of the Central Military Commission, led Chinese people to carry out Deng Xiaoping's theory. During this period, the

PRC gained sovereignty of Hong Kong and Macao in 1997 and 1999 respectively, and witnessed the PRC's accession into the World Trade Organization after 15 years of negotiations, and that Beijing was awarded to host the 2008 Summer Olympics.

In November 2002, Hu Jintao took the office, and persisted in and continued the policies and principles of "reform and opening to the outside world", making the country stable, economy developed and foreign relations promoted. China's cultural impact grows as well. The country is building Confucius Institutes, Chinese-language teaching institutes around the world, in an attempt to familiarize a far-wider range of people with Chinese language. And in fine art, China is making a dramatic impact. In 2007, the works of the artist Feng Xiaogang earned nearly $ 57 million, making him the second highest-earning artist in the world. On October 11th 2012, Mo Yan won the Nobel Prize in Literature, and he was the first Nobel Prize winner in Chinese history.

Xi Jinping was elected to be the General Secretary of the Chinese Community Party and Chairman of the Central Military Commission at the first plenum of the 18th CPC Central Committee on November 15th, 2013, who is the first top Party leader born after 1949. He now leads the 91-year-old CPC, the world largest political party with more than 82 million members, and sums up the CPC's mission as comprising three responsibilities: to the nation, the people and the Party. Besides, he

China Dream

points out that realizing the great renewal of the Chinese nation is the Chinese nation's greatest dream in modern history. To achieve this sacred "China Dream", he has clarified his positions on various aspects of the country's development.

Notes

1. **the Heptarchy**: The Heparchy means the period between the 6th century and the 9th century in the history of England in which one or other of the seven kingdoms of Anglo-Saxon origin was dominant. Finally in 829, the king of Wessex defeated the other kings and unified England.
2. **the Danelaw**: The Danelaw is also used to describe the set of legal terms and definitions created in the treaties between the English king, Alfred the Great, and the Danish warlord, Guthrum, written following Guthrum's defeat at the Battle of Edington in 878. In 886, the Treaty of Alfred and Guthrum was formalised, defining the boundaries of their kingdoms, with provisions for peaceful relations between the English and the Vikings.
3. **the Great Charter**: Its important provisions were as follows: (1) no tax should be made without the approval of the Grand Council; (2) no freemen should be arrested, imprisoned or deprived of their property; (3) the Church should possess all its rights, together with freedom of elections; (4) London and other towns should retain their traditional rights and privileges,

and (5) there should be the same weights and measures throughout the country.

4. the laissez faire policy: Laissez-Faire is an economic theory and policy that promotes a minimal to nonexistent amount of government interference and intervention into the private business sector. Proponents of the theory or model believe that the government not only should not interfere with everyday dealing of supply and demand, but that it should be, in a sense, entirely separated from the business world.

5. the Seven Years' War: The Seven Years War was one of the major wars of the 18th century. Britain, Hanover, Prussia and Portugal fought against Austria, France, Russia, Saxony, Spain and Sweden. The war began after Saxony and Bohemia were attacked by Prussia's King Frederick the Great. This was a time when major powers in Europe were also fighting for control of colonies in India and North America.

6. the Articles of Confederation: The Articles of Confederation was an agreement among the 13 founding states that established the U.S. as a confederation of sovereign states and served as its first constitution.

7. the Zimmermann Telegram: The Zimmermann Telegram was a 1917 diplomatic proposal from the German Empire for Mexico to join the Central Powers, in the event of the U.S. entering World War I on the side of the Entente Powers. The proposal was intercepted and decoded by British intelligence. Revelation of the contents outraged American public opinion and helped generate support for the U.S. declaration of war on Germany in April.

8. the Berlin Airlift: During the multinational occupation of post-World War II Germany, the Soviet Union blocked the Western Allies' railway, road, and canal access to the sectors of Berlin under Allied control. Their aim was to force the western powers to allow the Soviet zone to start supplying Berlin with food, fuel, and aid, thereby giving the Soviets practical control over the entire city. In response, the Western Allies organized the Berlin airlift to carry supplies to the people in West Berlin, flying over 200,000 flights in one year, and providing up to 4,700 tons of daily necessities such as fuel and food to the Berliners.

Glossary

legionnaire [li:dʒi'neə] *n.* 军团士兵
marauder [mə'rɔːdə] *n.* 掠夺者,抢劫者
keeled [ki:ld] *adj.* 备有龙骨的
homage ['hɔmidʒ] *n.* 效忠(仪式);顺从
bubonic [bju:'bɔnik] *adj.* 腺鼠疫
ravage ['rævidʒ] *vt.* 摧残;蹂躏;破坏;劫掠
papacy ['peipəsi] *n.* [the Papacy] 教皇制度
drastic ['dræstik] *adj.* 激烈的;(法律)严厉的
ostensible [ɔs'tensəbl, -sibl] *adj.* 表面上的

ardent [ˈɑːdənt] *adj.* 热心的；热情的

proletariat [ˌprəuleˈtɛəriət] *n.* 无产阶级

appeasement [əˈpiːzmənt] *n.* 绥靖主义

tenable [ˈtenəbl] *adj.* 守得住的；可保持的

decriminalization [diːkriminəlaiˈzeiʃən] *n.* 合法化

plc（Public Limited Company）股票上市公司

oust [aust] *vt.* 逐出；驱逐（from；of）；免职

indigenous [inˈdidʒinəs] *adj.* 土生土长的

normative [ˈnɔːmətiv] *adj.* 标准的，规范的

entice [inˈtais] *vt.* 引诱，怂恿

annexation [ˌænekˈseiʃən] *n.* 附加；合并

intercept [ˌintəˈsept] *vt.* 中途拦截；截获（情报）

retaliation [riˌtæliˈeiʃn] *n.* 报复；反击

disenchanted [ˌdisinˈtʃɑːntid] *adj.* 不再抱幻想的

escalate [ˈeskəleit] *vi.* （战争等）逐步升级

commandeer [ˌkɔmənˈdiə] *vt.* 强夺，强占

haven [ˈheivn] *n.* 港口；避难所；安息所

mortgage [ˈmɔːgidʒ] *n.* 抵押；抵押单据

anthropoid [ˈænθrəpɔid] *adj.* （猿等）似人类的

Neolithic [ˌniːəˈliθik] *adj.* 新石器时代的

agrarian [əˈgrɛəriən] *adj.* 耕地的；农业的

mausoleum [ˌmɔːsəˈliəm] *n.* 陵墓

augment [ɔːgˈment] *vt.，vi.* 增大，增加

seismograph [ˈsaizməgrɑːf] *n.* 地震仪

mutiny [ˈmjuːtini] *n.* 暴动，叛变

eunuch [ˈjuːnək] *n.* 太监，宦官

succumb [səˈkʌm] *vi.* 屈服；屈从（to）

relentless [riˈlentlis] *adj.* 残忍的，不留情面的

reinstate [ˈriːinˈsteit] *vt.* 使恢复（权利）；使复职

designate [ˈdezigneit] *vt.* 指定（出示），标明

Further Reading

1）**History of Canada**

http://en.wikipedia.org/wiki/History_of_Canada

http://www.historyofcanada.info/

2）**History of Australia**

http://en.wikipedia.org/wiki/History_of_Australia

http://gutenberg.net.au/ebooks02/0200471h.html

3) **History of New Zealand**

http://en.wikipedia.org/wiki/History_of_New_Zealand

http://www.historyofnations.net/oceania/newzealand.html

Group Tasks

Having read the accounts of history in relation to China, the U.K. and the U.S., choose one or more of the following quotes that interest you, to write a reflection upon how each of the countries has presented itself, through its history, to the world.

➤"History is not a succession of events, it is the links between them." (E. Evans-Pritchard)

➤"It is a mark of civilized man that he seeks to understand his traditions, and to criticize them, not to swallow them whole." (M. I. Finley)

➤"The love of liberty is the love of others; the love of power is the love of ourselves." (William Hazlitt)

➤"The disadvantage of men not knowing the past is that they do not know the present." (G. K. Chesterton)

➤"To be ignorant of what occurred before you were born is to remain always a child." (Cicero)

➤"That men do not learn very much from the lessons of history is the most important of all the lessons that history has to teach." (Aldous Huxley)

➤"The history of the world is the history of the privileged few." (Henry Miller)

➤"Human history becomes more and more a race between education and catastrophe." (H. G. Wells)

Chapter 3　Government and Politics

Section A　Government and Politics
of the United Kingdom

The U.K. is a constitutional monarchy: succession to the British throne is hereditary. The head of state is a king or a queen, but the king or queen is just the symbol of the whole nation, and the power to run the country rests with the elected Parliament, which is headed by a Prime Minister in association with his cabinet. The Parliament operates with the two-party system, and the two major parties play the roles as the Government and the Opposition.

1. The Constitution

The constitution of the U.K. is a set of laws and principles under which the U.K. is governed. Unlike many other nations, the British Constitution is not written down in one single official document. Much of the Constitution is written down, but it is not systematically codified into a single document.

The main components of the British Constitution are Statutory Law, Common Law, and Conventions. A statute is a formal written enactment of a legislative authority that governs a state, a city, or a county, and statutory laws are Acts of Parliament written down in actual laws and passed by Parliament at one time or another in the course of history. For example, the Bill of Rights in 1689 laid down a number of things that future monarchs could not do, and it extended the powers of the Parliament. The Parliament Act 1911 asserted the supremacy of the House of Commons by limiting the power of the House of Lords in law-making. Common law is deduced from custom or legal precedents and interpreted in court cases by judges. Conventions are rules which are not written down, but everyone agrees that those rules must be followed in practice, and are also regarded as vital to the working of government. Any attempt to flout this convention would be just as serious constitutionally as any attempt to ignore a written law.

2. The Parliament

　　The Parliament is the supreme legislative body in the U.K., and the Parliament alone possesses legislative supremacy and thereby ultimate power over all other political bodies in the U.K. and its territories. The British Parliament consists of three elements: the Monarch, the House of Lords, and the House of Commons. Before a Bill can become a law, it has to be passed by the House of Commons and the House of Lords, and finally go to the Monarch for his or her signature. The Parliament is an essential part of U.K. politics, and its main roles are examining and challenging the work of the government, debating and passing all laws, and enabling the government to raise taxes, etc..

▶ The Monarch

　　The British monarch is hereditary. Although the monarch's powers are limited by law and Parliament, the Monarch is a symbol of the tradition and unity of the British state, and still retains great government and state functions.

　　The present monarch is Queen Elizabeth Ⅱ, who has reigned since February 6th 1952. Queen Elizabeth Ⅱ is the constitutional monarch of 16 sovereign states (known as the Commonwealth realms) and their territories and dependencies, as well as head of the 53-member Commonwealth of Nations. The Queen is the symbol of the whole nation. In law, she is head of the executive, an integral part of the legislature, head of the judiciary, the commander-in-chief of all the armed forces and the "supreme governor" of the Church of England. The formal title of the U.K. government is Her Majesty's Government, all official letters and documents bear the initials OHMS (On Her Majesty's Service), the armed forces are called "Royal Army", and even the Opposition Party in the Parliament is named as "Her Majesty's Opposition".

　　The Queen participates in various important acts of government. For example, she summons, prorogues and dissolves Parliament; she confirms major public appointments such as government ministers, judges, diplomats, Church of England bishops and the new Prime Minister after the election. In international affairs, as Head of State, she has the power to declare war, make peace, recognize foreign states and conclude treaties. In all these instances, the Queen can only act on the advice which is arrived at after policies and decisions have been fully examined and debated in Parliament. The principal role of the Queen today is symbolic, and she must represent the nation's present-day hopes and ideals as well as its historical past.

Queen Elizabeth Ⅱ

▶ The House of Lords

The House of Lords is the upper house of the Parliament, which consists of the Lords Spiritual and the Lords Temporal. Members of the House of Lords are known as "Lords of Parliament", who are not elected but either inherit their title or are appointed by the Government or shadow cabinet. The Lords Spiritual includes archbishops and prominent bishops of the Church of England. The Lords Temporal refers to those lords who are either life peers or hereditary peers, although the hereditary right to the House of Lords was abolished for all but 92 peers in 1999.

The House of Lords and the House of Commons share the same building of the Westminster Palace in London, and up to the beginning of the 20th century, the House of Lords had equal power with the House of Commons; however, the Parliament Act 1911 effectively abolished the power of the House of Lords to prevent the passing of legislation approved by the House of Commons. Nowadays, the powers of the Lords in legislation are very limited. In addition, the House of Lords has undergone some major reforms in membership and orgnization after 1999 when the House of Lords Act was passed.

Palace of Westminster, London

The main function of the House of Lords is to bring the wide experience of its members into the process of lawmaking. It regularly reviews and amends bills from the Commons. In other words, the non-elected House is to act as a chamber of revision, complementing but not rivaling the elected House.

▶ The House of Commons

The House of Commons is the lower house of the Parliament, and it is the center of the parliamentary power. The Commons is a democratically elected body, consisting of 650 members (since the 2010 general election), who are known as Members of Parliament (MPs). Members are elected through the first-past-the-post system[1] by electoral districts known as constituencies. They hold their seats until Parliament is dissolved (a maximum of five years after the preceding election). Each member is elected by and represents an electoral district, and the number of seats varies a little because of changes in the population.

The House of Commons was originally far less powerful than the House of Lords, but today its legislative powers greatly exceed those of the Lords. Since the passage of Parliament Act 1911 and 1949, the House of Commons has become the dominant branch of the Parliament, both in theory and in practice. The party which holds the majority of "seats" in the House of Commons forms the government, its leader acting as the Prime Minister. The Government is primarily responsible to the House of Commons.

The House of Commons plays the key part in the activities of the Parliament as a whole, and it performs many important functions. For example, it considers, proposes and drafts new laws, and it can even restrain the actions of the government. Moreover, it has the power to supervise finance. The government cannot legally spend any money without permission from the House of Commons. In addition, it can influence future government policy.

3. The Government

The British government is the supreme administrative institution which manages state affairs, and it refers to the various departments and their agencies under the leadership of the Prime Minister. The Cabinet is the core of leadership of the government, and it is composed of the Prime Minister and heads of the most important departments. The Prime Minister and the Cabinet are collectively accountable for their policies and actions to the Monarch, to the Parliament, to their political party and ultimately to the electorate.

The Prime Minister is the learder of the majority party in the Parliament. After each general eletion, the monarch will ask the leader of the winning party to be the Prime Minister and form a new Cabinet. Ministers of the Crown, and especially Cabinet Ministers, are selected primarily from the elected members of the House of Commons, and also from the House of Lords, by the Prime Minister. The Prime Minister is the head of the government, and has the last word in deciding government policy. He or she can control the Parliament and influence other parties, and recently he or she is the most powerful leader in Britain.

4. The Judiciary

The Judiciary of the U.K. is not a single body, and it is rather complicated. Each of the separate legal systems in England and Wales, Northern Ireland and Scotland has their own judiciary. The legal system of Northern Ireland is similar to that of England and Wales, but Scotland has a distinct legal system based on Roman law.

▶ Justices of the Supreme Court

The judges of the Supreme Court of the U.K. are known as Justices of the Supreme Court, and they are also Privy Counsellors. Justices of the Supreme Court are granted the courtesy title Lord or

The U.K. Supreme Court

Lady for life.

The Supreme Court is a relatively new Court being established in October, 2009. Formerly, the Highest Court of Appeal in the U.K. was the House of Lords Appellate Committee made up of Law Lords. After the coming into force of the Constitutional Reform Act 2005, those Law Lords become judges of the Supreme Court. The Supreme Court is headed by the President and Deputy President of the Supreme Court and is composed of a further ten Justices of the Supreme Court.

▶ Tribunal Judiciary

The U.K. tribunal system is headed by the Senior President of Tribunals, and it is part of the national system of administrative justice with tribunals classed as non-departmental public bodies (NDPBs). They are not an integral part of any government department, and they carry out their work at arm's length from Ministers, although Ministers are ultimately responsible to the Parliament for the activities of bodies sponsored by their department.

5. Political Parties and Elections

▶ Political Parties

There are many parties in Britain, but three parties currently dominate the national political landscape: the Conservative Party, the Labour Party, and the Liberal Democrats.

The modern Conservative Party was founded in 1834 and is an outgrowth of the Tory movement or party which began in 1678. The Conservative Party is the main centre-right political party because the Conservatives are opposed to great changes in society and have a belief in private enterprise and freedom from state control. The Conservative Party is supported by those who have something to "conserve", such as landowners and businessmen, often from the middle and upper-middle class. Generally speaking, the more you have in society, the more likely you are to be a conservative.

The Labour Party was created by the growing trade union movement at the end of the 19th century, and at first it was called the Labour Representation Committee. The Labour Party was founded in 1900 and formed its first government in 1924. Since that time, the Labour and Conservative parties have been dominant, with the Liberal Democrats also holding a significant number of seats. The Labour Party is the party of the reformist, non-revolutionary left, because it believes in the pursuit of greater social and economic equality, and aims at the nationalization of the means of production, distribution and exchange. They see the government as the right body to act as a "redistributive" agent: transferring wealth from the richer to the poorer by means of taxing the richer part of the society and providing support to the poorer part, and to provide a range of public services available to all, such as health, education and public transport.

There are several minor parties, such as the Liberal Democrats, the Communist Party, the national parties of Wales, Scotland and Northern Ireland, etc., but they are rather weak. Of them, the Liberal Democrats won the 2010 general election and entered government for the first time as part of a coalition, and became the third largest party in the Parliament, focusing on Constitutional and Political Reforms. However, at the 2015 general election, the party was reduced to eight MPs, and at the 2017 general election, the party returned twelve MPs.

▶ Elections

Every five years a general election is held in Britain. Elections are held in every constituency to decide which individuals shall represent them in the House of Commons. The whole U.K. is usually divided into 650 electoral constituencies. Each constituency has approximately an equal size of population, and elects one member to the House of Commons.

Any citizen over the age of 18 (with a few exceptions, such as criminals, lunatics, and members of the House of Lords) can vote in the constituency where he or she usually resides, and no person may vote in more than one constituency. During the general election, the political parties launch electoral campaigns, such as advertisements in newspaper, leaflets, and party political broadcasts on radio and television.

On the day of the election, voters go to their local polling station, have their names checked in the register, and are given the ballot paper with the candidates' names listed on it. Then each voter puts a cross beside the name of the candidate for whom he or she wishes to vote, folds the paper, and puts it into the ballot-box. When the voting closes at the end of the day, the sealed ballot-boxes are taken to one center in the constituency and votes are counted in the presence of the candidates. The candidate who receives the largest number of votes wins the election, and will go to Westminster as MP for the constituency. The party which wins over half of the constituencies is the majority in the House of Commons, and forms the new government.

6. The Commonwealth

The Commonwealth of Nations is the successor of the British Empire, and it is not a political union, but an intergovernmental organization of 54 independent member states (one of whose membership is currently suspended), in which countries with diverse social, political and economic backgrounds are equal in status. The member states cooperate within a framework of common values and goals, such as the promotion of democracy, human rights, individual liberty, egalitarianism, free trade, multilateralism and world peace, etc.. Membership in the Commonwealth is expressed in cooperation, consultation, mutual assistance, and the periodic meeting of national leaders. The symbol of their free association is the Head of the Commonwealth, which is a ceremonial position currently held by Queen Elizabeth Ⅱ. On the second Monday in March each year, Commonwealth Day is celebrated, and it is an annual event during which all member countries of the Commonwealth celebrate their links.

Section B   Government and Politics of the United States of America

The United States is one of the youngest countries in the world and yet it has the world's oldest constitution and political party (the Democratic Party).

1. The Constitution

The Constitution of the U.S. is the supreme law of the land, which means that when state constitutions or laws passed by state legislatures or by the national Congress are found to conflict with the federal Constitution, these laws have no force. It was completed on September 17, 1787, and was later ratified by special conventions in each state. It created a federal union of sovereign states, and a federal government to operate that union. It was officially adopted on March 4, 1789 and has served as a model for the constitutions of other numerous nations.

The Constitution consists of a preamble, seven original articles, and twenty-seven amendments. The preamble states its purpose, and the first three Articles of the Constitution establish the rules and separate powers of the three branches of the federal government: a legislature, the bicameral Congress; an executive branch led by the President; and a federal judiciary headed by the Supreme Court. The last four Articles frame the principle of federalism. The first ten constitutional amendments ratified by three-fourths of the states in 1791 are known as the Bill of Rights, which contains such liberties as freedom of religion, freedom of speech, freedom of press, the right of peaceful assembly, and the right to petition the government to correct wrongs, etc.. The Constitution has been amended seventeen times (for a total of 27 amendments) and its principles are applied in courts of law by judicial review.

One of the obvious characteristics in the Constitution is "checks and balances". The government consists of three branches: the legislature, the executive, and the judiciary, and each branch has its distinct powers and can check or block the actions of the others. They maintain a balance and no branch can take action on the supposition that it is more powerful than the other two. Checks and balances prevent any one branch from accumulating too much power and encourage cooperation between branches as well as comprehensive debate on controversial policy issues. In addition, the Constitution specifies exactly which power the central government has and which power is reserved for the state government.

2. The American Government

The form of government is based on three main principles: federalism, the separation of powers and respect for the Constitution and the rule of law. Government, both at the federal and state level, is divided into three branches. The legislative branch makes law; the executive branch applies and enforces the law; the judicial branch interprets the law. The federal government is the central government of the U.S., and three equal and separate branches are checked and balanced by one another. The federal government and state governments keep independent from each other. The powers of the federal government are only exemplified in the Constitution, and the other powers are all given to the state governments. The state governments follow much the pattern as the federal government.

▶ The Legislative Branch

Congress is the legislative branch of the federal government, the law-making and the supreme legislative body of the nation, and it is composed of two houses: the Senate and the House of Representatives.

The Senate consists of 100 members, 2 from each of the 50 states regardless of population, which assures that the small states have an equal voice in one of the houses of Congress. The Senators must be at least 30 years old, citizens of the U.S. for at least 9 years, and residents of the state from which they are elected. Senators serve for six years after they are elected, and every two years one-third of the Senate stand for reelection.

The House of Representatives, commonly known as the House, has 435 voting members plus a non-voting representative from Puerto Rico, Guam and the District of Columbia respectively. The Representatives must be at least 25 years old, citizens of the U.S. for at least 7 years, and residents of the state from which they are elected. Each representative serves a two-year term of office. Besides, the number of representatives in each state depends on its population as reported in the most recent national census which is made every ten years. Therefore, states with a larger population have more representatives than states with a smaller one.

Congress convenes in regular session each January 3, and it holds two annual sessions each term. Sessions are held in the Capitol Building in Washington, and the chief function of Congress is to make laws. A bill becomes law after it is introduced and passed in Congress, and it has to

U.S. Capitol, Washington, D.C.

go through many procedures. Once the bill is approved by both houses, it goes to the President for approval. The President may either sign it into law or veto it. If the President vetoes a bill, but Congress still wants to have the law, then Congress can override the veto by a two-thirds majority.

▶ The Executive Branch

The executive branch consists of the President and those to whom the President's powers are delegated. The Constitution vests executive power in a president, and also provides for the election of a vice president, who succeeds to the presidency in case of the death, resignation, or incapacitation of the President. The President is the head of the executive branch of the government which includes 14 departments and many independent agencies. The heads of the departments, chosen by the President and approved by the Senate, form a council of advisers known as the President's "cabinet".

White House, Washington, D.C.

The President should be a native-born American citizen at least 35 years old and a resident of the U.S. for at least 14 years. He is elected by the people through the Electoral College to a four-year term, and limited to two terms. Throughout American history Franklin D. Roosevelt was the only president who served more than two successive terms (1933 – 1945). The President is the head of state and government, as well as the military commander-in-chief and chief diplomat. The President's status makes him the most important figure as the first citizen of the U.S., and his wife is called the First Lady.

The President has powers to manage national affairs and the working of the federal government. He can issue rules, regulations, and instructions called executive orders. He can also appoint the heads of all executive departments and agencies, together with hundreds of other high-ranking federal officials. As the Commander-in-Chief of the armed forces, he has the power to raise, train, supervise and deploy American armed forces. In addition, he is primarily responsible for foreign relations with other nations. Although Secretary of State is the official spokesperson for U.S. foreign policy, he or she just advises the President on foreign affairs, and the final decision is always made by the President. Besides, the President often represents the U.S. abroad in consultations with other heads of state through his officials, and negotiates treaties with other countries. However, the President's powers are not unlimited. For instance, his appointment of the head and senior officials of the executive branch agencies, and his treaties with other countries are subject to the confirmation by the Senate. The President cannot exercise his rights to do whatever he wants, and the President may be impeached by a majority in the House and removed from office by a two-thirds majority in the Senate for "treason, bribery, or other high crimes and misdemeanors". All these avoid the tyranny of a person or a group that is too powerful.

▶ The Judicial Branch

In the U.S. there are two sets of courts: the federal court and the state courts. The federal court usually settles disputes between the center and the units; while the state courts deal with subjects of state or local importance. The state courts and the federal court exist side by side.

The judicial branch of the federal government consists of a series of courts, the Supreme Court, the courts of appeals, and the district courts.

The American Supreme Court

The Supreme Court is the highest court of the U.S., and it is the only court specifically created by the Constitution. The Supreme Court consists of a Chief Justice and eight Associate Justices. They are appointed by the President with the approval of the Senate. Justices have their jobs for life, unless they resign, retire, or are impeached by the House and convicted by the Senate. The Chief Justice is the executive officer of the Court, and decisions are made by the majority, with each justice having one vote. The major powers of the Supreme Court are as follows: to interpret laws, to hear appeals from any federal court cases, to hear appeals from state court cases that involve the Constitution or national laws, to declare a law unconstitutional, and to declare a presidential act unconstitutional.

The courts of appeals (or circuit courts) are intermediate appellate courts of the federal court system, and it was created in 1891 to facilitate the disposition of cases and ease the burden on the Supreme Court. There are currently 13 courts of appeals, and they are considered among the most powerful and influential courts in the U.S., because the Supreme Court chooses to hear fewer than 100 of the more than 10,000 cases annually, and the courts of appeals serve as the final arbiter in most federal cases.

Below the courts of appeals are the district courts which are the general trial courts of the federal court system. Both civil and criminal cases are filed in the district court. The district courts do not have juries or witnesses to testify and present evidence. Rather than determine guilt or innocence, these courts evaluate arguments about legal questions arising in the cases.

3. Political Parties

Thomas Nast's Political Cartoon

American politics have been dominated by a two-party system, which consists of the Democratic Party and the Republican Party. In 1847, the famous American artist Thomas Nast drew a political picture with a donkey

representing the Democratic Party and an elephant representing the Republican Party, and then the donkey and the elephant became the symbols of the two parties. In general, since the 1930s, the Democratic Party positions itself left-of-center in American politics while the Republican Party positions itself as right-of-center, and the two parties took office by turns.

The Democratic Party is one of two major political parties in the U.S., and it is the oldest political party in the world. The Democratic Party grew out of the "Anti-Federalists" that appeared after 1787 when the Constitution was made. The name "Anti-Federalists" was changed into "Democratic-Republicans" by Thomas Jefferson in 1791, and it was then changed into "Democrat" during Andrew Jackson's administration (1829 – 1837). It was the leading party before the Civil War, and represented the interests of the slave-owners. Now it stresses government regulation on the economy, takes full employment as a matter of national concern, and gives priority to controlling inflation and economic programs for those in need. The Democrats favor civil rights laws, a strong social security system, and less restrictive abortion laws. The former president of the U.S., Barack Obama, was the 15th Democrat to hold the office.

The Republican Party is one of the two major contemporary political parties in the U.S., and it is often referred to as the Grand Old Party. Founded in 1854 by northern anti-slavery expansion activists and modernizers, the Republican Party rose to prominence with the election of Abraham Lincoln, the first Republican to campaign on the northern principles of anti-slavery. Today, the Republican Party mainly represents the interests of big businesses, and it places great emphasis on the private sectors and objects to government intervention in business. The republicans stress the need for law and order, and self-reliance, favor reduction of public spending as well as taxes, and oppose complete governmental social programs and free choice of abortion. Besides, they favor a strong military posture and assertive stand in international relations. President Donald Trump is the 20th Republican to hold the office.

Any person has the liberty to decide which party he would like to be in and he can also change his membership at any time. All the party expenditures are covered by donations from their party members.

4. Elections

The U.S. has a federal government, with elected officials at the federal (national), state and local levels. On a national level, the head of state, the President, is elected indirectly by the people, through an Electoral College. All members of the federal legislature, the Congress, are directly elected. There are many elected offices at the state level, each state having at least an elective governor and legislature. There are also elected offices at the local level in counties and cities.

The focal point of American political life is the presidential election which is rather complex, and there are several steps in the election of President: primaries and caucuses (primary election), national party conventions, the campaign (popular election), and the Electoral College.

Primaries are statewide intra-party pre-election. The purpose is to give voters the opportunity to select directly their party's candidates, and the major task is to select delegates to the national party convention. The nominating process usually occurs in February of the election year.

Following the intense campaigning for primaries and caucuses all over the nation, in the summer each party holds a national convention to finalize the selection of one presidential nominee. Delegates to these conventions, chosen within each state, are generally pledged to cast votes for a particular candidate. In order to secure a party's nomination, a candidate must receive a majority of the votes from the delegates. If nobody gets the absolute majority on the first ballot, a second, or a third ballot is held.

After the convention, each party is represented by one candidate, and the whole party will help its candidate run for election all over the country. The general election is held on the Tuesday following the first Monday of November each election year. Presidential candidates run separate campaigns in different states, and they travel throughout the country, making public appearance and giving speeches. They have to face the rival in debates on television, and make the best use of their tongue to arouse public confidence in them. When a candidate wins the majority of electoral votes in a state, he gains all the electoral votes of that state, which is known as the "winner-take-all" principle.

However, the President is not elected directly by the voters. Instead, they are elected by "electors" who are chosen by popular vote on a state-by-state basis. The number of "electors" from each state is equal to the number of members of Congress, and each elector casts one Electoral College vote. On the first Monday after the second Wednesday in December after Election Day, the electors assemble in their state capitals, cast their ballots, and offi-

Obama's Second Inauguration

cially select the President of the U.S.. With 538 Electors, the winner of the election is the candidate with at least 270 Electoral College votes.

On January 20, the newly-elected President enters office in a formal ceremony known as the inauguration. The inauguration ceremony is traditionally held on the steps of the U.S. Capitol. The President takes an oath of office, and makes an inaugural address to outline the policies and plans of his administration.

Section C Government and Politics of China

The People's Republic of China (PRC) is a socialist country led by the working class, based on the worker-peasant alliance and practicing people's democratic centralism. The primary system in China is the socialist system.

1. The Constitution

The Constitution of the PRC is nominally the supreme law within the PRC. Since the establishment of the PRC on October 1, 1949, the constitution had been adopted and amended respectively in 1954, 1975, 1978 and 1982. The current version was adopted on the fifth Plenary Session on the Fifth National People's Congress on December 4, 1982 with further revisions in 1988, 1993, 1999, 2004 and 2018. The Constitution has 5 sections which are the preamble, general principles, the fundamental rights and duties of citizens, the structure of the state[2], the national flag, the national anthem, the national emblem and the capital. There are 4 chapters and 143 articles in total. The fundamental features of the Constitution are setting the fundamental system and tasks, establishing the Four Basic Principles, and laying the basic rationales for reform. The Constitution stipulates that all activities undertaken by its citizens and organizations shall be subject to the Constitution. Any organization or individual cannot surpass the Constitution and law, and the Constitution is the highest law within the PRC.

2. The Chinese Government

◉ The National People's Congress (NPC)

The PRC practices the system of people's congress. China's Constitution stipulates that all power in the PRC belongs to the people, and the organs through which the people exercise state power are the National People's Congress (NPC) and the local people's congresses at different levels. All citizens of the PRC who are over the age of 18 years have the right to elect or be elected as NPC deputies, regardless of ethnic status, race, sex, occupation, family background, religious belief, education, property status or length of residence. Deputies of the people's congresses of the provinces, autonomous regions, and municipalities are directly under the Central Government. The term for deputies is five years, and the congress is held annually.

The basic functions and powers of the NPC are to amend the Constitution, to supervise the enforcement of the Constitution, to enact and amend basic laws of the state, and to decide on the major national leaders, including the President, Vice President, the Premier of the State Council and other component members of the State Council, the Chairman of the Central Military Commission and other component members of the Central Military Commission, the Director of National Supervisory Commission, the President of the Supreme People's Court and the Procurator-General of the Supreme People's Procuratorate. The NPC examines and approves the plan for national economic and social development and the report on its implementation;

examines and approves the state budget and the report on its implementation; and makes decisions on other important issues in national life.

The permanent organ of the NPC is its Standing Committee, which is responsible to the NPC. It serves the same term as the NPC, and it functions as the highest body of state power and accepts supervision by the NPC when it is not in session. Under normal circumstances, the NPC Standing Committee meets every two months, but extraordinary meetings can be convened as required.

▶ The President

The President of the PRC is the head of state of the PRC. According to the current Constitution of the PRC, the President must be a Chinese citizen who has the right to vote and stand for election and has reached the age of 45, and there are no term limits attached to this office from 2018. The President is elected by the NPC which also has the power to remove the President and other state officers from office. The President has the power to promulgate laws, select and dismiss the Premier as well as the ministers of the State Council, grant presidential pardons, declares a state of emergency, issue mass mobilization orders, and issue state honors. In addition, the President names and dismisses ambassadors to foreign countries, signs and annuls treaties with foreign entities. According to the Constitution, all powers mentioned above require the approval or confirmation of the NPC. Besides, the President also conducts state visits on behalf of the PRC.

▶ State Council

The State Council, or the Central People's Government, is the chief administrative authority of the PRC. It is comprised of a premier, vice-premiers, state councilors, ministers in charge of ministries and commissions, the auditor-general and the secretary-general. Currently, the council has 35 members: the premier, one executive vice premier, three vice premiers, five state councilors (of whom two are also ministers), and 25 additional ministers and chairs of major agencies. At present, the State Council includes 26 ministries, commissions and departments, such as Ministry of Foreign Affairs, Ministry of Defense, National Development and Reform Commission, Ministry of Education, Ministry of Science and Technology, People's Bank of China and National Audit Office, etc..

As the chief administrative organ of government, its main functions are to formulate administrative measures, issue decisions and orders, and monitor their implementation; draft legislative bills for submission to the NPC or its Standing Committee; and prepare the economic plan and the state budget for deliberation and approval by the NPC. The State Council is formally responsible to the NPC and its Standing Committee in conducting a wide range of government functions both at the national and at the local levels, and it is the executive body of the highest organ of state power and administration.

▶ The State Central Military Commission

The State Central Military Commission is the supreme leading organ of the armed forces of the PRC, and it directs and commands the national armed forces. The armed forces are the People's Liberation Army[3], People's Police Force (be responsible for keeping security of the country and order of the society), and Civilian Force (the civilian armed forces). The Chairman of the Central Military Commission is elected by the NPC, and the selection of other members is decided by the NPC and its Standing Committee on the basis of the nomination by the chairman. The State Central Military Commission is responsible to the NPC and its Standing Committee. The term for the State Central Military Commission is five years, but there is no limit to the number of terms.

The State Central Military Commission is considered the supreme military policy-making body and its chairman is the commander-in-chief of the armed forces. The Chairman is responsible to the NPC and has the right to make final decisions within its functions and powers.

▶ The National Supervisory Commission

The National Supervisory Commission is the highest anti-corruption agency of the PRC, at the same administrative ranking as Supreme People's Court and Supreme People's Procuratorate. The National Supervision Commission was formed at the first session of the 13th National People's Congress in 2018. The Commission includes the director, deputy director, and ordinary members, and the director is appointed by the NPC.

▶ The Supreme People's Court

The Supreme People's Court is the highest judicial organ and the highest trial organ in China, and it is responsible to the NPC and its Standing Committee. Its structure comprises a judicial committee, or the highest judicial organization, and courts. The appointment of the President and the Vice President of the Supreme People's Court and the members of its Judicial Committee are decided by the NPC.

The Supreme People's Court, Beijing

It independently exercises the highest judicial power according to the law and without any interruption by administrative organs, social organizations or individuals. According to the Constitution and statutes, the main responsibilities of the Supreme People's Court are trying cases that have the greatest influence in China, hearing appeals against the legal decisions of higher courts, and trying the cases the Supreme People's Court claims are within its original jurisdiction; supervising the work of local courts and special courts at every level, overruling wrong judgments they might have made, and deciding interrogations and reviewing cases tried by the lower courts; and giving judicial explanations of the specific utilization of laws in the judicial process that must be carried out nationwide.

▶ The Supreme People's Procuratorate

The Supreme People's Procuratorate is the highest procuratorial organ. It is mainly responsible for supervising regional procuratorates and special procuratorates to perform legal supervision by law and protecting the unified and proper enforcement of State laws. The Supreme People's Procuratorate has to report its work to the NPC and its Standing Committee to whom it is responsible, and accept their supervision.

3. Parties

China is a multi-party country. Apart from the ruling Communist Party of China (CPC), there are eight political parties. They were established long before the founding of the PRC. Every political party is independent in terms of organization, and they enjoy the rights of political freedom, organizational independence, and equality within the scope of the Constitution. Politically other eight political parties support the leadership of the CPC, and it is the historic choice they made during the long-term cooperation and efforts with the CPC.

▶ The Communist Party of China

The Communist Party of China is the vanguard of the Chinese working class, the faithful representative of the interests of the Chinese people of all ethnic groups and the core of leadership over the socialist cause of China. CPC's maximum program of long objective is to realize the Communist social system and the minimum program at present is to build socialism with Chinese characteristics. The CPC takes Marxism-Leninism, Mao Zedong Thought and Deng Xiaoping Theory as the guidance of its actions. The CPC's basic line for the primary stage of socialism is to unite with and lead the people of all ethnic groups in the endeavor to build China into a prosperous, strong, democratic and highly civilized modern socialist state by taking economic development as the central task, adhering to the Four Cardinal Principles[4], persisting in reform and opening up, developing the spirit of self-reliance and pioneering enterprises with painstaking efforts.

Chinese workers, farmers, soldiers, intellectuals and other revolutionaries, who have reached 18 years of age, accept the Party Program and Party Constitution, are willing to participate in one Party organization and actively work in it, carry out Party resolutions and pay regular Party dues, may apply for membership in the CPC. Party members must be admitted through a Party branch according to the principles of admitting members individually only, without exception. On the other hand, Party members are free to withdraw from the Party. When a Party member asks to withdraw from the Party, the matter shall be referred to the Party branch for discussion at a general meeting, and then his or her name must be declared struck from the rolls, and a report must be made to the Party organization at the next higher level for the record.

The central organizations of the CPC are the CPC's National Congress, its Central Committee, the General Secretary, the Central Political Bureau and its Standing Committee, the Central Secretariat, the Central Military Commission and the Central Commission for discipline inspection. The CPC's National Congress, held once every five years, is convened by the Central Committee. If the Central Committee deems it necessary, or over one-third of the provincial-level organizations express a demand, the congress may be held ahead of schedule; and if there is no special situation, its convening shall not be postponed. When the national congress is not in session, the Central Committee is the highest leading organ of the CPC, and the Central Committee is responsible to and reports its work to the National Congress.

Founded in 1921, the CPC helped establish the PRC in 1949 through years of armed struggles. After that, the CPC led Chinese people of all ethnic groups in defending the independence and security of the country, successfully completing the transition from new democracy to socialism. From 1979, the CPC began to carry out the reform and opening-up policy, and in the past three decades since the initiation of these reforms, China's economic and social development has been crowned with remarkable success and the country has taken on a new look.

**Deng Xiaoping's
Reform and Opening-up Policy**

▶ Other Political Parties

Apart from the CPC, other eight political parties are China Revolutionary Committee of the Kuomintang, China Democratic League, China Democratic National Construction Association, China Association for Promoting Democracy, China Peasants and Workers' Democratic Party, China Zhi Gong Dang, Jiusan Society, and the Taiwan Democratic Self-Government League. Most of them were founded during the anti-Japanese War and the national liberation war, and soon after their founding, these parties developed cooperative relations with the CPC at different levels.

According to the principles of "long-term coexistence, mutual supervision, sincere treatment with each other and the share of weal or woe", the political parties in China are not opposition parties, but parties giving full cooperation to the CPC to jointly strive for the socialist cause. At present, these political parties have their local and basic organizations in every province, municipalities directly under the Central Government, autonomous regions, and large and medium-sized cities. They are actually friendly parties of the CPC that participate in state administration.

Notes

1. **the first-past-the-post system**: a first-past-the-post election is one that is won by the candidate with more votes than any other(s).

2. **structure of the state**: the National People's Congress, the State Council, the Local People's Congress, Local People's Governments, the People's Courts, and the People's Procuratorates.

3. **People's Liberation Army**: the principal body of China's armed forces, which is made up of the reserve force and the country's standing army which consists of the Army, Navy, Air Force and the Second Artillery Force.

4. **Four Cardinal Principles**: the principle of upholding the socialist path, upholding the people's democratic dictatorship, upholding the leadership of the CPC and upholding Marxism-Leninism and Mao Zedong Thought.

Glossary

hereditary [hiˈreditəri] *adj.* 世袭的;承袭的

codify [ˈkəudifai] *vt.* 把(法律)编成法典

Statutory Law 成文法

Common Law 习惯法

conventions [kənˈvenʃnz] *n.* 惯例

statute [ˈstætjuːt] *n.* 法令;法规;成文法

flout [flaut] *vt.* 藐视,无视(规则,法律等)

prorogue [prəˈrəug] *vt.* 使(议会)休会

the Lords Spiritual (英国)上议院神职议员

the Lords Temporal (英国)上议院世俗议员

constituency [kənˈstitjuənsi] *n.* 选区

House of Lords Appellate Committee 上议院受理上诉委员会

Constitutional Reform Act 2005　2005 年宪制改革法案

tribunal [triˈbjuːnl, trai-] *n.* 仲裁机构

non-departmental public bodies(NDPBs) 非部委公共机构

merger [ˈməːdʒə] *n.* (企业等的)并吞;合并

coalition [ˌkəuəˈliʃən] *n.* 联合,联盟

ballot ['bælət] *n.* 选票，投票用纸

egalitarianism [iˌgæli'teriənizəm] *n.* 平等主义

multilateralism ['mʌlti'lætərəlism] *n.* 多边贸易

ratify ['rætifai] *vt.* 批准，认可

preamble [priː'æmbl] *n.* 序言，绪论

Bill of Rights 权利法案，人权法案

checks and balances 三权分立

Puerto Rico 波多黎各

Guam 关岛

convene [kən'viːn] *vi.* 集会，聚集

vest [vest] *vt.* 授予，给予（权力、权威等）

incapacitation ['inkəˌpæsi'teiʃən] *n.* 剥夺资格

Electoral College 选举团

deploy [di'plɔi] *vt.* （尤指军事行动）使展开；施展；部署

Secretary of State 国务卿

appellate [ə'pelit] *adj.* 受理上诉的

caucus ['kɔːkəs] *n.* [美]（政党选举候选人或决定政策的）预备会议

State Council 国务院

Central Military Commission *n.* 中央军事委员会

Supreme People's Court 最高人民法院

Supreme People's Procuratorate 最高人民检察院

stratum ['streitəm] *n.* (*pl.* -ta[-tə]) 阶层

plenary ['pliːnəri] *adj.* 全体出席的；全体大会

auditor-general 审计长

secretary-general 秘书长

Ministry of Foreign Affairs 外交部

Ministry of Defense 国防部

State Development Planning Commission 国家开发计划委员会

National Population and Family Planning Commission 国家人口和计划生育委员会

deliberation [diˌlibə'reiʃən] *n.* 审议，商讨，评议

interrogation [inˌterə'geiʃən] *n.* 询(讯，审)问

vanguard ['vænɡɑːd] *n.* 先锋；先进分子

CPC's National Congress 中国共产党全国代表大会

China Revolutionary Committee of the Kuomintang 中国国民党革命委员会

China Democratic League 中国民主同盟

China Democratic National Construction Association 中国民主建国会

China Association for Promoting Democracy 中国民主促进会

China Peasants and Workers' Democratic Party 中国农工民主党

China Zhi Gong Dang 中国致公党

Jiusan Society 九三学社

the Taiwan Democratic Self-Government League 台湾民主自治同盟

Further Reading

1）**The Government and Politics of Canada**

http://manage.eblcu.cn/specls/cls/200266/can02/guide02.asp.htm

http://en.wikipedia.org/wiki/Politics_of_Canada

2）**The Government and Politics of Australia**

http://en.wikipedia.org/wiki/Politics_of_Australia

3）**The Government and Politics of New Zealand**

http://en.wikipedia.org/wiki/Politics_of_New_Zealand

http://en.wikipedia.org/wiki/Outline_of_New_Zealand

http://newzealand.govt.nz

Group Tasks

It is believed that Plato said："There will be no end to the troubles of states, or of humanity itself, till philosophers become kings in this world, or till those we now call kings and rulers really and truly become philosophers, and political power and philosophy thus come into the same hands."

After revising the section on politics, first discuss with others what Plato's words might mean. Then, debate how the U.K., China and America might claim to have held to this idea that it is necessary for "kings to be philosophers" in the way they present their politics to the world.

Chapter 4   Philosophy

Section A   Philosophy in the United Kingdom

Philosophy refers to the study of fundamental nature of knowledge, reason, mind, language and traditions. British philosophy is the study of the philosophical tradition of the British people. The history of British philosophy is usually classified into four periods: medieval period, early modern period, 19th century, and 20th century and beyond. Since the medieval times, Britain has had a number of philosophers who have in their own ways greatly contributed to the British society. Francis Bacon, the father of empiricism, was one of the most influential philosophical advocates of the early modern period in British history. However, the discussion of the early modern period of British philosophy remains incomplete without the mention of the classic trio, John Locke, George Berkeley and David Hume. From the mid-19th century, the country witnessed the beginning of British idealism that remained influential until the early twentieth century. Key philosophers of this time include Thomas Hill Green and Francis Herbert Bradley. In the early 20th century, George Edward Moore and Bertrand Russell pioneered analytical philosophy that till date dominates the British philosophy. We will select some of them to introduce their works and philosophical ideas in this section.

1. British Empiricism

Empiricism is the idea that the origin of all knowledge is sense experience. It emphasizes the role of experience and evidence, especially sensory perception, in the formation of ideas, while discounting the notion of innate ideas, and argues that the only knowledge humans can have is a posteriori (i.e. based on experience). It relies on induction or inductive reasoning (making generalizations based on individual instances) in order to build a more complex body of knowledge from these direct observations. British Empiricism is a practical philosophical movement of empiricism which grew up, largely in Britain, during The Age of Enlightenment of the 17th and 18th Century. The major figures in the movement were Francis Bacon, John Locke, George Berkeley and David Hume, however, we just focus on Bacon and Hume in this section.

▶ Francis Bacon

Sir Francis Bacon (1561 – 1626) was an English philosopher, statesman, essayist and scientist of the late Renaissance
period. His philosophy is displayed in the vast and varied writings he left, which might be divided into three categories: scientific works, religious and literary works, as well as juridical
works.

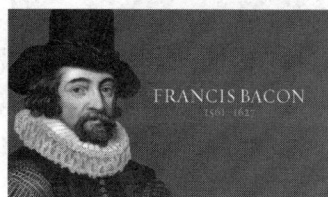

Francis Bacon

▶ *Scientific Works*

Bacon's notable writings in science are parts of a vast work which he left unfinished, his
"*Magna Instauratio*". In this book he calls for inductive reasoning (generalizations based on individual instances), the approach used by modern science. Classically, philosophers had a method wherein they would jump to general conclusions after examining only a few specific instances, and then work backwards for a thorough verification processes. Bacon challenged this
deductive method and argued that truth required evidence from the real world. He believed in going from very specific to general, over a rigorous period of research to confirm a hypothesis.

▶ *Literary and Religious Works*

Bacon's most literary works are collected in his popular *Essays*, published in three editions
in his lifetime, the first containing ten essays, in 1597; the second, with thirty-eight, in 1612;
and the third, in 1625. The essays are written in a wide range of styles, from the plain to the epigrammatic. They cover topics drawn from both public and private life, and in each case the essays cover their topics systematically from a number of different angles.

His religious works are collected in *Meditationes Sacrae* (*Sacred Meditations*), *The New
Atlantis* and other works. At first glance, Bacon's scientific humanism, most clearly expressed
in *The New Atlantis*, may seem compatible with the Christian faith, however, religion only
plays an illusory role subordinated to Bacon's true faith—science. Christianity supplements society with a cohesive structure, but it is mostly a means to the end of scientific advancement. Bacon composes a worldly faith fundamentally hostile to orthodox Christianity by depicting reason
as "light", education as "salvation", and by emphasizing the earthly utility of Christianity rather than any transcendent power that it possesses.

▶ *Juridical Works*

Bacon's ideas about law are collected in his book *The Elements of the Common Laws of*

England: *Maxims of the Law*. Bacon's propositions of legal reform, though not established in his lifetime, are considered to have been one of the influences behind the Napoleonic Code, which is regarded as one of the most influential legal documents in world history. Bacon is credited for the establishment of several features in the modern common law system including using cases as repositories of evidence about the "unwritten law". Some jurists consider Bacon as the father of modern jurisprudence, the science, study and theory of law.

▶ David Hume

David Hume (1711 – 1776) was a Scottish philosopher, historian, economist, and essayist, who is best known today for his highly influential system of philosophical empiricism, skepticism, and naturalism. Hume's empiricist approach to philosophy places him with John Locke, Francis Bacon and George Berkeley as a British Empiricist. Beginning with his *A Treatise of Human Nature* (1739), Hume strove to create a total naturalistic science of man that examined the psychological basis of human nature. Against philosophical rationalists, Hume held that passion rather than reason governs human behavior. Hume argued against the existence of innate ideas, positing that all human knowledge is founded solely in experience and that genuine knowledge must either be directly traceable to objects perceived in experience, or result from abstract reasoning about relations between ideas which are derived from experience.

David Hume

2. British Idealism

"Idealism" or "idealist" is used to describe a person having high ideals, sometimes with the connotation that those ideals are unrealisable or at odds with "practical" life. However in philosophy, idealism is used to refer to any metaphysical theory positing the primacy of mind, spirit, or language over matter. British idealism started from the mid 19th century to the early twentieth century. The leading figures in the movement were Thomas Hill Green and Francis Herbert Bradley.

▶ Thomas Hill Green

Thomas Hill Green (1836 – 1882) was an English philosopher and brought idealism into England. He firmly rejected the native British philosophical tradition: its empiricist theory of knowledge, in the introduction to his edition of Hume's Treatise of Human Nature. He argued against empiricism and held that the mind was active in knowledge. He was against

Thomas Green

hedonism and held that human action was free, not the causal outcome of natural desires, and that its end should be self-fulfillment instead of pleasure. This conception of man's moral agency led him in *Lectures on the Principles of Political Obligation* to assign to the state the task of creating the conditions for individuals to pursue their moral perfection freely.

▶ Francis Herbert Bradley

F. H. Bradley (1846 – 1924) was the most famous, original and philosophically influential of the British Idealists. He attacked the method of inductive logic by holding that judgment and inference cannot begin with isolated, particular facts. His most important work was *Appearance and Reality* (1893). He saw reality as a monistic whole, which is apprehended through "feeling", a state in which there is no distinction between the perception and the thing perceived.

Francis Bradley

3. Analytical Philosophy

Analytical philosophy is a branch of philosophy that was important in the 20th century. Analytical philosophy focuses on the philosophy of language, and on argumentation. The founders of this movement include Gottlob Frege, George Edward Moore, Bertrand Russell and Ludwig Wittgenstein. We just introduce Russel, the most influential philosopher among them.

▶ Bertrand Russell

Bertrand Arthur William Russell (1872 – 1970) was a mathematician, philosopher, and logician of the modern age, working mostly in the 20th century. He was also a popularizer of philosophy and a commentator on a large variety of topics, ranging from very serious issues to the mostly mundane. Russell's elegant prose, clarity of expression, and biting wit were widely admired. Millions looked up to Russell as a prophet of the creative and rational life; at the same time, his stances on many topics were extremely controversial. As one of the world's most well-known intellectuals, Russell's voice carried enormous moral authority, even into his late nineties. Among his other political activities, Russell was an influential proponent

Bertrand Russell

of nuclear disarmament and an outspoken critic of the American war in Vietnam. In 1950, Russell was made Nobel Laureate in Literature "in recognition of his varied and significant writings in which he champions humanitarian ideals and freedom of thought".

Russell is generally recognized as one of the founders of analytic philosophy. At the beginning of the 20th century, alongside G. E. Moore, Russell was largely responsible for the British "revolt against Idealism", a philosophy greatly influenced by Georg Hegel and his British apostle, F. H. Bradley. He and Moore strove to eliminate what they saw as meaningless and incoherent assertions in philosophy, and sought clarity and precision in argument by the use of exact language and by breaking down philosophical propositions into their simplest components. Russell, in particular, saw logic and science as the principal tools of the philosopher. The main task of the philosopher was to illuminate the most general propositions about the world and to eliminate confusion. In particular, he wanted to end what he saw as the excesses of metaphysics.

Section B Philosophy in the United States of America

American philosophy is the activity and tradition of philosophers affiliated with the United States. While it lacks a core of defining features, American philosophy can nevertheless be seen as both reflecting and shaping collective American identity over the history of the nation. In this section, we will select three branches of American philosophy to explain: Pragmatism, American Enlightenment and Transcendentalism.

1. Pragmaticism

As other philosophers, American philosophers have asked and tried to answer big questions about the way things are: What is true? What am I? How should I live? What is right? What is wrong? How do I know? The Puritans brought these questions with them from Europe and we still ask them today. American Philosophy first appeared in the late 1860s with the creation of a philosophical movement called Pragmatism (1870 – 1910).

Charles Pierce

Pragmatism is based on the idea that what is "true" is what works in practice: what has practical, observable consequences for our lives. It was created by Charles Sanders Pierce (1839 – 1914) and developed by William James (1842 – 1910), who famously claimed that "truth" is what "happens to an idea". Pragmatism is the first formal American philosophy, that is, the first philosophy created in America and recognized as a branch within the professional disciplines of philosophy in America, Europe, and around the world. Today it is experiencing a revival.

But Pragmatism didn't come from nowhere. It arose from earlier philosophical movements carried to America from Europe, and from early

William James

American discussions of philosophical questions among its religious, literary, scientific, and political leaders and everyday citizens themselves. The Puritans who came to America in the 1630s believed that humans were fallen from God's grace, but they also believed that they might be saved if they used their human ability to reason—or think—to examine the bible and the world around them in order to understand God's will.

2. American Enlightenment

The Puritans also brought with them from the Europe the ideas of the Enlightenment, primarily the notion that man is a creature capable of rational inquiry. In the 1700s, Americans adapted and used this philosophical idea as a political principle in the period that has come to be called the American Enlightenment (1680 – 1820). Thinkers and writers of this period believed in learning from tradition and the past, but they disdained blind acceptance of any kind of knowledge, especially of religious doctrines. This is because they held that rational beings are by definition innovative: they adapt what they have learned to respond to the demands of

Thomas Jefferson

present conditions. The writings of Thomas Jefferson (1743 – 1826) are products of the American Enlightenment. He drafted American *Declaration of Independence*, in which he supported the notion that human beings are rational thinkers capable of making their own choices based on the evidence available to them. This kind of human being is capable of being an active citizen in a democracy rather than a passive subject in a monarchy.

3. Transcendentalism

In the early to mid-nineteenth century, Ralph Waldo Emerson (1803 – 1882) inspired a religious, literary, and political movement called Transcendentalism (1820 – 1870). Emerson and his circle believed that human beings are not only innovative, but perfectible: their power to think enables them to develop their unique talents and become the best version of themselves that they can be. The Transcendentalists also rejected Enlightenment notions of rationality in the abstract and considered the actual experience of persons thinking. They focused on the whole individual: a thinker, but one with feelings who lives in a particular context and tries to make sense of his or her place in the universal order of things. Transcendentalism is often referred to as American Romanticism, an American

Ralph Emerson

form of European Romanticism.

Section C   Philosophy in China

Chinese Philosophy refers to several schools of philosophical thought in the Chinese tradition. It covers a long history of 5000 years.

1. History of Chinese philosophy

It is known that early Shang Dynasty (1600 B. C. – 1046 B.C.) thought was based on cyclicity, from observation of the cycles of day and night, the seasons, the moon, etc., a concept which remained relevant throughout later Chinese philosophy, and immediately setting it apart from the more linear Western approach. During this time, both gods and ancestors were worshipped and there were human and animal sacrifices.

Cyclicity

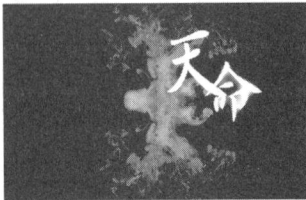

The Mandate of Heaven

During the succeeding Zhou Dynasty (1122 B.C.– 256 B.C.), the concept of the Mandate of Heaven was introduced, which held that Heaven would bless the authority of a just ruler, but would be displeased with an unwise ruler, and retract the Mandate.

The *Book of Changes* was traditionally compiled by the mythical figure Fu Xi in the 28th Century B.C., although modern research suggests that it more likely dates to the late 9th Century B.C. The text describes an ancient system of cosmology and philosophy that is intrinsic to

The Book of Changes

ancient Chinese cultural beliefs, centering on the ideas of the dynamic balance of opposites, the evolution of events as a process, and acceptance of the inevitability of change. It consists of a series of symbols, rules for manipulating these symbols, poems and commentary, and is sometimes regarded as a system of divination.

In about 500 B.C., the classic period of Chinese philosophy (known as the Contention of a Hundred Schools of Thought) flourished, and the four most influential schools (Confucianism, Taoism, Mohism and Legalism) were established.

The Contention of a Hundred Schools of Thought

During the Qin Dynasty, after the unification of China in 221 B.C., Legalism became ascendant at the expense of the Mohist and Confucianist schools, although the Han Dynasty (206 B.C.– A.D. 220) adopted Taoism and later Confucianism as official doctrine. Along with the gradual parallel introduction of Buddhism, these two schools have remained the determining forces of Chinese thought up until the 20th Century.

Neo-Confucianism (a variant of Confucianism, incorporating elements of Buddhism, Taoism and Legalism) was introduced during the Song Dynasty (A.D. 960 – 1279) and popularized during the Ming Dynasty (1368 – 1644).

During the Industrial and Modern Ages, Chinese philosophy also began to integrate concepts of Western philosophy. Sun Yat-Sen (1866 – 1925) attempted to incorporate elements of democracy, republicanism and industrialism at the beginning of the 20th century, while Mao Zedong (1893 – 1976) later added Marxism and other communist thought.

However, up to date the most influential schools of Chinese philosophy are Confucianism, Taoism, Mohism and Legalism. That is why we just center on them in this section.

2. Major Schools

▶ Confucianism

Confucianism is a collection of the thoughts and system of philosophy propounded by Confucius (551 – 479 B.C.) and his followers and supporters. It is rife with governmental morality, ethics in social relationships, social justice and the value of sincerity in all human activities. Confucius teachings and his conversations and exchanges with his disciples are recorded in the *Lunyu* or *Analects*. His influence on China is so great that he was hailed after his death as "The Uncrowned King". Fung Yu-lan, one of the great 20th century authorities on the history of Chinese thought, compares Confucius' influence in Chinese history with that of Socrates in the West.

Confucius

Benevolent Government

In politics, Confucianism advocates "internal saints and external kings" which emphasizes a man's personal integrity and virtues based on which he governs the whole nation. It can be summed up as "benevolent government" which is just like parents who need to take care of their children and always put the interest of the people first. This thought was applied by many later emperors, such as Emperor Taizong of the Tang Dynasty, who created one of the most peaceful and prosperous kingdoms in the world. Even today, Chinese leaders stress "morality" and "people oriented" policies.

In ethics, Confucianism advocates the Five Constant Virtues, that is benevolence, righteousness, ritual propriety, wisdom and integrity. To be a moral person or junzi, the ancient Chinese cultivated and monitored themselves according to the Five Constant Virtues. Confucianism also emphasizes Five Cardinal Relationships in society, that is the relationships between ruler and subject, husband and wife, father and son, elder brother and younger brother, and friend and friend. Each group had its corresponding duties to fulfill.

In education, many of Confucius' ideas concerning education correspond to the general laws of modern pedagogic, such as to provide students with education that matched their aptitude, to explain the present in the light of the past, to instruct oneself while teaching others, to combine theory and practice etc. Confucius also encourages people to be modest and learn from others' merits. He once said "When I walk along with two others, they may serve me as my teachers. I will select their good qualities and follow them, their bad qualities and avoid them."

In relations between human and nature, Confucianism proposes the perfect harmony between the two. Man is just one part of the nature and the two is a unity, a contrast with the thought that man should develop all kinds of techniques and weapons to conquer the nature. Confucius once said "Don't catch fish with a net when you go fishing; don't shoot a bird when it perches high in the tree". His emphasis on frugality in the use of resources and advice to people to restrain their desire are still enlightening in this fast developing and over-consuming world.

▶ Taoism

Taoism or Daoism is a philosophy which later developed into a religion. Tao literally means "path" or "way", although it is more often used as a metaphysical term that describes the flow of the universe, or the force behind the natural order. The Three Jewels of the Tao are compassion, moderation, and humility. Taoist thought focuses on wu wei (non-action), spontaneity, humanism, relativism, emptiness and the strength of softness (or flexibility). Nature and ancestor spirits are common in popular Taoism, although typically there is also a pantheon of gods, often headed by the Jade

Lao Tzu

Yin and Yang

Emperor. The most influential Taoist text is the "Tao Te Ching" (or "Daodejing") written around the 6th Century B.C. by Lao Tzu (or Laozi). The concept of Yin and Yang is important in Taoism. For Taoists, life is lived inside the interplay of opposites: up and down, hot and cold, male and female, dry and wet, outside and inside, high and low, joy and sadness, peace and war, exertion and rest, life and death, and so on. Yin and Yang symbolize this primal interplay of opposites in life and in the world-known as the Tao. They form the dynamism or energy of the Tao, and that is the way of all things.

▶ Legalism

Legalism is a pragmatic political philosophy, whose main motto is "set clear strict laws, or deliver harsh punishment", and its essential principle is one of jurisprudence. According to Legalism, a ruler should govern his subjects according to Fa (law or principle), Shu (method, tactic, art, or statecraft) and Shi (legitimacy, power, or charisma). Under Li Si in the 3rd century B.C., a form of Legalism essentially became a totalitarian ideology in China, which in part led to its subsequent decline.

Han Feizi

▶ Mohism

Mohism was founded by Mozi (c.470 – 390 B.C.). It promotes universal love with the aim of mutual benefit, such that everyone must love each other equally and impartially to avoid conflict and war. Mozi was strongly against Confucian ritual, instead emphasizing pragmatic survival through farming, fortification and statecraft. In some ways, his philosophy parallels Western utilitarianism. Although popular during the latter part of the Zhou Dynasty, many Mohist texts were destroyed during the succeeding Qin Dynasty, and it was finally supplanted completely by Confucianism during the Han Dynasty.

Mozi

▶ Buddhism

Buddhism is a religion, a practical philosophy and arguably a psychology, focusing on the teachings of Buddha (Siddhartha Gautama), who lived in India from the mid-6th to the early 5th Century B.C.. It was introduced to China from India, probably some time during the 1st Century B.C.. Chinese tradition focuses on ethics rather than metaphysics, and it developed several schools distinct from the originating Indian schools, and in the process integrated the ideas of Confucianism, Taoism and other indigenous philosophical systems into itself. The most prominent Chinese Buddhist schools are Sanlun, Tiantai, Huayan and Chán (known as Zen in Japan).

Siddhartha Gautama

Notes

1. **The Age of Enlightenment**: The Age of Enlightenment (or simply the Enlightenment or Age of Reason) was a cultural movement of intellectuals in the 18th century, first in Europe and later in the American colonies. Its purpose was to reform society using reason (rather than tradition, faith and revelation) and advance knowledge through science. It promoted science and intellectual interchange and opposed superstition, intolerance and some abuses by church and state.

2. **Renaissance**: Renaissance (French: "Rebirth") refers to a period in European history, covering the span between the 14th and 17th centuries. It is an extension of the Middle Ages, and is bridged by the Age of Enlightenment to modern history, and conventionally held to have been characterized by a surge of interest in Classical scholarship and values. The Renaissance also witnessed the discovery and exploration of new continents, the substitution of the Copernican for the Ptolemaic system of astronomy, the decline of the feudal system and the growth of commerce, and the invention or application of such potentially powerful innovations as paper, printing, the mariner's compass, and gunpowder. To the scholars and thinkers of the day, however, it was primarily a time of the revival of Classical learning and wisdom after a long period of cultural decline and stagnation.

3. **Declaration of Independence**: The United States Declaration of Independence is the statement adopted by the Second Continental Congress meeting in Philadelphia, Pennsylvania on July 4, 1776. The Declaration announced that the Thirteen Colonies then at war with the Kingdom of Great Britain would regard themselves as thirteen independent sovereign states no longer under British rule. Since then, it has become a well-known statement on human rights, particularly its second sentence: We hold these truths to be self-evident, that all men are created equal, that they are endowed by their Creator with certain unalienable Rights, that among these are Life, Liberty and the pursuit of Happiness.

4. **Hundred Schools of Thought**: The Hundred Schools of Thought is the name given to philosophers and schools that flourished from 770 to 221 B.C., an era of great cultural and intellectual expansion in China. Even though this period, known in its earlier part as the Spring and Autumn period and the Warring States period in its latter part, was characterized by chaos and bloody battles, it is also known as the Golden Age of Chinese philosophy because a variety of thoughts and ideas were freely developed and discussed. This phenomenon has been called the Contention of a Hundred Schools of Thought. The thoughts and ideas of this period have profoundly influenced lifestyles and social consciousness in East Asian countries through the present day.

Glossary

philosophy [fə'lɔsəfi] *n.* 哲学

medieval [ˌmedi'iːvl] *adj.* 中古的,中世纪的

empiricism [im'pirisizəm] *n.* 实证论,经验论

analytical [ˌænə'litikl] *adj.* 分析的

induction [in'dʌkʃn] *n.* 归纳(法)

deduction [di'dʌkʃn] *n.* 推理,演绎(法)

generalization [ˌdʒenrəlai'zeiʃn] *n.* 归纳;概论

renaissance [ri'neisns] *n.* 文艺复兴

juridicial [dʒuə'ridikl] *adj.* 裁判的,司法的

verification [ˌverifi'keiʃn] *n.* 证明;证实

hypothesis [hai'pɔθəsis] *n.* 假设,假说

epigrammatic [ˌepigrə'mætik] *adj.* 警句的

compatible [kəm'pætəbl] *adj.* 兼容的;和谐的

subordinate [sə'bɔːdinət] *vt.* 使服从

orthodox ['ɔːθədɔks] *adj.* 普遍赞同的;正统的

transcendent [træn'sendənt] *adj.* 超然的

repository [ri'pɔzətri] *n.* 仓库;贮藏室

jurisprudence [ˌdʒuəris'pruːdns] *n.* 法学

skepticism ['skeptisizəm] *n.* 怀疑态度,怀疑论

rationalist ['ræʃnəlist] *n.* 理性主义者

metaphysical [ˌmetə'fizikl] *adj.* 形而上学的

hedonism ['hiːdənizəm] *n.* 享乐主义

monistic [mɔ'nistik] *adj.* 一元论的

mundane [mʌn'dein] *adj.* 世俗的

prophet ['prɔfit] *n.* 预言家,先知;主张者

proponent [prə'pəunənt] *n.* 支持者,拥护者

disarmament [dis'ɑːməmənt] *n.* 解除武装

apostle [ə'pɔsl] *n.* 提倡者

apall [ə'pɔːl] *vt.* 使惊骇,使充满恐惧

incoherent [inkəu'hiərənt] *adj.* 思想不连贯的

affiliate [ə'filieit] *vt.* 使隶属于

pragmatism ['prægmətizəm] *n.* 实用主义

discipline ['disəplin] *n.* 学科

disdain [dis'dein] *vt.* 鄙视;不愿意做

democracy [di'mɔkrəsi] *n.* 民主;民主国家

monarchy ['mɔnəki] *n.* 君主政体;君主政治

perfectible［pəˈfektəbl］*adj.* 可使完美的

cyclicity［saiˈklisiti］*n.* 循环性，周而复始

retract［riˈtrækt］*vt.* 撤回或撤销

cosmology［kɔzˈmɔlədʒi］*n.* 宇宙学

divination［ˌdiviˈneiʃn］*n.* 预言；占卦

variant［ˈveəriənt］*n.* 变体

reconcile［ˈrekənsail］*vt.* 使和好，使和解

spontaneity［ˌspɔntəˈneiəti］*n.* 自发性

legitimacy［liˈdʒitiməsi］*n.* 合法（性）

charisma［kəˈrizmə］*n.* 魅力；感召力

fortification［ˌfɔːtifiˈkeiʃn］*n.* 筑垒；防御工事

totalitarian［təuˌtæləˈteəriən］*adj.* 极权主义的

supplant［səˈplɑːnt］*vt.* 取代；代替

indigenous［inˈdidʒənəs］*adj.* 土生土长的

Further Reading

1）**Western philosophy**

https：//www.britannica.com/topic/Western-philosophy

2）**Canadian philosophy**

https：//www.thecanadianencyclopedia.ca/en/article/philosophy

https：//en.wikipedia.org/wiki/List_of_Canadian_philosophers

3）**Australian philosophy**

https：//en.wikipedia.org/wiki/Australian_philosophy

https：//www.rep.routledge.com/articles/thematic/australia-philosophy-in/v-1

4）**New Zealand philosophy**

https：//en.wikipedia.org/wiki/Category：New_Zealand_philosophers

Group Tasks

1. There are some common topics in both Chinese and western philosophy，such as some fundamental questions on the nature of knowledge，morality and human nature，society and government. Choose one topic that you are interested in and compare the similarities and differences in Chinese and western philosophy. Share your findings and ideas with your classmates.

2. Discuss the implications of ancient Chinese philosophy for the modern world.

Chapter 5   Education

Section A   Education in the United Kingdom

British education has achieved a worldwide reputation for quality. Its educational traditions have developed over centuries, and led by outstanding universities such as Oxford and Cambridge University and by the world famous Independent Schools like Eton, Harrow and Winchester.

1. The Goal of British Education

The goal of British education is to provide children with literacy and other basic skills they will need to become active members of society. British education is renowned for concerning itself with the development of the whole personality. Learning is important, but not the whole thing. Young people need to develop their potential to explore and discover the world around them, to think for themselves and form opinions, to relate to others, to develop their bodies through sport and physical education, and to gain experience in taking responsibility.

2. Educational Policy

Before 1870, education was voluntary and many of the existing schools had been set up by churches. Only 40% of children aged 10 went to school regularly. From then on, in response to changes brought about by the Industrial Revolution and social and political movements, the government started to take responsibility for education. Education in Britain is compulsory for all children between the ages of 5 and 16. This is a fundamental policy since 1944 when the Education Act passed in that year implemented free education for all children throughout the country. An examination, known as the Eleven-plus test, was given to all children after they have finished primary education at age 11 to test children's knowledge in English and arithmetic. However, this system is criticized for reinforcing the incorrect assumption that children of lower social class had lower intelligence and for dividing the children into different trends at an early age. So in the 1960s, comprehensive system was introduced, which ended the division between grammar schools, where the most academically capable pupils were sent to prepare for university, and vocational schools, where the less successful ones were sent to learn a trade. Children study at comprehensive primary schools between age 5 and 11 and then go on to comprehensive secondary schools without the Eleven-plus test and study there until the age of 16.

The Education Reform Act 1988 provided for the establishment of a National Curriculum, which divides the primary and secondary education into four key stages and sets the minimum learning requirements for all children at each stage. The national curriculum occupies no less than 70% of the school timetable, the rest of the time being used for subjects of the school's choice. At each of the stages the core subjects of English, mathematics, science, technology, physical education and religious education are taught. History, geography, music and art are also compulsory subjects up to 16 years old, but they become optional in Key Stage 4.

In November 2000, a new National Curriculum was launched to help students to become more competent in coping with challenges of the 21st century. The new curriculum adds Information and Communication Technology to the existing curricula for primary and secondary education. It also advocates a shift of focus on primary and secondary education from knowledge-based approaches to skill-based ones. Parallel to the practical skills, the new curriculum also lays emphasis on the enhancement of students' "thinking skills", such as the abilities to collect, sort out and analyze information, and to reason logically on the basis of evidence.

3. Education System

The education system in the U.K. is very complicated. Generally speaking, it includes primary education, secondary education, further education, and higher education. Besides, there are two systems of primary and secondary education—the state school and the independent or "public" school. The former is in the majority; the latter are few in number but of great influence. All British children are required by law to have a full-time education from the age of 5 to 16. Any child may attend, without paying fees, the state schools until they are eighteen. Education at this stage is compulsory, but school is not. Parents can educate the child themselves if they show their timetable, methods and equipment for an inspector to approve.

▶ Primary Education

The system of state primary education is from the age of five to eleven, while the system of private schools at elementary level is perhaps from three to thirteen including preschool education. Actually there are several different systems in operation.

In the state primary schools, there are two sections—an infant section, from five to seven and a junior section, from seven to eleven. Before their primary schooling some children have an opportunity to attend one of the few kindergartens from the age of three to five, officially called

"Nursery Schools". But most small children stay at home with their mothers. The great majority of parents send their children to state schools, where education is provided free of charge. These schools are co-educational or mixed schools, because they admit both boys and girls. The academic year begins in September, and is divided into three terms, with holidays at Christmas, Easter, and in the summer. The exact dates of the holidays vary from area to area. Religion, English, Math, History, Geography, Nature Studies, Hygiene, Art Handicraft, Music and Physical Education are taught in the primary schools.

There is also private education in Britain at this stage. Before a child begins his education in a preparatory school at the age of seven or eight, his or her parents may send him or her to a small private school which charges fees. The preparatory schools, which are popularly known as prep schools, are independent schools for children from seven or eight up to thirteen. Their curriculum differs considerably from that of the primary school, since its main purpose is the "common entrance" examination at the age of thirteen, for admission to a "public school". Prep schools usually have very small classes and the better prep schools have the benefits of ample space, good playing fields and pleasant surroundings.

▶ Secondary Education

State secondary schools take in students aged 11 and education continues for five years until they have reached the age of 16. Independent secondary schools teach students aged between 13 and 16.

About 90% of secondary schools are comprehensive schools, which provide a general education. Students study both academic subjects like literature and science and more practical ones like cooking and carpentry.

When children finish their schooling at 16, they are required to take a national examination, the General Certificate of Secondary Education (GCSE), which certifies that they have achieved the standard expected after 11 years of compulsory education. Having completed their GCSE, students may choose to leave school and begin working, or to continue full-time education in what is called "the sixth form", which lasts for a period of two years, and then take a further set of standardized exams, known as the A-levels[1] (General Certificate of Education-Advanced), in three or four subjects. Since admittance to universities depends largely on A-level results, the two years spent in the sixth form are crucially important and stressful for students. Other students who decide not to go to university may choose to take vocational training. The vocational equivalent of the A-levels is the General National Vocational Qualifications (GNVQs), which provides a broad vocational education.

In the private sector, independent schools or public schools receive their funding through the private sector and tuition fees, with minimal government assistance, and they are generally much better funded than most state schools and are thus in a position to recruit the best teachers and provide superior facilities. As a result, graduates of independent schools are more likely than those of state schools to be accepted by famous universities. These schools aim at shaping characters as well as individuality. Traditionally they emphasize two factors in education. One is the study of classics and science, the other is the development of what is called "character". The so-called public school spirit is founded on the development simultaneously of both team spirit and leadership and it is through games that these qualities of character are first developed. Most independent schools, particularly the

Eton College

most eminent ones, are called by the name of the town or village in which they are located; some are called "College" and some are not. The four most famous of all are Eton College, Harrow school, Winchester College and Rugby School. Eton College, often informally referred to as Eton, is a British independent boarding school located in Eton, near Windsor in England. It educates over 1,300 pupils, aged between 13 to 18 years old and was founded in 1440 by King Henry VI. Following the public school tradition, Eton is a full boarding school, which means all pupils live at the school, and is one of four such remaining single-sex boys' public schools in the U.K. (the others being Winchester College, Harrow School and Radley College) to continue this practice. It has educated nineteen British Prime Ministers and generations of aristocracy, and has been referred to as "the chief nurse of England's statesmen".

▶ Higher Education

Higher education has a long history in Britain. According to their history, universities in the U.K. are sometimes classified into the Old Universities, the Red-brick Universities, and the New Universities.

The Old Universities refer to those founded before the year 1600. The first universities in Britain were Oxford and Cambridge which were established in 12th and 13th centuries respectively, and the Scottish universities of St. Andrews, Glasgow, Edinburgh and Aberdeen were founded in 15th and 16th centuries. England, at this period, had no other universities besides Oxford and Cambridge until the 19th century.

It was not until the beginning of the 19th century that the creation of more universities was seen to be either necessary or desirable. One of the first new foundations was London University, following the organizational structure of the ancient foundations, which also consists of a number of constituent colleges. This was followed by the foundation of several universities such as Manchester and Birmingham, which developed from provincial colleges. These provincial universities of the period 1850 – 1930 as well as

London University

London University are usually referred to by the slightly contemptuous term "the Red-brick Universities", which defines this group of universities all built in the favorite building material of the period—red brick, which is contrasted with the more dignified and solid-looking ancient stone architecture of "Oxbridge".

The New Universities are those that sprang up after World War Ⅱ in the not-too-large, but not-too-small industrial towns. A group of post-war universities, such as Lancaster, York, Warwick and East Anglia, try to break away from the traditional specialist courses and to teach a more balanced mixture of subjects. Much more emphasis of these modern universities is placed on advanced studies in science and technology and the newer social science disciplines than on the arts and humanities, and many students now choose the new universities because of their more "modern" approach.

Formally higher education was age-restricted and for economic or social reasons many people may not get the opportunity. The Open University was initiated from Britain in 1969, and it offers a non-traditional route for people to take university level courses and receive a university degree. People can register without having any formal education qualifications, and they can follow university courses through textbooks, TV and radio broadcasts, correspondence, video, and a network of study centers. Tens of thousands of British people, from housewives to coal miners, from teachers to ballet dancers, "attend" the Open University each year.

There's no national entrance examination of any sort in Britain. Universities select and admit students mainly on the basis of the grades of their A-levels, or AS-levels or GNVQs, usually in conjunction with school references plus an interview. Students spend three years studying full-time for the first degree, Bachelor of Arts or Bachelor of Science. Then, if they want to obtain a Master's Degree in Arts or Science, they will need another one year of full-time or two years of part-time study. To obtain a doctoral degree requires from three to five years of additional study and research.

4. Two Famous Universities

▶ Oxford University

The University of Oxford is a collegiate research university located in Oxford, England. It is the oldest university in the English-speaking world, and it grew rapidly from 1167 when Henry Ⅱ banned English students from attending the University of Paris.

The University is a "city university" in that it does not have a main campus; instead, colleges, departments, accommodation, and other facilities are scattered throughout the city centre. The Science Area, in which most science departments are located, is the area that bears the closest resemblance to a campus.

The University has the largest university library system in the U.K.. With over 11 million volumes housed on 120 miles of shelving, the Bodleian group is the second largest library in the U.K., after the British Library. The Bodleian is a legal deposit library, which means that it is entitled to request a free copy of every book published in the U.K.. Besides, Oxford maintains a number of museums and galleries, open for free to the public. The Ashmolean Museum, founded in 1683, is the oldest museum in the U.K. and the oldest university museum in the world.

The University Parks are a 70-acre parkland area in the northeast of the city, which is open free of charge to the public during daylight hours. As well as providing beautiful gardens and rare and exotic plants, the parks contains numerous sports fields, used for official and unofficial fixtures. The Botanic Garden on the High Street is the oldest botanic garden in the U.K. and the third oldest scientific garden in the world. It is one of the most diverse yet compact collections of plants in the world and includes representatives from over 90% of the higher plant families.

The Oxford Botanic Garden

Undergraduate teaching is centered on the tutorial, and students usually have one or two tutorials a week, and can be taught by academics at any other college—not just their own. These tutorials are complemented by lectures, classes and seminars, which are organized on a departmental basis. Graduate students are usually instructed through classes and seminars, though there is more focus upon individual research. There are many opportunities for students at Oxford to receive financial help during their studies. For graduate study, there are many scholarships attached to the university, available to students from all sorts of backgrounds, from Rhodes Scholarships to the relatively new Weidenfeld Scholarships.

The academic year is divided into three terms. Within each of the terms, Council determines an 8-week period called Full Term, during which undergraduate teaching takes place. These teaching terms are shorter than those of many other British universities, and the total duration of Full Terms amounts to less than half the year.

According to the 2012 Times Higher Education World Reputation Rankings based on a survey of 17,554 academics over 149 countries, Oxford belongs to the elite group of six universities touted as the globally recognized "super-brands".

▶ Cambridge University

The University of Cambridge is a public research university located in Cambridge, England. It is the second oldest university in the English-speaking world, and it is considered to be one of the most prestigious institutions of higher learning in the world.

The institute grew out of an association of scholars that was formed in 1209 by scholars leaving Oxford after a dispute with townsfolk. The two "ancient universities" have many common features and are often jointly referred to as Oxbridge. Today, Cambridge is a collegiate university with 31 colleges and 6 academic schools. All these university institutions occupy different locations in the town. Cambridge is also a member of a myriad of academic associations and forms part of "the golden triangle" of British universities. A total of 89 Nobel Prizes winners are affiliates of the university.

The university occupies a central location within the city of Cambridge, with the students taking up a significant proportion (nearly 20%) of the town's population. Most of the older colleges are situated nearby the city centre and river Cam, along which it is traditional to punt in order to appreciate the buildings and surroundings. Examples of notable buildings include King's College Chapel, the history faculty building designed by James Stirling, and the Cripps Building at St John's College.

King's College Chapel

The university has 114 libraries. The Cambridge University Library is the central research library, which holds over 8 million volumes. It is a legal deposit library, therefore it is entitled to request a free copy of every book published in the U.K. and Ireland. In addition to the University Library and its dependents, every faculty has a specialized library. Furthermore, every college has a library as well, partially for the purposes of undergraduate teaching, and the older colleges often possess many early books and manuscripts in a separate library.

The Fitzwilliam Museum

Cambridge University operates eight arts, cultural, and scientific museums, and a botanic garden. For instance, the Fitzwilliam Museum, is the art and antiquities museum; the Kettle's Yard is a contemporary art gallery; the Cambridge University Museum of Zoology houses a wide range of zoological specimens from around the world and is known for its iconic finback whale skeleton that hangs outside; the Sedgwick Museum of Earth Sciences is the geology museum of the University; the Cambridge University Botanic Garden created in 1831 is the botanic garden of the University.

Cambridge is a collegiate university, meaning that it is made up of self-governing and independent colleges, each with its own property and income. Most colleges bring together academics and students from a broad range of disciplines, and within each faculty, school or department within the university, academics from many different colleges will be found. There are also several theological colleges in Cambridge, separate from Cambridge University, including Westcott House, Westminster College and Ridley Hall Theological College, which are, to a lesser degree, affiliated to the university and are members of the Cambridge Theological Federation.

The academic year is divided into three terms, determined by the Statutes of the

University. Within these terms undergraduate teaching takes place within eight-week periods called Full Terms. Like Oxford, these terms are also shorter than those of many other British universities.

In the last two British Government Research Assessment Exercise in 2001 and 2008 respectively, Cambridge was ranked first in the country. In 2006, a Thomson Scientific study showed that Cambridge has the highest research paper output of any British university, and is also the top research producer (as assessed by total paper citation count) in 10 out of 21 major British research fields analyzed.

Section B   Education in the United States of America

Education has been greatly respected throughout the history of the U.S.. Even before the Revolution, several outstanding colleges were founded, such as Harvard College, Yale College, College of New Jersey, etc.. Education is like a big opening window, and Americans are proud of the fact that the window of knowledge is never slammed shut for any of the nation's citizens. In this nation of rapid change, there can be no age limit on learning, and everyone must study, in classrooms or independently, to keep in touch with the changing life around them.

1. The Goal of American Education

The national goal of education today is to achieve universal literacy and to provide individuals with educational opportunities. Education for all, "its emphasis on education of the masses rather than on education of the intellectuals", is one of the most ambitious undertakings in American history. However, this principle cannot be and has never been truly carried out in America. Before the 1960's, many Negroes had not been given the right to receive education.

School education in America is compulsory. All states have compulsory school attendance laws. Children must go to school until they are at least 16 years old unless they are severely handicapped. Schools are expected to meet the needs of every child, regardless of ability, and also the needs of society itself. The underlying goal is to develop every child to the utmost of his or her own possibilities, however great or small these may be, and to give each one a sense of civic and community consciousness. Americans believe that, through education, an individual acquires knowledge, skills, attitudes, and abilities which will enable them to fit into society and improve their social status. Americans hold the view that the future of the nation depends largely on education.

2. Education System

Though far from uniform, the structure of American education system generally embraces three levels: elementary, secondary and higher education. The system requires that students complete 12 years of primary and secondary education prior to attending university or college. This may be accomplished either at public (government-operated) schools, or at private schools.

Public school systems are supported by a combination of local, state, and federal government funding. Because a large portion of school revenues come from local property taxes, public schools vary widely in the resources they have available per student. Class size also varies from one district to another. Curriculum decisions in public schools are made largely at the local and state levels; the federal government has limited influence. Admission to individual public schools is usually based on residency.

Private schools in the U.S. include parochial schools (affiliated with religious denominations), non-profit independent schools, and for-profit private schools. Private schools charge varying rates depending on geographic location, the school's expenses, and the availability of funding from sources, other than tuition. Private schools have various missions: some cater to college-bound students seeking a competitive edge in the college admissions process; others are for gifted students, students with learning disabilities or other special needs, or students with specific religious affiliations. Unlike public school systems, private schools have no legal obligation to accept any interested student. Admission to some private schools is often highly selective. Private schools offer the advantages of smaller classes, under twenty students in a typical elementary classroom. According to elite private schools themselves, the investment in faculty development helps maintain the high quality program that they offer.

▶ Elementary Education

Historically, in the U.S., local public control (and private alternatives) have allowed for some variation in the organization of schools. Elementary school includes kindergarten to 5th grade (or sometimes, to 4th grade, 6th grade or 8th grade). Basic subjects are taught in elementary school, and students often remain in one classroom throughout the school day, except for physical education, library, music, and art classes.

Public Elementary School teachers typically instruct between twenty and thirty students of diverse learning needs. In general, a student learns basic arithmetic and sometimes rudimentary algebra in mathematics, English, and fundamentals of other subjects. Typically, the curriculum in public elementary education is determined by individual school districts. The school district selects curriculum guides and textbooks that reflect a state's learning standards and benchmarks for a given grade level. Learning Standards are the goals by which states and school districts must meet adequate yearly progress (AYP) as mandated by No Child Left Behind (NCLB). Curricular decisions within private schools are often made differently from those in public schools, and in most cases without consideration of NCLB.

Elementary School teachers are trained with emphases on human cognitive and psychological development and the principles of curriculum development and instruction. Teachers typically earn either a Bachelor's or Master's Degree in Early Childhood and Elementary Education. Certification standards for teachers are determined by individual states, and some states require content area tests, as well as instructional skills tests for teacher certification in that state.

Secondary Education

Middle school and Junior high school include the grade levels intermediate between elementary school and senior high school. "Middle school" usually includes 6th, 7th and 8th grades; "Junior high" typically includes 7th, 8th, and 9th grades. The range defined by either is often based on demographic factors, such as an increase or decrease in the relative numbers of younger or older students, with the aim of maintaining stable school populations. At this time, students are given more independence, moving to different classrooms for different subjects, and being allowed to choose some of their class subjects (electives).

Senior high school is a school attended after junior high school. High school is often used instead of senior high school and distinguished from junior high school. High school usually runs either from 9th to 12th, or 10th to 12th grade.

Generally, at the high school level, students take a broad variety of classes without special emphasis in any particular subject. Students are required to take a certain minimum number of mandatory subjects, but may choose additional subjects to fill out their required hours of learning.

Many states require a "health" course in which students learn about anatomy, nutrition, first aid, sexuality, drug awareness and birth control. Foreign language and some forms of art education are also a mandatory part of the curriculum in some schools.

Many high schools provide Advanced Placement (AP) or International Baccalaureate (IB) courses. These are special forms of honors classes where the curriculum is more challenging and lessons more aggressively paced than standard courses. AP or IB courses are usually taken during the 11th or 12th grade of high school, but may be taken as early as 9th grade. Most post-secondary institutions take AP or IB exam results into consideration in the admissions process. Because AP and IB courses are intended to be the equivalent of the first year of college courses, post-secondary institutions may grant unit credit, which enables students to graduate earlier.

Higher Education

Higher education can be divided into undergraduate and graduate education. The higher education comprises four categories of institutions: the university, the four-year undergraduate institution(the college), the technical training institution, and the two-year community college. The university may contain several colleges for undergraduates seeking a bachelor's (4-year) degree, and one or more graduate schools for those continuing in specialized studies beyond the bachelor's degree to pursue a master's or a doctoral degree. Most of the four-year undergraduate institutions are not part of a university. In the technical training institution, high school graduates may take courses ranging from six months to four years and learn a wide variety of technical skills. The community college awards the associate's degree, from which students may enter many professions or transfer to four-year colleges or universities.

The four undergraduate grades are commonly called freshman, sophomore, junior, and senior years. Students traditionally apply for admission into colleges. Schools differ in their competitiveness and reputation; generally, the most prestigious schools are private, rather than public. Admission criteria involve the grades earned in high school courses taken, the students' GPA (grade point average), class ranking, and standardized test scores (Such as the SAT[2] or the ACT[3] tests). Most colleges also consider more subjective factors such as a commitment to extracurricular activities, a personal essay, and an interview.

Once admitted, students engage in undergraduate study, which consists of satisfying university and class requirements to achieve a bachelor's degree in a field of concentration known as a major. Some students enroll in double majors or "minor" in another field of study.

Professional degrees, such as law, medicine, pharmacy, and dentistry, are offered as graduate study after earning at least three years of undergraduate schooling or after earning a bachelor's degree depending on the program. These professional fields do not require a specific undergraduate major, though medicine, pharmacy, and dentistry have set prerequisite courses that must be taken before enrollment.

Some students choose to attend a community college for two years prior to further study at another college or university. In most states, community colleges are operated either by a division of the state university or by local special districts subject to guidance from a state agency. Community colleges may award Associate of Arts or Associate of Science degree after two years. Those seeking to continue their education may transfer to a four-year college or university.

Graduate study, conducted after obtaining an initial degree and sometimes after several years of professional work, leads to a more advanced degree such as a master's degree. Entrance into graduate programs usually depends upon a student's undergraduate academic performance or professional experience as well as their scores on a standardized entrance exam like the Graduate Record Examination (GRE), the Medical College Admission Test (MCAT), or the Law School Admission Test (LSAT). Many graduate and law schools do not require experience after earning a bachelor's degree to enter their programs; however, business school candidates are usually required to gain a few years of professional work experience before applying.

After additional years of study and sometimes in conjunction with the completion of a master's degree, students may earn a Doctor of Philosophy (Ph.D.) or other doctoral degrees, such as Doctor of Medicine, Doctor of Psychology, etc.. Some programs, such as medicine and psychology, have formal apprenticeship procedures, such as residencies and internships, which must be completed after graduation and before one is considered fully trained. Other professional programs like law and business have no formal apprenticeship requirements after graduation (although law school graduates must take the bar exam to legally practice law in nearly all states).

3. Two Famous Universities

⊙ Harvard University

Harvard University is an American private Ivy League research university located in Cambridge, Massachusetts. It was established in 1636, being the oldest institution of higher learning in the country and one of the most prestigious universities in the world.

Harvard was named after its first benefactor, John Harvard. Although never formally affiliated with a church, the college primarily trained Congregationalist and Unitarian clergy. Following the American Civil War, President Charles W. Eliot's forty-year tenure (1869 – 1909) transformed the college and affiliated professional schools into a centralized research university, and Harvard became a founding member of the Association of American Universities in 1900. Drew Gilpin Faust was elected the president in 2007 and is the first woman to lead the university.

Harvard Yard in Winter

The university comprises 11 separate academic units, 10 faculties and the Radcliffe Institute for Advanced Study, with campuses throughout the Boston metropolitan area. Harvard's main campus is centered on Harvard Yard in Cambridge, approximately 3.4 miles northwest of downtown Boston.

Eight U.S. presidents have been graduates, and 130 Nobel Laureates have been students, faculty, or staff affiliates. Harvard is also the alma mater of 62 living billionaires, the most in the country. The Harvard University Library is the largest academic library in the U.S., and one of the largest in the world.

Harvard has an intense athletic rivalry with Yale University culminating in "the Game", although the Harvard-Yale Regatta predates the football game. This rivalry, though, is put aside every two years when the Harvard and Yale Track and Field teams come together to compete against a combined Oxford University and Cambridge University team, a competition that is the oldest continuous international amateur competition in the world.

▶ Yale University

Yale University is a private Ivy League research university located in New Haven, Connecticut. Founded in 1701 in the Colony of Connecticut, the university is the third oldest institution of higher education in the U.S..

The institution traces its roots to 17th century clergymen who sought to establish a college to train clergy and political leaders for the colony. In 1718, the College was renamed "Yale College" to honor a gift from Elihu Yale, a governor of the British East India Company. In 1861, the Graduate School of Arts and Sciences became the first U.S.

Yale University

institution to award the Ph.D.. Yale became a founding member of the Association of American Universities in 1900. Yale College was transformed, beginning in the 1930s, through the establishment of residential colleges: 12 now exist and two more are planned.

49 Nobel Laureates have been affiliated with the University as students, faculty, and staff. Yale has produced many notable alumni, including five U.S. Presidents, 19 U.S. Supreme Court Justices, and several foreign heads of state. Yale Law School is particularly well-regarded and the most selective law school in the country.

Section C　Education in China

China has attached great importance to education since the ancient time. Respecting teachers and valuing education have been a tradition of Chinese people. Now, China has set up a modern education system with government as the major investor so that every person is allowed to gain knowledge legally.

1. Ancient Chinese Education

There were beginnings of education as early as in the eras of Yao, Shun and Yu in the Prehistoric Times (from 1.7 million years ago to 21st century B.C.). In the Shang Dynasty, the development of Chinese characters entered a more advanced stage, and some books made of heavy materials appeared. In this situation, formal schools emerged with the names like "Xiao" (school), "Xue" (study) and "Daxue" (higher school). Teachers then were all government officials and students were all children of the nobility, which was the earliest "Guan Xue" (official education). In the golden era of the slavery society—Western Zhou Dynasty, the six classical arts—rites, music, archery, riding, writing and mathematics became the content of the education. At that time, the government paid equal attention to cultivating the students in every aspect, including thoughts, morals, practical skills, culture, etiquette and inner feeling. That kind of teaching methods had far-reaching influence on the form of the traditional Chinese education. In the Spring and Autumn and Warring States Periods, "Guan Xue" began to decline and private schools rose in importance.

In the Han Dynasty, the government attached great importance to those knowledgeable people and encouraged people to write and copy books, which made the education unprecedentedly prosperous. Schools at that time were divided into official and private ones, and official schools were subdivided into local and central. Emperor Wudi started the highest grade official school—the Great Academy, which was set up in the northwestern suburban area of the capital city Chang'an (Xi'an). The teaching materials of the official schools were classical books of Confucius. Students who were admitted to the Great Academy were destined for careers in the civil service after they passed the exams and were competitively selected for various positions. Private schools were much more widespread than official schools, most of which mainly taught students to recognize and write Chinese characters, similar to present day elementary schools.

In the Sui and Tang Dynasties, the official and private schools were both further developed with the establishment and development of the Imperial Exam System. In the end of the Tang Dynasty, private academies (shuyuan) appeared out of the private schools. Since the Song Dynasty, China was ruled by different ethnic groups one after another, and all the ethnic groups desired to cultivate ruling brains of their own nations. Wars broke out frequently at that time and official schools couldn't easily operate, so private schools flourished.

With the coming of the Ming Dynasty, the imperial examination system reached its period of full bloom. The provincial and metropolitan examiners tested only "eight-part essays". Candidates were required to write in a fixed style with a fixed word count—it had to be eight paragraphs, while imitating the tone of the classics. This method neglected other forms and contents, and thus it was harmful as it stifled both creativity and imagination. It was the Opium War that made the intelligentsia start to advocate the education reforms, and after the May Fourth Movement, schools emerged in a state similar to the way they are today in China.

2. Present Education System

The education of China entered a new era after 1949. Along with the need for social development, the Chinese government has from that time given priority to the development of education, implementing a policy of invigorating the country through science, technology and education. At the same time, the Chinese government has been carrying out education reforms based on the principle that education should be geared to the needs of modernization and the world and of the future. The Chinese government increases input to science, technology and education year by year. Through uninterrupted efforts in the past six decades, China has made great progress in education. Nine years of compulsory education (from primary school to junior middle school) has been implemented nationwide. Higher education, occupational and polytechnic education, diversified adult education and ethics education have been developed rapidly.

China has set up an education system with government as the major investor and social partners as co-investors. In the current stage, local governments are playing key roles in compulsory education, while central and provincial governments are dominant in higher education. The national Ministry of Education is the supreme education administrative body, and is responsible for carrying out relevant laws, regulations and policies, activating and guiding education reforms and integrating and coordinating educational initiatives and programs nationwide.

In addition, the Chinese government pays attention to guaranteeing citizens' rights to get education especially the right of the minorities, women and disabled people, by making appropriate laws. To assist needy students, the Chinese government adopted a series of measures to prevent them from dropping out from education, including scholarships, subsidies, student loans and tuition fee reduction.

▶ Elementary Education

The institution of primary education in a country as vast as China has been an impressive accomplishment. Under the Law on Nine-Year Compulsory Education, primary schools were to be tuition-free and reasonably located for the convenience of children attending them; students would attend primary schools in their neighborhoods or villages.

Children usually enter primary school at the age of seven for six days a week, which after 1997 were changed to five days. The two-semester school year consists of 9.5 months, and begins on September and March, with a summer vacation in July and August and a winter vacation in January and February.

The primary-school curriculum consists of Chinese, mathematics, physical education, music, drawing, and elementary instruction in nature, history, and geography, combined with practical work experiences around the school compound. Besides, the Ministry of Education requires that all primary schools offer courses on morality and ethics. A foreign language, often English, is introduced in about the third grade.

▶ Secondary Education

Public secondary schools include junior middle schools and senior middle schools, both for three years of study. Students graduating from junior middle schools usually go to senior middle schools, and some of them go to vocational high schools or secondary professional schools for three to five years.

Junior secondary education is more commonly known as (junior) middle school education, and it consists the last three years of nine years compulsory education. The Senior High School Entrance Examination (Zhongkao) is the academic examination held annually in China to distinguish junior graduates. Generally speaking, students will be tested in Chinese, Mathematics, English, Physics, Chemistry, Political Science and PE. However, the scoring system may change and vary in different areas. Admission for senior high schools, especially selective high schools, is somewhat similar to the one for universities in China. However, the severe competition only occurs in the very top high schools, and normally, most students will have sufficient results for them to continue their secondary education if they wish to.

Senior secondary education is not compulsory because junior graduates have freedom to choose to continue a three-year academic education in academic high schools, which will eventually lead to university, or to switch to a vocational course in vocational high schools. Generally speaking, Chinese, Mathematics and English are considered as three main subjects as they will definitely be tested in College Entrance Examination (Gaokao). In most provinces, students also need to be examined in either natural sciences, which incorporate Physics, Chemistry and Biology, or social sciences, which incorporate Geography, History and Ideology and Political Science.

In China, a senior high school graduate will be considered as an educated person, although the majority graduates will go to universities or vocational colleges. Given the fact that the intensity of the competition for limited university places is unimaginable, most high schools are evaluated by their academic performance in College Entrance Examination.

Vocational education embraces higher vocational schools, secondary skill schools, vestibule schools, vocational high schools, and other adult skill and social training institutes. To enable vocational education to better accommodate the demands of economic re-structuring and urbanization, in recent years the government has remodeled vocational education, oriented towards obtaining employment, and focusing on two major vocational education projects to meet society's ever more acute demand for high quality, skilled workers. These are cultivating skilled workers urgently needed in modern manufacture and service industries.

▶ Higher Education

Higher education in China has played an important role in the economic construction, science progress and social development by bringing up large scale of advanced talents and experts for the construction of socialist modernization.

Higher education is performed by universities, colleges, institutes and vocational colleges. These institutions bear three major tasks of teaching, conducting scientific research and providing social services. Two-year and three-year colleges, typically awarding associate degrees, exist next to typical four-year colleges and universities which offer academic as well as vocational courses leading to bachelor's degrees or higher. Master's degrees and doctoral degrees are offered by universities and research institutions which are accredited by the State Council.

Higher education used to be "elite education", with only very few students lucky enough to enter the system. In 1999, however, China began to dramatically expand its higher education system. Since then, more and more Chinese students have access to higher education.

As the economic development of China, private school system has been gradually built up. Some public colleges and universities cooperated with investors to run secondary college by using public running and being sponsored by private enterprises, which promotes the development of education. On the other hand, the Technical and Vocational Education in China has developed rapidly, and become the focus of the whole society. There was also a renewed interest in television, radio, and correspondence classes (distance learning and electronic learning).

Nowadays, as the educational level of Chinese has increased, getting into college is no longer a remarkable achievement among the Chinese students. Instead, having a degree of an ordinary Chinese university already can't satisfy the increasingly competitive society. Chinese parents and students have begun to place a high value on overseas education, especially at top American and European institutions such as Harvard University, Oxford University, and Cambridge University. Since 1999, the number of Chinese applicants to top schools overseas has increased tenfold. Much of the interest in overseas schools has been attributed to the release of how-to parenting books such as Harvard Girl, which spawned a "national obsession" with admissions to overseas schools. After 2005, the number of overseas students from China not only has shown a rising trend, but also presented a trend of lowering age.

3. Two Famous Universities

▶ Peking University

Peking University is a major research university located in Beijing, and a member of the C9 League[4]. It is the first established modern national university of China, founded as the "Imperial University of Peking" in 1898 to replace the ancient Guozijian. In 1902, the Faculty of Education was spun off to become today's Beijing Normal University, the best teacher's college in China. In 1912, following the Xinhai Revolution, the Imperial University was renamed "National Peking University". By 1920 it had

Peking University

become a center for progressive thought. Today, Peking University is frequently placed as one of the best universities in China by many national and international rankings. Besides academics, Peking University is especially renowned for its campus grounds, and the beauty of its traditional Chinese architecture.

The campus of Peking University was originally located north of the Forbidden City in the center of Beijing, and was later moved to the former campus of Yenching University in 1952. The main campus is in northwest Beijing, in Haidian district. The university campus is in the former site of the Qing Dynasty royal gardens and it retains a lot of traditional Chinese-style landscape including traditional houses, gardens, pagodas as well as many notable historical buildings and architectures. Weiming Lake is in the north of the campus and is surrounded by walking paths and small gardens.

Weiming Lake

With 4.5 million holdings, Peking University library is the largest of its kind in Asia. Besides, the university hosts many museums, such as the Museum of University History and the Arthur M. Sackler Museum of Art and Archaeology. Notable items in these museums include funerary objects that were excavated in Beijing and date back thousands of years from the graves of royalties of the Warring States period. There are ritual pottery vessels as well as elaborate pieces of jewelry on display. There are also human bones set up in the traditional burial style of that period.

The university has made an effort to combine the research on fundamental scientific issues with the training of personnel with high level specialized knowledge and professional skills as demanded by the country's development.

Throughout its history, the university has educated and hosted many prominent modern Chinese thinkers, such as Mao Zedong, Lu Xun, Hu Shi, Li Dazhao, Chen Duxiu, etc.. Over the past century, more than 400 Peking University alumni had become presidents of other major Chinese universities.

▶ Tsinghua University

Tsinghua University is a national key university located in Beijing. With a motto of Self-Discipline and Social Commitment, Tsinghua University describes itself as being dedicated to academic excellence, the well-being of Chinese society and to global development. Nowadays, the university is one of the nine tertiary institutions in the C9 League and has been frequently regarded as one of the top universities in mainland China.

Tsinghua University

The campus of Tsinghua University is also located in northwest Beijing, in the Haidian district. It is located on the former site of the Qing Dynasty royal gardens and retains Chinese-style landscapes as well as traditional buildings, but some of its buildings are also in the Western-style. T. Chuang, a 1914 graduate of the University of Illinois, helped design the campus grounds of Tsinghua University under the influence of American architectural styles and architectures. Tsinghua

University's campus was named as one of the most beautiful college campuses in the world by a panel of architects and campus designers in Forbes in 2010, and it was the only university in Asia on the list.

　　Tsinghua University Library's collection focuses on Science and Technology and also covers broad subjects of Humanities, Social Sciences and Management. Tsinghua university library system includes the university library, 6 subject branch libraries and more than 10 school or department reading rooms. In the past few years, the library has expanded its collection very fast especially in the e-resources. It is undergoing the transformation from a traditional library based on physical collections preservation and service to a modern library abundant in digital resources, with a rapid developing network service. A collection of old documents, pictures, artworks, maps, graphics, videos and music in the Tsinghua History Museum tells the visitors the history of Tsinghua University.

　　Tsinghua University has produced many notable graduates, especially in political sphere. These include former General Secretary and President Hu Jintao, the current Party General Secretary Xi Jinping, the former chairman of the National People's Congress Wu Bangguo, the former Premier Zhu Rongji, and so on.

Notes

1. **A-levels**: A-levels require studying an offered A-level subject over a two-year period and sitting for an examination at the end of each year, proctored by an official assessment body. A-levels are recognized by many universities as the standard for assessing the suitability of applicants for admission in England, Wales, and Northern Ireland, and many such universities base their conditional admissions offers on a student's predicted A-level grades.
2. **the SAT**: The SAT is a standardized test for most college admissions in the U.S.. The SAT is owned, published, and developed by the College Board, a non-profit organization in the U.S.. The test is intended to assess a student's readiness for college. It was first called the Scholastic Aptitude Test, then the Scholastic Assessment Test. The current SAT Reasoning Test, introduced in 2005, takes three hours and forty-five minutes to finish, and costs $50 ($81 International), excluding late fees. Possible scores range from 600 to 2400, combining test results from three 800-point sections (Mathematics, Critical Reading, and Writing).
3. **the ACT**: The ACT (American College Testing) college readiness assessment is a standardized test for high school achievement and college admissions in the U.S. produced by ACT, Inc. The ACT has historically consisted of four tests: English, Mathematics, Reading, and Science Reasoning. In February 2005, an optional Writing test was added to the ACT, mirroring changes to the SAT that took place later in March of the same year. In the Spring of 2015, the ACT will start to be offered as a computer-based test that will incorporate some optional Constructed Response Questions; the test content, composite score and multiple choice format will not be

affected by these changes. The test will continue to be offered in the paper format for schools that are not ready to transition to computer testing.

4. the C9 League: The C9 League is an alliance of nine Chinese universities. It was established in 2009. On May 4, 1998, Project 985 was initiated by the Chinese government in order to advance the higher education system. In the first phase, nine universities were selected and allocated funding for an initial period of three years: Fudan University, Harbin Institute of Technology, Nanjing University, Peking University, Shanghai Jiao Tong University, Tsinghua University, University of Science and Technology of China, Xi'an Jiao Tong University and Zhejiang University. On October 10, 2009, these nine universities made up the C9 League. The league was self-organized, attempting to create a group that is pitched as China's equivalent of Ivy League.

Glossary

arithmetic [ə'riθmətik] *n.* 算术,计算

contemptuous [kən'temptjuəs] *adj.* 轻蔑的; 傲慢的,贬义的

collegiate [kə'liːdʒiət] *adj.* 学院的,大学的,大学生的

fixture ['fikstʃə] *n.* 运动会举行日; (预先规定日期的)比赛项目

compact ['kɔmpækt] *adj.* 小巧的,袖珍的; 矮小结实的

tout [taut] *vt.* 竭力称许,推荐; 兜售

myriad ['miriəd] *n.* 无数,极大数量

punt [pʌnt] *vt.* 用篙撑(船); 用平底船运载 *vi.* 坐(撑)平底船

finback ['finbæk] *n.* 长须鲸

parochial [pə'rəukjəl, -kiəl] *adj.* 教区的,属教区管辖的; 乡镇的; 地方性的

benchmark ['bentʃ,mɑːk] *n.* 基准

mandatory ['mændətəri] *adj.* 命令的; 强制的; 义务的

anatomy [ə'nætəmi] *n.* 解剖学; 解剖

International Baccalaureate 进入某些国家大学所要求的国际大学入学考试

benefactor ['benifæktə] *n.* 恩人; 施主; 保护人; 捐助人

Congregationalist [,kɔngri'geiʃənəlist] *n.* 公理会的教友

Unitarian [,juːni'tɛəriən] *n.* 唯一神论者

tenure ['tenjuə] *n.* (职位的)占有(权),任期

alma mater [,ælmə 'mɑːtə(r)] *n.* 母校

regatta [ri'gætə] *n.* 赛船; 赛艇会

predate ['priː'deit] *v.* 提早日期,居先

stifle ['staifl] *vt.* 使窒息; 镇压,阻止(反叛等)

intelligentsia [in,telə'dʒentsiːə] *n.* (总称)知识界,知识阶层

invigorate [in'vigəreit] *vt.* 使精力充沛,使强壮; 鼓舞,激励

itinerant [i'tinərənt] *adj.* 巡回的,流动的

vestibule［'vestibju:l］ *n.* 门厅,通道

vestibule schools（工厂的）新工人培训学校

revere［ri'viə］ *vt.* 尊敬,崇敬

spawn［spɔ:n］ *vt.* 产生,引起

spin off 创造新的事物而不影响原物的大小（稳定性）

Further Reading

1）**Education in Canada**

http：//en.wikipedia.org/wiki/Education_in_Canada

http：//www.edwiseinternational.com/study-in-canada/education-system-in-canada.asp

2）**Education in Australia**

http：//en.wikipedia.org/wiki/Education_in_Australia

http：//australianadvice.co.uk/education-system-in-australia.html

https：//secure.australia-migration.com/page/Education/239

3）**Education in New Zealand**

http：//en.wikipedia.org/wiki/Education_in_New_Zealand

http：//www.educationzing.com/new-zealand/

http：//www.newzealandeducationguide.com/index.htm

Group Tasks

Summarizing an American report picked at random from the Internet about the U.S. and Chinese education systems, we read such conclusions as：

1. Teachers in China are given more respect than teachers in the U.S.. For example, teachers receive their own national holiday, Teachers' Day.

2. Chinese schools have a hard work ethic, resulting in student success.

3. Chinese schools do not segregate high achieving students from lower achieving students through tracking levels, like in the U.S.. This is mostly due to the belief that all students can succeed if they put in the effort.

One negative aspect of the Chinese education system is that high stakes testing in order to pass into the next grade results in many students left with no other choice but to drop out of the school system all together.

One negative aspect of the U.S. system is that：

While American students have the same amount of allocated time as Chinese students, the amount of engaged time spent in school is dramatically less than their Chinese counterparts.

Review the information on education and consider these points in discussion. Are they true? How would you see the education system in the U.K. in comparison with those of China and the U.S.? Perhaps you might form three panels to debate the three systems, with each of three groups "championing" one country, to see who can make the best case for their system.

Chapter 6 Literature and Art

Section A Literature and Art in the United Kingdom

1. English Literature

English literature has a long history and a secure position in world literature. This chapter tries to make a brief introduction to fiction, poetry and drama respectively.

▶ Fiction

We are familiar with English literature chiefly through novels, though poems and songs are the earliest forms of writing in English literature. Fables are probably the earliest forms of story-telling. Legends come later and are more serious so far as the themes are concerned. The best-loved story is about Robin Hood who was a popular hero living under the greenwood with his men, taking from the rich and giving to the poor.

In the 16th century, Thomas More (1478 – 1535), one of the greatest English humanists, issued his masterpiece *Utopia*. In the book, he exposed the poverty of the laboring class and the greed and luxury of the rich, and described an ideal communist society in which the only principle of Utopia is "from every one according to his capacities, to every one according to his need".

During the puritan period, John Bunyan (1628 – 1668) was a commanding prose writer. His *The Pilgrim's Progress* appeals to people of every age and condition. It is a religious allegory which depicts the spiritual pilgrimage of a Christian, who files from the City of Destruction, meets with perils and temptations at the Slough of Despond, Vanity Fair and Doubting Castle, faces and conquers the demon Appollyon, and finally reaches the Delectable Mountains and the Celestial City.

It was not until the 18th century that the modern novel began to

John Bunyan

appear. Daniel Defoe (1661 – 1731) and his *Robinson Crusoe* and Jonathan Swift (1667 – 1745) and his *Gulliver's Travels* belong to this period. Defoe was the first writer who made studies of the lower-class people. His language was smooth, easy, colloquial and mostly vernacular, and he was the founder of realistic novel. *Robinson Crusoe* praises the fortitude of the human labor and the Puritan, and it is representative of the English bourgeoisie. Swift was a master satirist. *Gulliver's Travels* is a satirical novel which is similar to *Robinson Crusoe* in many ways. It records four voyages of Lemuel Gulliver and his adventures in four astounding countries, by means of which Swift severely criticized the vices of the age. Samuel Richardson (1689 – 1761) was another novelist renowned as a story-teller. He chose the expostulatory form and wrote the first modern novel, and he was often called the founder of the English domestic novel.

The 19th century was the golden age of the novel. There were a lot of novelists, the greatest of whom was Charles Dickens (1812 – 1870). He was an outstanding critical realist writer and wrote more about the working class than most contemporary novelists. He created many well-known novels, such as *Oliver Twist*, *Hard Times*, *A Tale of Two Cities*, and so on. Walter Scott (1771 – 1832) was a famous Scottish historical novelist, and his language is difficult, deliberately old-fashioned, using the Scottish dialect sometimes. Jane Austen (1775 – 1817) was the earliest woman novelist in this age. She

Charles Dickens

wrote about middle-class family life. Her most widely-read novel was *Pride and Prejudice*. Charlotte Bronte (1816 – 1855) and Emily Bronte (1818 – 1848) were noted for their novels *Jane Eyre* and *Wuthering Heights*. *Jane Eyre* is noted for its sharp criticism of the existing society, such as the charity institution Logwood School. It is a successful introduction to the first governess heroine in the English novel, which represents those middle-class working women struggling for recognition of their basic rights and equality as a human being. *Wuthering Heights* is a story about two families and an intruding stranger.

Charlotte and Emily Bronte

The 20th century has produced many first-rate novelists, some of whom have written traditionally, describing various aspects of society and the individual; some have experienced new style of writing while others have dealt with mental processes. Thomas Hardy (1840 – 1928) was also influenced both in his novels and poetry by romanticism, especially by William Wordsworth and Charles Darwin. Like Charles Dickens, he was also highly critical of much in Victorian society, though Hardy focused more on a declining rural society. He gained fame as the author of such novels as, *Far from the Madding Crowd* (1874), *Tess of the d'Urbervilles* (1891), and *Jude the Obscure* (1895). David Herbert Lawrence (1885 – 1930) was one of the first novelists to introduce themes of psychology into his works. He believed that the healthy way of the individual's psychological development lay in the primacy of the life impulse, and he opened up a wide new territory to the novel. John Galsworthy (1867 – 1933) was one of the most prominent British novelists and dramatists of the 20th century, and he won the Nobel Prize for Literature in 1932. In the later decades of the 20th century, the genre of science fiction began to be taken more seriously because of the works of writers such as Arthur C. Clarke, Isaac Asimov and Michael Moorcock. Mainstream novelists like Doris Lessing also wrote works in this genre, while Scottish novelist Ian M. Banks achieved a reputation as both a writer of traditional and science fiction novels.

▶ Poetry

Much Old English verse in the extant manuscripts is probably adapted from the earlier Germanic war poems from the continent. When such poetry was brought to England it was still being handed down orally from one generation to another.

The most significant Middle English author was Geoffrey Chaucer who was active in the late 14th century, often regarded as "the Father of English Literature". Chaucer was widely credited as the first author to demonstrate the artistic legitimacy of the vernacular English language, rather than French or Latin. His main contribution to English poetry was the introduction of rhyming stanzas of various types from France to English poetry.

English poetry began to blossom in the Elizabethan and post-Elizabethan periods. The sonnet was introduced into English by Thomas Wyatt in the early 16th century. One of the most important poets of this period was Edmund Spenser, author of *The Faerie Queene*, an epic poem and fantastical allegory celebrating the Tudor dynasty and Elizabeth I. Sir Philip Sidney (1554 – 1586) was an English poet and was remembered as one of the most prominent figures of the Elizabethan Age. John Milton, one of the greatest English poets, wrote at this time of religious flux and political upheaval. Milton was best known for his epic poem *Paradise Lost* (1671). Milton's poetry and prose reflected deep personal convictions, a passion for freedom and self-determination, and the urgent issues and political turbulence of his day. Milton was called the "greatest English author" in William Hayley's 1796 biography, and he was generally regarded as "one of the preeminent writers in the English language and as a thinker of world importance".

The largest and most important poetic form of the era was satire. In general, publication of satire was done anonymously. There were great dangers in being associated with a satirist. John Dryden (1631 – 1700) was set upon for being merely suspected of having written *The Satire on Mankind*. He was an influential English poet, literary critic, translator, and playwright who dominated the literary life of Restoration England to such a point that the period came to be known

John Dryden

in literary circles as "the Age of Dryden". He established the heroic couplet as a standard form of English poetry by writing successful satires, religious pieces, fables, epigrams, compliments, prologues, and plays with it.

The graveyard poets[1] were a number of pre-Romantic English poets, writing in the 1740s and later, whose works were characterized by their gloomy meditations on mortality. They were often considered precursors of the Gothic genre. A notable poet of this period was Thomas Gray (1716 – 1771), whose *Elegy Written in a Country Churchyard* (1751) was "the best known product of this kind of sensibility".

The Romantic movement in English literature had its beginnings in the pre-Romantic poets. The early Romantic Poets brought a new emotionalism and introspection, and their emergence was marked by the first romantic manifesto in English literature, *Preface to Lyrical Ballads* (1798). The poems in *Lyrical Ballads* were mostly written by Wordsworth. The second generation of Romantic poets includes Lord Byron (1788 – 1824), Percy Bysshe Shelley (1792 – 1822) and John Keats (1795 – 1821). Byron, however, was still influenced by the 18th-century satirists and was perhaps the least "romantic" of the three. His amours with a number of prominent but married ladies were also a way to voice his dissent on the hypocrisy of a high society that was only apparently religious but in fact largely libertine, the same that had derided him for being physically impaired. Shelley was

Ode to the West Wind

perhaps best known for poems such as *Ozymandias*, *Ode to the West Wind*, and *To a Skylark*. Shelley's early profession of atheism led to his expulsion from Oxford and branded him as a radical agitator and thinker, setting an early pattern of marginalization and ostracism from the intellectual and political circles of his time. John Keats's cult of pantheism was as important as Shelley's. Keats's great attention to art, especially in his *Ode on a Grecian Urn* (1818) was quite new in romanticism.

The leading poets during the Victorian period were Alfred Tennyson (1809 – 1892), Robert Browning (1812 – 1889), Elizabeth Browning (1806 – 1861), and Matthew Arnold (1822 – 1888). The poetry of this period was heavily influenced by the Romantics, but also went off in its own directions. Particularly notable was the development of the dramatic monologue, a form used by many poets in this period, but perfected by Browning. Browning's main achievement was in dramatic monologues such as *My Last Duchess*, *Andrea del Sarto* and *The Bishop Orders his Tomb*.

Towards the end of the 19th century, English poets began to take an interest in French Symbolism. W. B. Yeats (1865 – 1939) went on to become an important modernist in the 20th century. A pillar of both the Irish and British literary establishments, in his later years he served as an Irish Senator for two terms. In 1923 he was awarded the Nobel Prize for Literature as the first Irishman. His works include *The Tower* (1928), *The Winding Stair* and *Other Poems* (1929).

T. S. Eliot (1888 – 1965) was one of the important early modernists. He was born in America but became a British citizen in 1927. His most famous works are: *Prufrock* (1915), *The Waste-land* (1921) and *Four Quartets* (1935 – 1942).

There are many poets today who have introduced many new ideas and who write in different styles. New poets starting their careers in the 1950s and 1960s included Philip Larkin (1922 – 1985) (*The Whitsun Weddings*, 1964), Ted Hughes (1930 – 1998) (*The Hawk in the Rain*, 1957) and Seamus Heaney (1939—2013) (*Death of a Naturalist*, 1966). Northern Ireland has also produced a number of other significant poets, including Derek Mahon and Paul Muldoon.

◉ Drama

English drama is completely dominated by William Shakespeare (1564 – 1616). He was not a man of letters by profession, and probably had only some grammar school education. He was neither a lawyer, nor an aristocrat as "the university wits" that had monopolized the English stage when he started writing. But he was very gifted and incredibly versatile. Though most dramas met with great success, it was in his later years, marked by the early reign of James I, that he wrote what have been considered his greatest plays: *Hamlet*, *Romeo and Juliet*, *Othello*, *King Lear*, *Macbeth*, *Antony and Cleopatra*, and *The Tempest*. Shakespeare also popularized the English sonnet which made significant changes to Petrarch's model.

After Shakespeare's death, the poet and dramatist Ben Jonson was the leading literary figure of the Jacobean era[2]. Jonson's aesthetics harked back to the middle Ages and his characters embodied the theory of humors. Jonson therefore tended to create types or caricatures. He was a master of style, and a brilliant satirist. Jonson's famous comedy *Volpone* (1605 or 1606) shows how a group of scammers are fooled by a top con-artist, vice being punished by vice, virtue meting out its reward. Other major plays by Jonson were *Epicoene* (1609), *The Alchemist* (1610), and *Bartholomew Fair* (1614).

Others who followed Jonson's style include Beaumont and Fletcher, who wrote the brilliant comedy, *The Knight of the Burning Pestle*, a mockery of the rising middle class and especially of those nouveau riches who pretend to dictate literary taste without knowing much literature at all. In the story, a couple of grocers wrangle with professional actors to have their illiterate son play a leading role in a drama.

After a sharp drop in both quality and quantity in the 1680s, the mid-1690s saw a brief second flowering of the drama, especially comedy. The playwrights of the 1690s set out to appeal to more socially mixed audiences with a strong middle-class element, and to female spectators, for instance by moving the war between the sexes from the arena of intrigue into that of marriage.

The premier ghost story writer of the 19th century was Sheridan Le Fanu. His works included the macabre mystery novel *Uncle Silas* (1865) and his Gothic novella *Carmilla* (1872). Bram Stoker's horror story *Dracula* (1897), belongs to a number of literary genres, including vampire literature, horror fiction, gothic novel and invasion literature.

A change came in the Victorian era with a profusion on the London stage of farces, musical burlesques, extravaganzas and comic operas. Oscar Wilde became the leading poet and dramatist of the late Victorian period. Wilde's 1895 comic masterpiece, *The Importance of Being Earnest*, holds an ironic mirror to the aristocracy and displays a mastery of wit and paradoxical wisdom. Wilde's plays, in particular, stood apart from the many now forgotten plays of Victorian times and had a much closer relationship to those of the Edwardian dramatists such as Irish playwright George Bernard Shaw(1856 – 1950). G.B. Shaw was influential in British drama, and his career began in the last decade of the 19th century. Shaw turned the Edwardian theatre into an arena for debate about important political and social issues, like marriage, class, and the rights of women.

G. B. Shaw

An important cultural movement in the British theatre which developed in the late 1950s and early 1960s was Kitchen sink realism, a term coined to describe art, novels, film and television plays, whose "heroes" usually could be described as angry young men. It used a style of social realism which depicts the domestic lives of the working class, to explore social issues and political issues. The drawing room plays of the post war period were challenged in the 1950s by these Angry Young Men, in plays like John Osborne's *Look Back in Anger* (1956). Again in the 1950s, the absurdist play *Waiting for Godot* (1955) by the Irishman Samuel Beckett profoundly affected British drama. Other important playwrights whose careers began later in the century are: Alan Ayckbourn (*Absurd Person Singular*, 1975) and Caryl Churchill (*Top Girls*, 1982).

After 1956, many English playwrights published plays, some absurd, some angry, some cruel and many mixing all of these ingredients, and they continued to write on various subjects. English plays have been occupying an important place in Western Culture.

2. English Art

Anglo-Saxon Carvings

English art introduced in this section mainly refers to the visual arts made in England. Although medieval English painting, mostly religious, had a strong national tradition and was at times influential on the rest of Europe, it was in decline from the 15th century. The Protestant Reformation, which was especially destructive of art in England, not only brought the tradition to an abrupt stop but resulted in the destruction of almost all wall-paintings. Only illuminated manuscripts[3] now survive in good numbers.

The oldest art in England can be dated to the Neolithic period, including the large ritual landscapes such as Stonehenge. In the Iron Age, a new art style arrived as Celtic culture spread across the British Isles. The arrival of the Romans brought the Classical style, glasswork and mosaics. In the 4th century, a new element was introduced as the first Christian art was made in Britain. Several mosaics with Christian symbols and pictures have been preserved.

In Medieval period, Anglo-Saxon sculpture was outstanding for its time. By the first half of the 11th century, English art was being lavishly patronized by the wealthy Anglo-Saxon elite, who valued above all works in precious metals, but the Norman Conquest in 1066 brought a sudden halt to this art boom, and instead works were melted down or removed to Normandy. After a pause of some decades, manuscript painting in England soon became again the equal of any in Europe.

The artists of the Tudor court in the Renaissance and their successors until the early 18th century were mostly imported talents, often from Flanders. By the following century, a number of significant English painters of full-size portraits began to emerge, and towards the end of the century the other great English specialism, of landscape painting, also began to be practiced by natives. One of the most important native painters of this period was William Dobson.

In the 18th century, English painting finally developed a distinct style and tradition again, still concentrating on portraits and landscapes, but also attempting, without much success, to find an approach to history painting. William Hogarth, his satirical works, full of black humor, pointed out to contemporary society the deformities, weaknesses and vices of London life.

The English tradition continued to draw of the relaxed elegance of the portrait style developed in England by Van Dyck, although there was little actual transmission from his work via his workshop. By the end of the century, the English swagger portrait was much admired abroad, and had largely ceased to look for inspiration abroad.

The early 19th century also saw the emergence of the Norwich school of painters. The Norwich School was the first provincial art-movement outside London.

The Pre-Raphaelite movement, established in the 1840s, dominated English art in the second half of the 19th century. Its members, William Holman Hunt, Dante Gabriel Rossetti, John Everett Millais and others, concentrated on religious, literary, and genre works executed in a colorful and minutely detailed almost photographic style.

In many respects, the Victorian era continued until the outbreak of World War I in 1914, and the Royal Academy became increasingly ossified. Modernist movements were both cherished and vilified by artists and critics; impressionism was initially regarded as a "subversive foreign influence", but became "fully assimilated" into British art during the early 20th century.

In the 1950s, the London based Independent Group formed, from which pop art emerged in 1956 with the exhibition at the Institute of Contemporary Arts. The Independent Group is regarded as the

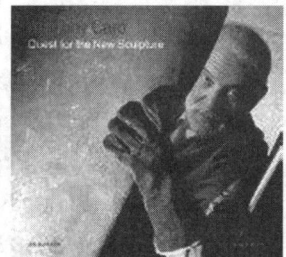

Anthony Caro

107

precursor to the Pop Art movement in Britain and the U.S.. In the 1960s, Sir Anthony Caro became a leading figure of British sculpture along with a younger generation of abstract artists including Isaac Witkin, Phillip King and William Tucker. During the 1960s, another group of British artists, including Bruce McLean, Barry Flanagan, Richard Long, and Gilbert and George, offered a radical alternative to the conventional art making.

Post-modern, contemporary British art, particularly that of the Young British Artists[4], has been said to be perceived as a post-imperial cultural anxiety. The Sensation exhibition of works from the Saatchi Collection was controversial in both the U.K. and the U.S., though in different ways. At the Royal Academy press-generated controversy centered on Myra, a very large image of the murderer Myra Hindley by Marcus Harvey. In 1999, the Stuckists figurative painting group which includes Billy Childish and Charles Thomson was founded as a reaction to the YBAs. In 2004, the Walker Art Gallery[5] staged The Stuckists Punk Victorian, the first national museum exhibition of the Stuckist art movement[6].

Section B Literature and Art in the United States of America

1. American Literature

The history of American literature is comparatively short, roughly about 250 years. During its early history, America was a series of British colonies on the eastern coast of the present-day U.S.. Therefore, its literary tradition began as linked to the broader tradition of English literature. American literature showed its own characteristics only until the war of independence and the founding of the U.S.. At the beginning of the 19th century, American literature showed great importance on the stage of world literature. American literature is the production of the development of the American society, reflecting the social life of American.

▶ Fiction

It was in the late 18th and early 19th centuries that the nation's first novels were published. These fictions were too lengthy to be printed as manuscript or public reading. Among the first American novels are Thomas Attwood Digges' *Adventures of Alonso*, published in London in 1775 and William Hill Brown's *The Power of Sympathy* published in 1791.

American did not have its real fiction until Washington Irving who completed his first major book in 1809 entitled *A History of New York from the Beginning of the World to the End of the Dutch Dynasty*. Irving was the first to write the local color of America, and he was often considered the first writer to develop a unique American style.

In 1832, Poe began writing short stories that explored previously hidden levels of human psychology and pushed the boundaries of fiction toward mystery and fantasy. Cooper's *Leather-stocking Tales about Natty Bumppo* was popular both in the new country and abroad. In 1837, the young Nathaniel Hawthorne (1804 – 1864) collected some of his stories as *Twice-Told Tales*, a volume rich in symbolism and occult incidents. Hawthorne went on to write full-length "romances" that explored such themes as guilt, pride, and emotional repression in his native New England. His masterpiece, *The Scarlet Letter*, was the stark drama of a woman cast out of her community for committing adultery. Hawthorne's fiction had a profound impact on his friend Herman Melville (1819 – 1891), who first made a name for himself by turning material from his seafaring days into exotic and sensational sea narrative novels. In *Moby-Dick*, an adventurous whaling voyage becomes the vehicle for examining such themes as obsession, the nature of evil and human struggle against the elements. Anti-transcendental works from Melville, Hawthorne, and Poe all comprised the Dark Romanticism subgenre of literature popular during this time.

Mark Twain (the pen name used by Samuel Clemens, 1835 – 1910) was the first major American writer to be born away from the East Coast—in the border state of Missouri. His regional masterpieces were the memoir *Life on the Mississippi* and the novels *Adventures of Tom Sawyer* and *Adventures of Huckleberry Finn*. Twain's style, influenced by journalism and wedded to the vernacular, direct and unadorned but also highly evocative and irreverently humorous, changed the way Americans write their language.

Mark Twain

At the beginning of the 20th century, American novelists were expanding fiction's social spectrum to encompass both high and low life and sometimes connected to the naturalist school of realism. In her stories and novels, Edith Wharton (1862 – 1937) scrutinized the upper-class, Eastern-seaboard society in which she had grown up. At about the same time, Stephen Crane (1871 – 1900), best known for his Civil War novel *The Red Badge of Courage*, depicted the life of New York City prostitutes in *Maggie: A Girl of the Streets*. And in *Sister Carrie*, Theodore Dreiser (1871 – 1945) portrayed a country girl who moves to Chicago and becomes a kept woman. More directly political writings discussed social issues and power of corporations. Some like Edward Bellamy in *Looking Backward* outlined other possible political and social frameworks.

Experimentation in style and form soon joined the new freedom in subject matter. In 1909, Gertrude Stein (1874 – 1946), by then an expatriate in Paris, published *Three Lives*, an innovative work of fiction influenced by her familiarity with cubism, jazz, and other movements in contemporary art and music. Stein labeled a group of American literary notables who lived in Paris in the 1920s and 1930s as the "Lost Generation"[6].

American writers also expressed the disillusionment following upon the war. The stories and novels of F. Scott Fitzgerald (1896 – 1940) captured the restless, pleasure-hungry, defiant mood of the 1920s. Fitzgerald's characteristic theme, expressed poignantly in *The Great Gatsby*, was the tendency of youth's golden dreams to dissolve in failure and disappointment.

Ernest Hemingway (1899 – 1961) saw violence and death first-hand as an ambulance driver in World War I, and the carnage persuaded him that abstract language was mostly empty and misleading. He cut out unnecessary words from his writing, simplified the sentence structure, and concentrated on concrete objects and actions. He adhered to a moral code that emphasized grace under pressure, and his protagonists were strong, silent men who often dealt awkwardly with women. *The Sun Also Rises* and *A Farewell to Arms* are generally considered his best novels; in 1954, he won the Nobel Prize for Literature. His style of writing is striking. His sentences are short; words are simple, yet they are filled with emotion and deep meaning.

Depression era literature was blunt and direct in its social criticism. Henry Miller assumed a unique place in American Literature in the 1930s when his semi-autobiographical novels, written and published in Paris, were banned from the U.S.. Although his major works, including *Tropic of Cancer* and *Black Spring*, would not be free of the label of obscenity until 1962, their themes and stylistic innovations had exerted a major influence on succeeding generations of American writers.

The period in time from the end of World War Ⅱ up until, roughly, the late 1960s and early 1970s saw the publication of some of the most popular works in American history such as *To Kill a Mockingbird* by Harper Lee. In the postwar period, the art of the short story again flourished. Among its most respected practitioners was Flannery O'Connor (1925 – 1964).

Though its exact parameters remain debatable, from the early 1970s to present day, the most salient literary movement has been postmodernism. Thomas Pynchon, a seminal practitioner of the form, drew in his works on modernist fixtures such as temporal distortion, unreliable narrators, and internal monologue. In 1973, he published *Gravity's Rainbow*, a leading work in this genre, which won the National Book Award and was unanimously nominated for the Pulitzer Prize for Fiction[7] that year. Toni Morrison, the most recent American recipient of the Nobel Prize for Literature, writing in a distinctive lyrical prose style, published her controversial debut novel, *The Bluest Eye*, to spread critical acclaim widely in 1970.

Toni Morrison

Other notable writers at the turn of the century include Michael Chabon, a Pulitzer Prize winner forthe novel *The Amazing Adventures of Kavalier & Clay* (2000), Denis Johnson, known for the novel *Tree of Smoke* (2007) and Louise Erdrich, nominated for the Pulitzer Prize for her novel *The Plague of Doves* (2008) and awarded National Book Award for The *Round House* (2012).

▶ Poetry

The Colonial period saw the birth of African American literature, through the poetry of Phillis Wheatley and shortly after the Revolution, the slave narrative of Olaudah Equiano, *The Interesting Narrative of the Life of Olaudah Equiano*. This era also saw the birth of Native American literature, through the two published works of Samson Occom: *A Sermon Preached at the Execution of Moses Paul* and a popular hymnbook, *Collection of Hymns and Spiritual Songs*.

Bryant wrote early romantic and nature-inspired poetry, which evolved away from their European origins. The New England Brahmins were a group of writers connected to Harvard University and its seat in Cambridge, Massachusetts. The core included James Russell Lowell, Henry Wadsworth Longfellow, and Oliver Wendell Holmes, Sr. Henry Longfellow was America's most beloved 19th century poet, and in his best known poems, Longfellow created myths and classic epics from American historical events and materials. He reminded Americans of their roots and in the process he became an American icon himself. Everyone read his poems, and his face was instantly recognizable. Many companies used his image to enhance the appeal of their products. Today, Longfellow's face and words still appear on a variety of consumer goods.

America's two greatest 19th-century poets could hardly have been more different in temperament and style. Walt Whitman (1819 – 1892) was a working man, a traveler, a self-appointed nurse during the American Civil War, and a poetic innovator. His magnumopus was *Leaves of Grass*, in which he used a free-flowing verse and lines of irregular length to depict the all-inclusiveness of American democracy. Whitman was also a poet of the body—"the body electric", as he called it. Emily Dickinson (1830 – 1886), on the other hand, lived a sheltered life of a genteel unmarried woman in small-town Amherst, Massachusetts. Within its formal structure, her poetry was ingenious, witty, exquisitely wrought, and psychologically penetrating. Her work was unconventional for its day, and little of it was published during her lifetime.

Leaves of Grass

American poetry arguably reached its peak in the early-to-mid-20th century, with such noted writers as Wallace Stevens and his *Harmonium* (1923) and *The Auroras of Autumn* (1950), T. S. Eliot and his *The Waste Land* (1922), Robert Frost and his *North of Boston* (1914) and *New Hampshire* (1923), Hart Crane and his *White Buildings* (1926) and so on. The poetry of Robert Frost combined pastoral imagery with solitary philosophical themes and was often associated with rural New England. Frost was one of the most popular poets in America during his lifetime and was frequently called the country's unofficial poet laureate. His first two books of verse, *A Boy's Will* (1913) and *North of Boston* (1914) were immediate successes. In 1915, he returned to the U.S. and continued to publish poems that were both popular and critical successes. Frost

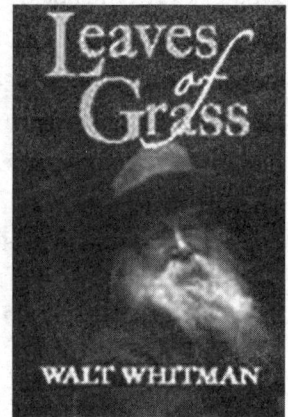

preferred traditional rhyme in poetry; his famous dismissal of free verse was, "I'd just as soon play tennis with the net down". Frost was awarded the Pulitzer Prize four times, and he read his poem *The Gift Outright* at the 1961 inauguration of John F. Kennedy.

At the beginning of the 20th century, Stein, Pound and Eliot, along with Henry James before them, demonstrated the growth of an international perspective in American literature, and not simply because they spent long periods of time overseas. The poet Ezra Pound (1885 – 1972) was born in Idaho but spent much of his adult life in Europe. His work was complex, sometimes obscure, with multiple references to other art forms and to a vast range of literature, both Western and Eastern. He influenced many other poets, notably T. S. Eliot, another expatriate. Eliot wrote spare, cerebral poetry, carried by a dense structure of symbols. In *The Waste Land*, he embodied a jaundiced vision of post-World War I society in fragmented, haunted images. In 1948, Eliot won the Nobel Prize for Literature.

In the postwar period, among the most respected American poets are John Ashbery, his celebrated *Self-portrait in a Convex Mirror* (Pulitzer Prize for Poetry, 1976); Elizabeth Bishop and her *North & South* (Pulitzer Prize for Poetry, 1956); Richard Wilbur and his *Things of This World*, winner of both the Pulitzer Prize and the National Book Award for Poetry in 1957; John Berryman and his *The Dream Songs* (Pulitzer Prize for Poetry, 1964; National Book Award, 1968); A.R. Ammons, whose *Collected Poems: 1951 – 1971* won a National Book Award in 1973; Theodore Roethke and his *The Waking* (Pulitzer Prize for Poetry, 1954); James Merrill and his *The Changing Light at Sandover* (Pulitzer Prize for Poetry, 1977); Louise Glück for her *The Wild Iris* (Pulitzer Prize for Poetry, 1993); W.S. Merwin for his *The Carrier of Ladders* (Pulitzer Prize for Poetry, 1971) and *The Shadow of Sirius* (Pulitzer Prize for Poetry, 2009); Mark Strand for *Blizzard of One* (Pulitzer Prize for Poetry, 1999); Robert Hass for his *Time and Materials*, which won both the Pulitzer Prize and National Book Award for Poetry in 2008 and 2007 respectively.

▶ Drama

America did not have its own drama until the turn of the 20th century. In the late 18th and early 19th centuries, American dramatic literature, by contrast, remained dependent on European models, although many playwrights did attempt to apply these forms to American topics and themes, such as immigrants, westward expansion, temperance, etc.. Among the best plays of the period are James Nelson Barker's *Superstition*, Anna Cora Mowatt's *Fashion*, Nathaniel Bannister's *Putnam, the Iron Son of 76*, Dion Boucicault's *The Octoroon*, and Cornelius Mathews's *Witchcraft*.

Realism also influenced American drama of the period, in part through the works of Howells and the works of such Europeans as Ibsen and Zola. Although realism was most influential in terms of set design and staging and in the growth of local color plays, it also showed up in the more subdued, less romantic tone that reflected the effects of the Civil War and continued social turmoil on the American psyche. The most ambitious attempt at bringing modern realism into the drama was James Herne's *Margaret Fleming*, which addressed issues of social determinism through realistic dialogue, psychological insight and symbolism.

American drama attained international status only in the 1920s and 1930s, with the works of Eugene O'Neill, who won four Pulitzer Prizes and the Nobel Prize. O'Neill (1888 – 1953), one of the greatest American playwrights, was the only dramatist to win Nobel award for literature. Actually, his family life was painful. His mother was a drug addict, so this had some effects on his life. In the early time, he drank heavily and had a number of romantic affairs with women. In 1920, he published his first long play, *Beyond the Horizon*, which established his fame as a creative playwright. In 1936, he won the Nobel Prize for literature. His plays had great influence on Tennessee Williams, William Inge, Edward Albee and Cao Yu, etc..

Eugene O'Neill

In the middle of the 20th century, American drama was dominated by the work of playwrights Tennessee Williams and Arthur Miller, as well as by the maturation of the American musical, which had found a way to integrate script, music and dance in such works as *Oklahoma*! and *West Side Story*. Tennessee Williams (1911 – 1983) was an American author who worked principally as a playwright in the American theater. He also wrote short stories, novels, poetry, essays, screenplays and a volume of memoirs. He received virtually all of the top theatrical awards for his works of drama, including a Tony Award for best play for *The Rose Tattoo* (1951) and the Pulitzer Prize for Drama for *A Streetcar Named Desire* (1948) and *Cat on a Hot Tin Roof* (1955). Between 1948 and 1959, seven of his plays were performed on Broadway. In 1980, he was honored with the Presidential Medal of Freedom by President Jimmy Carter and is today acknowledged as one of the most accomplished playwrights in the history of English-speaking theater.

Arthur Miller (1915 – 2005) was universally recognized as one of the greatest dramatists of the 20th century. Miller's father had moved to the U.S. from Austria Hungary, drawn like so many others by "the Great American Dream". Miller's most famous play, *Death of a Salesman*, was a powerful attack on the American system, with its aggressive way of doing business and its insistence on money and social status as indicators of worth. When it was first staged in 1949, the play was greeted with enthusiastic reviews, and it won the Tony Award for Best Play, the New York Drama Critics' Circle Award, and the Pulitzer Prize for Drama. It was the first play to win all three of these major awards. Miller died of heart failure at his home in Roxbury, Connecticut, on the evening of February 10, 2005, the 56th anniversary of the first performance of *Death of a Salesman* on Broadway.

2. American Art

In the 17th century, the North American colonies enjoyed neither the wealth nor the leisure to cultivate the fine arts extensively. Colonial artisans working in pewter, silver, glass, or textiles closely followed European models. In the first half of the 18th century, a growing demand for portrait painting attracted such artists as John Smibert, Peter Pelham, Joseph Blackburn from England, and Gustavus Hesselius from Sweden.

Of all the arts, sculpture was probably the least cultivated in the colonies. Apart from the anonymous carvers of tombstones and ships' figureheads, William Rush was almost the only known native sculptor to have practiced in pre-Revolutionary and early Federalist times.

The period from the birth of the republic to the Civil War did not see much increase in the demand for the fine arts. Such early painters as Washington Allston, Samuel Morse, John Vanderlyn, and John Trumbull, who sought a market in America for historical painting in the neoclassical manner of Jacques-Louis David, were quickly disillusioned. This period saw the gradual rise of a number of excellent genre painters—Henry Inman, William Mount, Richard Woodville, David Blythe, Eastman Johnson, and George Caleb Bingham, and they were the earliest painters of the American scene.

The first half of the 19th century witnessed development of the first school of American landscape painting. In sculpture, portraiture provided the main source of patronage. John Frazee and Hezekiah Augur with little training produced forceful and original work in marble and wood. Horatio Greenough began the long tradition of the American sculptor trained in Italy. In painting, among the many outstanding artists of this period, James Whistler, Albert Ryder, Thomas Eakins, and Winslow Homer created works that ranked among the finest achievements in American art. This period also saw the further development of the romantic landscape in the works of George Inness, Alexander Wyant, Homer Martin, and Ralph Blakelock.

Among the early 20th century, American sculptors Paul Bartlett, Karl Bitter, Frederick Mac-Monnies, George Barnard, and Lorado Taft exhibited a continuing conflict between naturalistic and idealized modes of representation. A significant cultural development of the era was the founding and expansion of American museums, whose collections were important to the art students and the public.

Most importantly, in the 20th century, American art turned to the exploitation of new techniques and new modes of expression. The functional design aesthetic of the machine strongly influenced all the arts. Meanwhile, the development of photography forced a reevaluation of the representational nature of painting, and the formal and expressive capacities of modern European art opened fresh fields for

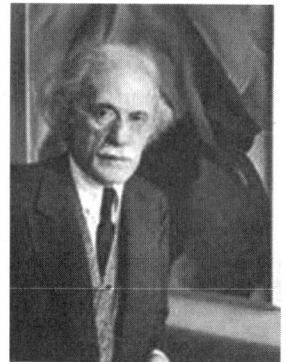

Alfred Stieglitz

the American artists.

Early in the 20th century a vigorous movement toward realism in subject matter and freedom in technique was headed by Robert Henri, John Sloan, and George Luks. With William Glackens, Everett Shinn and others, they formed the Eight, a group also known as the "Ash-can School". They sought to communicate something of the reality of everyday life through art. At the same time, Alfred Stieglitz offered America early glimpses of fauve and cubist works from Europe and exhibited abstract paintings by such Americans as Max Weber, Marsden Hartley, and John Marin at his revolutionary 291 Gallery for contemporary photographs and paintings.

Government sponsorship of the arts during the years of the Great Depression enabled many artists to continue working, embellishing many public buildings with murals and creating smaller works for display in public institutions.

The pop art movement of the 1950s and 1960s utilized an aesthetic based on the mass-produced artifacts of urban culture, rejecting the concepts of beauty and ugliness. Its major practitioners included Andy Warhol, Roy Lichtenstein, Jasper Johns, and Robert Rauschenberg. Other nonobjective styles of painting and sculpture flourished concurrently with pop art during the 1960s, including Op Art, minimalism, and color-field painting. No single school or style has dominated American art in the latter half of the 20th century, as artists have sought numerous avenues of individual expression.

The ascendancy of women and minority artists since the 1970s has been marked by essentialism, the assertion of the artist's distinctive heritage or social circumstance, favoring a point of view typically presented as outside the mainstream of contemporary art. Imagery suggestive of female anatomy and sexuality has been central to the works of Judy Chicago; an awareness of stereotypes of African-American women has informed drawings and installations by Adrian Piper. Jenny Holzer in her works has made extensive use of the printed word.

No single trend can be said to have dominated American art in the closing decades of the 20th century. However, in general, American art in the 1980s and 1990s saw an increased occurrence of words as statement and image as well as a widened use of photography, collage, and a variety of other media. Also characterizing these decades was eclecticism in materials and imagery, combinations of painting and sculpture in single works, a trend toward use of the ironic, a resurgence of realism, and a heightened use of "borrowings" from other periods and works of art.

Section C   Literature and Art in China

1. Chinese Literature

Chinese literature can be roughly divided into two parts, traditional literature and modern literature, with the New Culture Movement[9] (1917) and May Fourth Movement (1919) as its boundary line.

▶ Traditional Literature

Poetry

Poetry is one of the earliest genres of Chinese literature. *The Book of Songs*(*Shi Jing*), the earliest collection of Chinese poems, consists of 305 poems from the late period of the Western Zhou Dynasty to the middle ages of the Spring and Autumn Period. These poems can be divided into three kinds: *Feng*, *Ya*, and *Song*. *Feng* refers to the local poems in 15 states and areas. *Ya* includes the Minor Festal Odes (*xiao ya*) and the Major Festal Odes (*da ya*), basically written by the nobles. *Song* consists of the sacrificial hymns and songs in the courts.

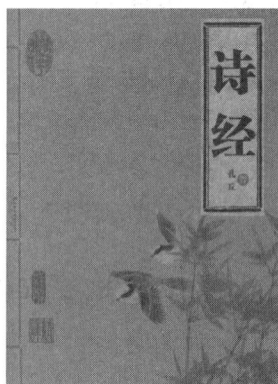

The Book of Songs

In the late period of the Warring States, poetry experienced its second prosperity—the occurrence of *The Songs of Chu*(*Chu Ci*), which originated in a southern state, Chu. It was written by Qu Yuan, one of the great Chinese poets, who was a reformer in politics. The poem was with free lines that made it easier to show its unrestrained and flowing emotion. *Li Sao* was the masterpiece of Qu Yuan, which portrayed the character of the poet himself and showed the conflicts between the reformists and conservatives.

In the Han Dynasty, the Musical Bureau, an official institute in charge of the songs and poems, was founded during the time of Emperor Wu of Han. It collected many folk songs and produced Musical Bureau poems, in which *Mo Shang Sang* (a story of a beautiful girl named Qin Luofu) and *Peacock Flies to the Southeast* (a tragic love story of Jiao Zhongqing and Liu Lanzhi) were the most famous poems. In the course of the development of Musical Bureau poems, the five-word verse and seven-word verse came into being. In Wei, Jin and the Southern and Northern Dynasty, the important poets are Cao Cao, Cao Zhi and the seven poets of Jian'an. Tao Yuanming was a famous pastoral poet in the Eastern Jin Dynasty.

Tao Yuanming

Li Bai

The next important period of traditional poetry is the Tang Dynasty, the most prosperous period in the history of Chinese poetry. Of the many poets, Li Bai, Du Fu, Bai Juyi and Wang Wei were the most noted. Li Bai was one of the well-known romantic poets. Du Fu was a realistic poet and he composed many famous poems such as *Three Officials*, showing his sympathy for the poor and his dissatisfaction with the reality. Bai Juyi was greatly influenced by Du Fu.

His poems described the sorrows of the poor. Wang Wei was a poet famous for his descriptions of the beautiful scenery in his poems. He was versatile and his poems were rewarded with the comment that "in his painting there is poetry and in his poetry there is painting".

The last period in poetry development is the Song Dynasty. *Ci*, a kind of musical poetry, which appeared in the Tang Dynasty, was flourished. Among a lot of famous *Ci* writers, Su Shi, Xin Qiji, and Li Qingzhao were the most outstanding. Su Shi was also well-known as Su Dongpo. His works can be described as powerful, vigorous and uninhibited. He was considered as one of the representatives of the "heroic" school at that time. Xin Qiji was a famous patriotic poet. His poems, which were also classified into the heroic school, were full of patriotic emotions. Li Qingzhao was regarded as the representative poet of the "sentimental"

Li Qingzhao

school. Her poems were noted for their grace and the tenderness and were full of sentimental feelings.

Prose

Prose is another important genre in the traditional Chinese literature. The earliest prose was collected in *Shang Shu* which was also a history book. A prominent period of the development of prose writing was the Warring States Period. The representing historical proses of this period were *The Spring and Autumn Annals* (*Chun Qiu*), *Discourses of the States* (*Guo Yu*) and *Stratagems of the Warring States* (*Zhan Guo Ce*). *Chun Qiu* was the chronicle of the state of Lu between 722 B.C. and 479 B.C.. *Guo Yu* and *Zhan Guo Ce* maily wrote about the history of the Spring and Autumn period and the Warring States period respectively. The Confucian writing (*Lun Yu*, *Mengzi* and *Xunzi*) and Taoist books (*Laozi* and *Zhuangzi*) are philosophical prose.

The second period of prose development is the Han Dynasty. The greatest achievement in prose writing was the appearance of *Records of the Grand History of China*, the first bibliographical book written chronologically by Sima Qian. It recorded the history from Huang Di to the early period of the Han Dynasty. Pianwen became very popular during the period of the Wei, Jin and the Southern and Northern Dynasty. Pianwen was a literary genre between poetry and

Sima Qian

prose, and attached more importance to forms than to contents. Then in the Tang Dynasty, pioneered by famous writers Han Yu and Liu Zongyuan, an ancient prose movement was started. The movement advocated that the prose should be written in plain words. This movement was carried on in the Song Dynasty by Ouyang Xiu, Zeng Gong, Su Shi, Su Xun, Su Zhe and Wang Anshi. Together they were called Eight Great Prose Writers.

Novels

In traditional Chinese literature, novels and operas flourished around the late time of Yuan, Ming and Qing Dynasties.

The Yuan Dynasty is called the golden age of traditional operas, the popular of which was Zaju. Zaju was based on the northern dialects and songs of China. Its main musical instrument was Pipa, a kind of 4-stringed lute. The best Zaju works were *Injustice Suffered by Dou'E* by Guan Hanqing, *Parasol Rain* by Bai Renfu, *Romance of the Western Chamber* by Wang Shifu and *Han Gong Qiu* by Ma Zhiyuan.

There were two great dramas in the Qing Dynasty, saying "southern Hong and northern Kong". Hong Sheng and Kong Shangren were very popular playwrights in that period. Hong Sheng's work was *The Palace of Eternal Life*, describing the true love between Emperor Tang Minghuang and Princess Yang Yuhuan. The drama also described the monopolization of Yang Guozhong and rebellion of An Lushan which brought sufferings to the nation and its people. The masterpiece of Kong was *The Peach Blossom Fan*, a love story about Li Xiangjun and Hou Fangyu. At the end of the Qing Dynasty, Beijing opera had become an independent drama and obtained a national status. Modern drama began to appear and became popular in a later time.

Novel as a kind of literary genre has a long history in China. It germinated in the Wei, Jin and Northern and Southern Dynasties, and grew quickly during the Ming and Qing Dynasties. Zhanghui Novels appeared in the Ming Dynasty. Zhanghui means that the novels are written in chapters respectively with specific topics. Novels and fictions in this period could be classified into three kinds—historical novels, vernacular novels and novels of deity and spirit. The most famous are *The Romance of the Three Kingdoms* (about historical events in Three Kingdoms: Wei, Shu and Wu), *Water Margin* (105 men and 3 women who were forced to rebel against the cruel and fatuous feudal rulers) and *Journey to the West* (based on the true story of a famous monk Tang Xuanzang who traveled on foot to the birthplace of Buddhism to seek for the Sutra).

In the history of Chinese literature, the Qing Dynasty was prominent for its fictions. A large number of novels were created during this period. Among them *Strange Stories from a Chinese Studio* and *A Dream of Red Mansions* were the most reputed. The former one described the world through imaginary stories by the author, Pu Songling, exposing social evils and the harmful effects of the Civil Service Exam, and it also depicted people's revolt against feudal marriage rites and their rebellions against the evil society. The latter one is world famous and has been translated into many languages. The cruel

A Dream of Red Mansions

penalties for "subversive" writing forced the author to express his ideas in a veiled and indirect manner. On the surface, this novel dealt largely with the love between Pao-yu and Tai-yu, but actually through this story as well as many other episodes in the book, the author penetratingly exposed the evils of the feudal system and the crimes of the feudal ruling class. It also described the sufferings and revolt of the laboring masses, truthfully reflecting the social contradictions in the last period of feudalism as well as the actual political struggle of that time. Only eighty chapters written by Tsao Hsueh-chin were extant in manuscript form, and he wrote more than this but unfortunately the manuscripts of the later chapters were lost. The last forty chapters in the present novel were the work of Kao Er, who lived after Tsao Hsueh-chin and carried out his plan of making the love story between Pao-yu and Tai-yu ended in tragedy.

Modern Chinese Literature

The New Cultural Movement of 1917, along with the May Fourth Movement in 1919, brought China into a new era. As a result of the social revolution, Chinese literature developed into the modern era with its modern poetry, prose, drama, novel and some other new genres.

The history of modern Chinese literature can be divided into four parts based on the change in time, originated from the late Qing Dynasty then flourished in the new literature. With some break down, it welcomed a new future after 1980s, then joins contemporary world literature as a further advanced and rational expression.

Late Qing Period

It was believed that modern Chinese literature erupted suddenly in the New Culture Movement. However, the origin of modern literature should date back to the late Qing period. At this time, a lot of translated works of Western expository writing and literature were introduced into China, which enriched the readers' ideas. Most outstanding works were the translations of Yan Fu and Lin Shu.

There was a rapid increase of fictions in the late Qing, especially after the 1905 abolishment of the Civil Service Examination. Some of the important novelists of the period included Wu Woyao, Li Boyuan, Liu E, and Zeng Pu. The content of those fictions focused highly on the temporal social problems.

Republican Era (1911 - 1949)

In the course of the New Culture Movement (1917 - 1923), the vernacular language largely displaced the classical in all areas of literature and writing. Though often said to be less successful than their counterparts in fiction writing, poets also experimented with the vernacular in new poetic forms, such as free verse and the sonnet. Modern poetry flourished especially in the 1930s, with famous poets Zhu Xiang, Dai Wangshu, Li Jinfa, Wen Yiduo, and Ge Xiao. May Fourth radicalism, combined with changes in the education system, made possible the emergence of a large group of women writers. These writers generally tackled domestic issues, such as relations between the sexes, family, and friendship, but they were revolutionary in giving direct expression to female subjectivity. Ding Ling's story *Diary of Miss Sophie* exposed the thoughts and feelings of its female diarist in all their complexity.

Other styles of literature at odds with the highly-political literature promoted by The League of Left-Wing Writers were founded in 1930. The "New Sensationists" —a group of writers based in Shanghai who were influenced, to varying degrees, by Western and Japanese modernism—wrote fiction that was more concerned with the unconscious and aesthetics than with politics or social problems. Lu

Lu Xun

Xun (1881 – 1936), pen name of Zhou Shuren, the most excellent author during that time, was a leader of The League of Left-Wing Writers. His works *The Madman's Diary* and *The True Story of Ah Q* shaped models for the modern Chinese novels. Ah Q, the humble, ignorant but stubborn and defiant farmer, has maintained his allure to writers for 79 years since his creation by Lu Xun in his novel.

Other famous writers during and after the war (the war of resistance against Japan and the war of liberation period, 1937 – 1949) were Lao She, Ba Jin, Cao Yu and Guo Moruo.

Maoist Era (1949 – 1976)

After 1949, socialist realism, based on Mao's famous 1942 "Yan'an Talks on Literature and Art", became the uniform style. Conflict, however, soon developed between the government and the writers. The open atmosphere of literary creation enabled literature to satirize and expose evils in contemporary society. This conflict came to a head in the Hundred Flowers Campaign. During the Cultural Revolution (1966 – 1976), the repression and intimidation led by Jiang Qing, succeeded in drying up all cultural activities except a few "model" operas and heroic stories. Although it has been learned that some writers continued to produce in secret, no significant literary work was published during that period. When the 10-year disaster was brought to an end, a new era of creativity in Chinese literature started.

Post-Mao (1976 – present)

The arrest of Jiang Qing and the other members of the Gang of Four in 1976, and especially the reforms initiated at the Third Plenum of the Eleventh National Party Congress Central Committee in 1978, led writers to take up their pens again. During this period, a large number of novels and short stories were published. Literary magazines from before the Cultural Revolution were revived, and new ones were established to satisfy the appetite of the reading public. There was a special interest in foreign works. Linguists were commissioned to translate recently published foreign literature, often without carefully considering its interest for the Chinese reader. Literary magazines specializing in translations of foreign short stories became very popular, especially among the young. Besides, the reportage literature, a hybrid of journalism and fiction became very popular. Novelists experimented with stream of consciousness and other narrative techniques, while the Misty School of poets developed a fusion of various modernist styles.

After the liberal 1980s, the 1990s saw a strong commercialization of literature due to an opening of the book market. There were many kinds of literature, such as cult literature (Guo Jingming's *Cry Me a Sad River*), vagabond literature (Xu Zechen's *Peking Double Quick* and Liu Zhenyun's *The Pickpockets*), underground literature (Mian Mian's *Panda Sex*), women's literature (Bi Shumin's *Women's Boxing* and *The Female Psychologist*), and master narratives by narrators (Mo Yan's *Life and Death are Wearing Me Out*).

Furthermore, Chinese literature showed signs of overcoming the commercialization of literature at the beginning of the 21st century. An example was Han Han's novel *His Land*, which was written in a social critical surrealistic style against the uncritical mainstream, ranked the 1st in 2009 Chinese bestseller list. In the new century, online literature in China plays a much more important role, and almost all books are available online. More and more people started posting their stories, poems, articles and other works on various BBS or literary websites.

Living and writing in France but continuing to write primarily in Chinese, Gao Xingjian became the first Chinese writer to receive the Nobel Prize for Literature in 2000; while in 2012 Chinese author Mo Yan, who left school to make a living at the age of 12, became the

Mo Yan

first Chinese citizen to win the Nobel prize for literature. His novel *Red Sorghum* was filmed in 1987, directed by Zhang Yimou. His other representative works include *Big Breasts and Wide Hips*, *The Republic of Wine*, and *The Garlic Ballads*, etc..

Liu Cixin

Liu Cixin is a Chinese modern science fiction writer. Liu's most famous work, *The Three-Body Problem*, was published in 2007. It was translated into English by Ken Liu and published by Tor Books in November 2014, and won the 2015 Hugo Award[10] for Best Novel. He was the first Asian writer to win the award. Liu has won both domestic and international popularity today.

2. Chinese Art

▶ Chinese Painting and Calligraphy

As an important part of the country's culture heritage, traditional Chinese painting is distinguished from Western painting in that it is executed on Xuan paper or silk with Chinese brush, Chinese ink and mineral and vegetable pigments. Most Chinese brushes are made from animal hairs glued into a bamboo handle. There are two main types of brushes: hard brushes which are typically made from brown wolf hairs, and soft brushes which are typically made from white goat hairs. Before setting a brush to paper, the painter must conceive a well-composed draft in his or her mind, drawing on his or her imagination and store of experience. Once one starts to paint, he or she will normally have to complete the work at one go, without any alteration of wrong strokes.

Writing Brushes, Ink Sticks, Paper and Ink Stones

Peony Painted with Gong-bi Technique

The two main techniques in Chinese painting are "gong-bi" and "ink and wash painting". Gong-bi, meaning "meticulous", uses highly detailed brushstrokes that delimit details very precisely. It is often highly colored and usually depicts figural or narrative subjects. It is mostly practiced by artists working for the court or in independent workshops. Ink and wash painting, in Chinese Shui-mo, is also loosely termed watercolour or brush painting, and also known as "literati painting". This style is also referred to as "xie-yi" or freehand style.

It is difficult to tell how long the art of painting has existed in China. Pots of 5,000 - 6,000 years ago were painted in color with patterns of plants, fabrics, and animals, reflecting various aspects of the life of primitive clan communities. These may be considered the beginnings of Chinese painting. China entered the slave society about 2000 B.C., and no paintings of that period have ever come to light, but society witnessed the emergence of a magnificent bronze culture, and bronzes can only be taken as a composite art of painting and sculpture.

Peony Painted in Freehand Style

In 1949, a painting on silk of human figures, dragons and phoenixes was unearthed from a tomb of the Warring States Period, which was the earliest work on silk ever discovered in China. From this and other early paintings on silk it may be easily seen that the ancients were already familiar with the art of the writing or painting brush, and paintings of that period were strongly religious or mythological in themes.

Paintings on paper appeared much later than those on silk for the simple reason that the invention of silk preceded that of paper by a long historical period. In 1964, when a tomb dating to the Jin Dynasty (265 - 420 A. D.) was excavated at Astana in Turpan, Xinjiang, a colored painting on paper was discovered, which was the only known painting on paper of such antiquity in China.

Zhou Fang's Painting of Court Ladies

There were many famous painters in different dynasties. The scroll paintings of Gu Kaizhi, known as the founder of traditional Chinese painting, represented the painting style of Northern and Southern Dynasties. Paintings of Zhang Xuan and Zhou Fang in Tang Dynasty, depicting the life of noble women and court ladies, exerted an eternal influence on the development of Painting of Beautiful Women. During the Yuan Dynasty, the "Four Great Painters" (Huang Gongwang, Wu Zhen, Ni Zan and Wang Meng) represented the highest level of landscape painting. Many well-known painters gathered in Suzhou in the Ming Dynasty which saw the rise of the Wumen Painting School, and the four Wumen masters Shen Zhou, Wen Zhengming, Tang Yin and Qiu Ying blazed new trails and developed their own unique styles. The eight painters of Yangzhou used freehand brushwork in their paintings with the main subjects of flowers and birds, bringing a pleasant change in painting style. The Shanghai Painting School played a vital role in the transition of Chinese traditional painting from a classical art form to a modern one.

Chinese calligraphy has a long history. There are five main styles in Chinese Calligraphy art. They are Seal script (Zhuanshu), Clerical script (Lishu), Semi-cursive script (Xingshu), Cursive script (Caoshu), and Regular Script (Kaishu). Different from paintings, it is in essence an abstract art. It uses Chinese characters as its vehicles of communication to communicate the spiritual world of the artist. It is believed among a large number of people that we can know about a person's character through his or her handwriting. Calligraphy is also considered an active way of keeping oneself fit and healthy for the practice is relaxing and self-entertaining.

◉ Chinese Sculpture

Chinese sculpture, with its earliest form as ritual bronzes from the Shang and Western Zhou dynasties, has exerted a continuing influence over Chinese art.

Chinese sculpture at Shang and Zhou dynasties is cast with complex patterned and zoomorphic decoration, but avoids the human figure, unlike the huge figures only recently discovered at Sanxingdui[11]. The spectacular Terracotta Army was assembled for the tomb of Qin Shi Huang, the first emperor of a unified China, as a grand imperial version of the figures long placed in tombs to enable the deceased to enjoy the same lifestyle in the afterlife as when alive, replacing actual sacrifices of very early periods. Smaller figures in pottery or wood were placed in tombs for many centuries afterwards, reaching a peak of quality in the Tang Dynasty.

Buddhism is also the context of all large portrait sculpture. The practice started in rock-cut cave temples where carvings, mostly in relief, of images enveloped chambers and complexes illustrating the beliefs associated to the Buddha's teachings. Creating these temples and sculptures not only garnered merit aligned to their own personal growth, but gave devotees a reference for worship and meditative inspiration. Major rock-cut sites, with large groups of excavated caves, include the Yungang Grottoes, Longmen Grottoes, Maijishan Grottoes, and Mogao Caves.

Media for these sculptures also ranged from sandstone, limestone, wood, ceramic, gilt bronze to copper alloy. Despite the monotone appearances of remaining sculptures today, these works were once brightly painted with an array of pigments.

◉ Chinese Ceramics (Pottery and Porcelain)

Chinese ceramic ware shows a continuous development since the pre-dynastic periods, and is one of the most significant forms of Chinese art.

The first types of ceramics were made during the Palaeolithic era, and in later periods range from construction materials such as bricks and tiles, to hand-built pottery vessels fired in bonfires or kilns, to the sophisticated Chinese porcelain wares made for the imperial court. Most later Chinese ceramics, even of the finest quality, were made on an industrial scale, thus very few individual potters or painters are known. Many of the most renowned workshops were owned by or reserved for the Emperor, and large quantities of ceramics were exported as diplomatic gifts or for trade from an early date.

▶ *Pottery*

Pottery may be the oldest artwork of human beings. As far back as the Neolithic Age, people began mixing clay and water then baking it until it held its shape. Ancient people attached the word "pottery" to their discovery and used it to create various vessels and tools to improve the quality of life. Over the course of thousands of years, they became dominant wares in people's daily life: used to cook, to store things, and to hold cuisine or waters.

A Basin in Neolithic Age

As time passed, the technique became more and more consummate. Different kinds of pottery appeared in different times and regions. Yangshao Culture, 5,000 – 7,000 years ago to today, developed a technique for painted ceramic wares. Qujialing Culture and Longshan Culture, dating back about 4,000 years ago, were known for their black ceramic wares. During the Shang Dynasty bronze vessels grew into somewhat of a status symbol; common people, though, still used traditional clay ceramic wares. Workshops of grey and white potters took the artistic features of bronze wares and decorated their articles ornately.

From the Warring States Period through the Han Dynasty, the art and culture of pottery thrived. In addition to creating everyday pieces, ceramic beasts and warriors were created and buried with the grandees. The Terracotta Warriors, discovered in Xi'an, are the finest representatives of artworks of that time. Visitors to the Warriors are continually amazed by the grandeur and elaborate displays of the well-preserved army. During the Three Kingdoms Period, the forging technique of porcelain gradually replaced traditional ceramic handiwork.

Another fine example of beautifully crafted pottery is the tricolor glazed pottery of the Tang Dynasty. The pieces were created by adding various metals oxide and baking at a low temperature. The glazed pottery would appear to be light yellow, reddish brown, shamrock or light green. The most popular were those of yellow, brown and green. The sculpting of figures, animals or daily appliances was amazingly in accord with the characteristics of Tang art – graceful and lively. Preferred by many foreigners to the region, the tricolor glazed pottery had been transported all over the world.

Tri-color Glazed Pottery

Another pottery that won great reputation for hundreds of years is purple clay pottery. It is well-known for its mild color, condensed structure, high intensity and fine particles. As early as the Song Dynasty, people found purple clay teapots to look much more graceful than those of other materials. In the Ming and Qing Dynasties, tea developed as a simple and tasteful art. People who liked drinking tea held firm to the belief that tea in the purple clay pot smelled balmier and could retain the original quality; these teapots transferred heat slower and were more endurable of heat; after long time's use, the teapot would not fade but become more lustrous. Modern people still delight in this classic fashion ideal.

Purple Clay Teapot

▶ Porcelain

Porcelain, also called "fine china", featuring its delicate texture, pleasing color, and refined sculpture, has been one of the earliest artworks introduced to the western world through the Silk Road. They are made in the form of all kinds of items, such as bowls, cups, tea sets, vases, jewel cases, incense burners, musical instruments and boxes for stationary and chess, as well as pillows for traditional doctors to use to feel one's pulse.

The earliest one was found made of Kaolin in the Shang Dynasty, and possessed the common aspects of the smoothness and impervious quality of hard enamel, though pottery wares were more widely used among most of the ordinary people.

The development of porcelain in the Han Dynasty began to accelerate and before long the artworks were introduced westward. Celadon and black porcelain wares were the dominant types at that time. Styles had formed and differed based on regions by then. The Yue Kiln in Zhejiang Province, which has enjoyed a good reputation for over 2,000 years up to now, produced delicate and hard celadon porcelain; while the De Kiln became the earliest kiln that baked black porcelain.

During the Tang Dynasty, a large number of porcelain wares were in daily use having been substituted for the ones made of gold, silver, jade and other materials. With export, Chinese patterns on these wares also took on more exotic appeal. The Yue and De Kilns of Zhejiang Province had features that were the most popular ones, and another one, Xing Kiln in Hebei Province was greatly prized for its white porcelain. Kilns baking porcelain for the royalty sprang up producing elegant and dainty works.

Stepping into the Song Dynasty, a variety of genres of porcelain appeared and it became a fashion that people showed great interest in purchasing and collecting certain wares suitable to their tastes. Ru, Ding, Ge, Jun and the official kilns had been the representatives of that age. Official kilns advocated concise patterns of decoration; Ru Kiln in Hebei Province added treasured agate into glaze so that the color and texture appeared to be uniquely daintily creamy and could be compared with jade. Ding Kiln boasted its white porcelain which had a texture as delicate as that of ivory with an adornment of black and purple glaze. While Ge Kiln produced articles with various grains and produced an amount of artworks greater than those of the other four.

Well developed in the Yuan Dynasty, the blue and white porcelain, in the main stream of porcelain, was the stylish artistic ware in the Ming and Qing Dynasties and promoted this period to be the most prolific in the field of feudal art. First it painted on the basic body with brush natural cobalt which would be turned blue after being in the forge. Set off by the white glaze and covered by the other level of clear glaze, the blue flowers and other patterns showed their comely charm and were widely welcomed among both refined and popular tastes. With the diversity of cobalt, theme, and style of painting, the blue and white porcelains differed constantly, each being unique.

The famille-rose porcelain was another highlight that appeared during the reign of Emperor Kangxi. The finished article appears more stereoscopic, colorful, gentle and clean. Nearly all the refined colored pigments were utilized like ancient purple, magenta, ochre, emerald, and so on.

Through the development of 4,000 years, now porcelain is still a brilliant art that attracts many people's interest. The Porcelain Capital, Jingdezhen in Jiangxi Province which has been praised for thousands of years, will be certain to satisfy your esthetic appetite.

Famille-Rose Porcelain

▶ Chinese Decorative Arts

As well as porcelain, a wide range of materials that were more valuable were worked and decorated with great skill for a range of uses or just for display. Chinese jade was attributed with magical powers, and was used in the Stone and Bronze Ages for large and impractical versions of everyday weapons and tools. Later a range of objects and small sculptures were carved in bronze, gold and silver, rhinoceros horn, Chinese silk, ivory, cloisonné, lacquer and many other materials.

▶ *Chinese Jade*

Jade has a history in China of at least 4,000 years, and it has influenced all walks of life. In ancient times, people expressed abstract notions with different patterns, which were influenced by Taoism and Buddhism. Jade craftworks were among the most precious and luxurious ones; people wore and decorated rooms with jade to indicate loyalty, elegance, beauty, and eternity. The most popular patterns were: peach (longevity), mandarin duck (love), deer (high official ranks), bat (blessing), fish (affluence), double phoenixes (thriving), bottle (safety), lotus (holiness), bamboo (lofty conduct), and fan (benevolence), etc.

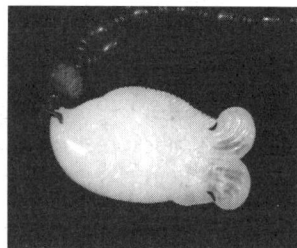

Chinese Jade

In Chinese, jade is pronounced as "Yu", and most words related to moral include this word such as "Unpolished jade never shines", indicating that one cannot be a useful person if he is not educated. It also implies honor and conviction. Many girls in ancient times were also named with jade to reflect the love of their parents. One of the Four Beauties in Chinese history, Yang Yuhuan, the beloved concubine of Emperor Xuanzong in the Tang Dynasty, was their representative. Yang is her surname and her given name Yuhuan means simply "jade ring".

Chinese jade can also be divided into several sub-classifications according to its color: white, grey, green, topaz, and black jade.

In China, the most reputable jade producing area is Hetian in Xinjiang Province. Hetian jade is so hard that it can scratch glass.

◎ Chinese Cloisonné

Cloisonné is a unique art form that originated in Beijing during the Yuan Dynasty. In the period titled "Jingtai" during the Ming Dynasty, the emperor who was very much interested in bronze-casting techniques, improved the color process, and created the bright blue that appealed to the Oriental aesthetic sense.

During the reigns of Emperors Kangxi and Qianlong of the Qing Dynasty, cloisonné improved and reached its artistic summit. Colors were more delicate, filigrees more flexible and fluent, and scope was enlarged beyond the sacrifice-process wares into snuff bottles, folding screens, incense burners, tables, chairs, chopsticks, and bowls.

Chinese Cloisonné

Cloisonné manufacture is comprehensive and sophisticated, combining the techniques of making bronze and porcelain ware, as well as those of traditional painting and sculpture.

Today this technique is associated with the sculpture of wood, jade, ivory and lacquer. Cloisonné art is exported to many countries as a favorite medium for ornaments.

◎ Chinese Lacquer

Radiating a serene luster, lacquer ware is an exquisite Chinese craft. As the earliest users, the Chinese have enjoyed its beauty since the Neolithic Age. During the past hundreds of years, it has played an important role in the development of Chinese arts and crafts as well as having a large influence on the world's art.

The original Chinese ancient lacquer ware was made using a natural lacquer obtained from sumac. The sumac should be about 10 years old. The liquid lacquer should curdle under damp

Chinese Lacquer Ware

conditions then become firm and resistant to heat, acid and alkali. As a whole, the manufacture process is very complex.

Nowadays, Chinese lacquer ware has become more delicate, spreading in Beijing, Yangzhou, Shanghai, Fujian and other areas. Distinctive features are well reflected in various lacquer ware: Those produced in Beijing is of sumptuous style; Fujian's is light, high-temperature-proof, corrosion-free and waterproof; Sichuan's is delicately carved and is famous for its rubbing patterns. Besides, pieces made in Yangzhou are well-known for their elegance, delicacy and a unique creative technique: whorl filling (Dianluo in Chinese) which uses shells as material, processes them into sheets as thin as cicada wings, and pastes them carefully onto lacquer objects. With this process, people even insert treasures like crystal, jade, pearls and coral onto lacquer furniture, tea wares, and calligraphy brushes. Lacquer ware produced in Pingyao Ancient City of Shanxi Province features a luster polished by the craftsmen's palms. This is considered to be the most refined because of its simple but radiant artwork.

▶ *Chinese Paper-cut*

Paper-cut is a very distinctive visual art of Chinese handicrafts. It originated from the 6th century when women used to paste golden and silver foil cuttings onto their hair at the temples, and men used them in sacred rituals. Later, they were used during festivals to decorate gates and windows. After hundreds of years' development, now they have become a very popular means of decoration among country folk, especially women.

Chinese Paper-cuts

The main cutting tools are simple: paper and scissors or an engraving knife. Clever and deft craftspeople are remarkably good at cutting in the theme of daily life. When you look at items made in this method carefully, you will be amazed by the true to life expressions of the figure's sentiment and appearance, or portrayal of natural plants and animals' diverse gestures. Patterns of chrysanthemum display the curling petals, pied magpies show their tiny feathers and others such as a married daughter returning to her parents' home, or young people paying a New Year call to their grandparents.

People find hope and comfort in expressing wishes with paper cuttings. For example, for a wedding ceremony, red paper cuttings are a traditional and required decoration on the tea set, the dressing table glass, and on other furniture. A big red paper character "Xi" (happiness) is a traditional must on the newlywed's door. Upon the birthday party of a senior, the character "Shou" represents longevity and will add delight to the whole celebration; while a pattern of plump children cuddling fish signifies that every year they will be abundant in wealth.

Chinese Embroidery

Embroidery is a brilliant pearl in Chinese art from the magnificent Dragon Robe worn by Emperors to the popular embroidery seen in today's fashions, and it adds so much pleasure to Chinese life and culture.

The oldest embroidered product in China on record dates from the Shang Dynasty. Embroidery in this period symbolized social status. It was not until later on, as the national economy developed, that embroidered products entered the lives of the common people.

Chinese Embroidery

The Chinese word for embroidery is "Xiu", a picture or embroidery of five colors. It implies beauty and magnificence. For example, name for "Splendid China" in Shenzhen, Guangdong was Jin Xiu Zhonghua. "Jin" is brocade; "Xiu" is embroidery; "Zhonghua" is China. In ancient China, embroidery was an elegant task for fair ladies who were forbidden to go out of their home, and it was also a good pastime to which they might devote their intelligence and passion.

There are four major traditional styles in Chinese embroidery: Su, Shu, Xiang, and Yue.

Su Embroidery

Su is the short name for Suzhou. A typical southern water town, Suzhou and everything from it reflects tranquility, refinement, and elegance. So does Su Embroidery. Embroidery with fish on one side and kitty on the other side is a representative of this style.

Favored with the advantaged climate, Suzhou with its surrounding areas is suitable for raising silkworms and planting mulberry trees. As early as the Song Dynasty, Su Embroidery was already well known for its elegance and vividness. In the Ming Dynasty, influenced by the Wu School of painting, it began to rival painting and calligraphy in its artistry.

In history, Su Embroidery dominated the royal wardrobe and walls. Even today, it occupies a large share of the market in China as well as in the world.

Shu Embroidery

Originated from Shu, the short name for Sichuan, Shu Embroidery, influenced by its geographic environment and local customs, is characterized by a refined and brisk style. The earliest record of Shu Embroidery was during the Western Han Dynasty. At that time, embroidered products were a luxury enjoyed only by the royal family and was strictly controlled by the government. During the Han Dynasty and the Three Kingdoms, Shu Embroidery and Shu Brocade were exchanged for horses and used to settle debts.

In the Qing Dynasty, Shu Embroidery entered the market and an industry was formed. Workshops and governmental bureaus were fully devoted to it, promoting the development of the industry. It became more elegant and covered a wider range. From the paintings by masters, to patterns by designers, to landscape, flowers and birds, dragons and phoenix, tiles and ancient coins, it seemed all could be the topic of embroidery. Folk stories like the Eight Immortals Crossing the Sea, Kylin Presenting a Son and other auspicious patterns such as magpie on plum and mandarin ducks playing on the water were also favorite topics. Patterns with strong local features, including lotus and carp, bamboo forest and pandas, were very popular among foreigners at that time.

Xiang Embroidery

As art from Hunan, it was a witness of the ancient Xiang (Hunan) and Chu (Hubei) culture. It was a gift to the royal family during the Spring and Autumn Period. The most persuasive evidence is the articles unearthed in Mawangdui Han Tomb.

Developing over two thousand years, Xiang Embroidery became a special branch of the local art. It gained popularity day by day. Besides the common topics seen in other styles, it absorbed elements from calligraphy, painting and inscription.

Its uniqueness is that it is patterned after a painting draft, but is not limited by it. Perhaps because of this technique, a flower seems to send off fragrance, a bird seems to sing, a tiger seems to run, and a person seems to breathe.

Yue Embroidery

Yue embroidery, which encompasses Embroidery of Guangzhou and Chaozhou, has the same origin as Li Brocade. People generally agree that it started from the Tang Dynasty since Lu Meiniang, who embroidered seven chapters of Buddhist sutra, was from Guangdong. Portrait and flowers and birds are the most popular themes as the subtropical climate favors the area with abundant these plants that are rarely seen in central China. In addition, it uses rich colors for strong contrast and a magnificent and bustling effect.

Since Cantonese take to fortunes in an almost superstitious attitude, attaching a lucky implication to everything, red and green, and auspicious patterns are widely used. The most famous piece is Hundreds of Birds Worshiping Phoenix. Fish, lobsters, bergamots and lychee are also common patterns.

Chinese Folding Screens

Folding screens are often decorated with beautiful art; major themes include mythology, scenes of palace life, and nature. Materials such as wood panel, paper and silk are used in making folding screens. They were considered ideal ornaments for many painters to display their paintings and calligraphy. Many artists painted on paper or silk and applied it onto the folding screen.

◗ Chinese Opera

Chinese opera together with Greece tragic-comedy and Indian Sanskrit opera are the three oldest dramatic art forms in the world. During the Tang Dynasty, the Emperor Taizong established an opera school with the poetic name Liyuan (Pear Garden). From that time on, performers of Chinese opera were referred to as "disciples of the pear garden". Since the Yuan Dynasty it had been encouraged by court officials and emperors and had become a traditional art form. During the Qing Dynasty, it became fashionable among ordinary people. Performances were watched in tearooms, restaurants, and even around makeshift stages.

Chinese opera evolved from folk songs, dances, talking, antimasque, and especially distinctive dialectical music. Gradually it combined music, art and literature into one performance on the stage. Accompanied by traditional musical instruments like the Erhu, the gong, and the lute, actors present unique melodies (which may sound strange to foreigners), as well as dialogues which are beautifully written and of high literary value. These dialogues also promoted the development of distinct literary styles, such as Zaju in the Yuan Dynasty. For Chinese, especially older folks, to enjoy this kind of opera is a real pleasure.

Over the past 800 years, Chinese opera has evolved into many different regional varieties based on local traits and accents. Today, there are over 300 dazzling regional opera styles. Kun Opera, which originated around Jiangsu Province, is a typical ancient opera style and features gentleness and clearness. This enables it to be ranked among the World Oral and Intangible Heritages. Qinqiang Opera from Shaanxi, known for its loudness and wildness, and Yu Opera, Yue Opera, and Huangmei Opera are all very enjoyable. Beijing Opera, the best-known Chinese opera style, was formed from the mingling of these regional styles.

◗ *Beijing Opera*

Beijing Opera is a purely Chinese opera which dates back to the year of 1790, when four local opera troupes of Anhui province came to Beijing on a performance tour. The artists of Beijing Opera absorbed the tunes of Anhui local opera Er Huang and Hubei local opera Xi Pi and drew on the best of Kun Qu, Qin Qiang and Bang Zi as well as other local operas. Through a period of more than half a century of combination and integration of various

The Facial Makeup in Peking Opera

features of operas, there evolved the present Beijing Opera. In Beijing Opera, there are four main types of roles: Sheng, Dan, Jing, Chou. Sheng is the male role; Dan is the female role; Jing is a supporting male role with striking character; Chou is the clown. Every type has its telltale facial makeup and decoration.

The facial makeup in Peking Opera is very interesting. It represents different characters. Facial makeup has obtained the reputation as "painting of heart and soul". There are certain makeup patterns for certain stereotype roles in the opera. It implies complimentary and derogatory connotations and enables audience to get a glimpse of the inner world of actors or actresses. For the painted role, the different colors of the faces represent different characters and personalities. Yellow and white represent cunning. Red stands for uprightness and loyalty. Black means valor and wisdom. Blue and green indicate the vigorous and enterprising character of rebellious heroes. Opera facial makeup has become one of the masterpieces in the thousand years of Chinese culture and art.

▶ *Kun Opera*

Kun Opera is one of the oldest operas in China, and it is also one of the treasures of Chinese traditional culture and art. Kun Opera integrates singing, dialogue, acting, acrobatics, dancing and material arts. It is praised as "the origin of all operas" for its elegant tunes and lines, melodious aria and delicate performance.

In 2001, UNESCO (the United Nations Educational, Scientific and Cultural Organization) proclaimed Kun Opera as a masterpiece of "the oral and intangible heritage of humanity".

The greatest features of Kun Opera include strong lyricism, delicate acting and harmonious combination of singing and dancing. Kun Opera is an integrated art that integrates multiple means of performance such as singing, dancing, emotional expression and speaking. With the long-term development of performing operas, simultaneous singing and dancing becomes a feature of Kun Opera, especially illustrated by body movements.

During the long-term practice, Kun Opera has accumulated an abundant repertoire, some of which are quite influential and frequently performed: *The Roaring Phoenix* written by Wang Shizhen, *The Peony Pavilion*, *The Purple Hairpin*, *Record of Handan*, and *Record of Southern Bough* written by Tang Xianzu, *The Jade Pin* written by Gao Lian, *The Kite* written by Li Yu, *Fifteen Strings of Cash* written by Zhu Suchen, *The Peach Blossom Fan* written by Kong Shangren, and *The Palace of Eternal Youth* written by Hong Sheng.

▶ *Huangmei Opera*

Huangmei Opera or Huangmei tone originated as a form of rural folksong and dance that had been in existence for the last 200 years and possibly longer. The original Huangmei Opera was sung by women when they were picking tea, and the opera was called the *Picking Tea*

Song. In the late Qing dynasty, the songs came into Anhui Province—Huaining County adjacent regions, combined with the local folk art, Anqing dialect with singing and chants, and gradually developed into a newborn opera.

As a matter of fact, Huangmei Opera wasn't recognized by people over the country till the founding of the People's Republic of China. With the encouragement of the government, Huangmei Opera got a great development in the late 1950s as the play *Tian Xian Pei* (*Marriage of the Fairy Princess*) was performed in Capital's Theater as well as its film was finished. Both the play and the film won a universal praise, and Huangmei Opera became a household name and spread to dozens of foreign countries. Even today, almost every Chinese can hum the classical song in the film, *the Couple Back Home Together*.

Today, the opera has also spread its fame both at home and abroad with its sweet melodies and lyrics, graceful sounds and movements, and beautiful costumes and sets. Huangmei fans can be found not only in the Chinese mainland but also in Hong Kong, Macao, Taiwan, Malaysia, Japan, and even Europe.

◉ *Sichuan Opera*

Sichuan Opera originated at the end of the Ming and the beginning of the Qing Dynasty. With immigrants flooding into Sichuan, different dramas were brought in to blend with the local dialect, customs, folk music and dances. Gradually, brisk humorous Sichuan Opera, reflecting Sichuan culture, came into being.

Face changing is the highlight of Sichuan Opera. It is said that ancient people painted their faces to drive away wild animals. Sichuan Opera absorbs this ancient skill and perfects it into an art.

◉ Chinese Shadow Play

Shadow Play was very popular during the Tang and Song Dynasties in many parts of China. Shadow puppets were first made of paper sculpture, later from the leather of donkeys or oxen. That's why their Chinese name is *pi ying*, which means shadows of leather.

Chinese Shadow Play

Shadow puppetry wins the heart of an audience by its lingering music, exquisite sculpture, brisk color and lively performance.

One mouth tells stories of thousands of years; a pair of hands operates millions of soldiers. This is how the shadow puppeteer works. Nicknamed the business of the five, a shadow puppet troupe is made up of five people. One operates the puppets, one plays a horn, a suo-na horn, and a yu-kin, one plays banhu fiddle, one is in charge of percussion instruments, and one sings.

This singer assumes all the roles in the puppet show, which is very difficult. That is not all; the singer also plays several of the over 20 kinds of musical instruments in a puppet show. These ancient musical instruments enhance this ancient folk art.

The stage for the play is a white cloth screen on which the shadows of flat puppets are projected. Shadow puppet looks similar to paper-cut except that their joints are connected by thread so that they can be operated freely. The figures all have a large head and a small body, which tapers down. The design of the figures follows traditional moral evaluation and aesthetics. A man has a big head and a square face, broad forehead and a tall strong body without being too masculine. A woman has a thin face, a small mouth and slim body without being too plump. Effeminacy and tenderness are the norm for Chinese beauty. Scholars wear long robes with an elegant demeanor, while generals in martial attire bring to mind bravery and prowess.

Besides the figures needed in a certain drama, the shadow puppets include heroes from folklore and history, such as the four ancient beauties (Xi Shi, Wang Zhaojun, Diao Chan, and Yang Yuhuan), the Monkey King, Emperor Qin Shi Huang, etc.

Notes

1. **graveyard poets**: A term applied to the 18th-century poets who wrote meditative poems, usually set in a graveyard, on the theme of human mortality, in moods which range from pensiveness to profound gloom.

2. **the Jacobean era**: Jacobean Era refers to the period of time in which James I ruled England and Scotland from 1603 to 1625. Following the illustrious reign of Queen Elizabeth I, this 22-year period is remarkable for its advances in literature and philosophy, and its dramatic changes to the nation as a result of imperialism.

3. **illuminated manuscript**: An illuminated manuscript is a manuscript in which the text is supplemented by the addition of decoration, such as decorated initials, borders (marginalia) and miniature illustrations. The term is now used to refer to any decorated or illustrated manuscript from the Western traditions.

4. **the Young British Artists**: The Young British Artists, or YBAs, is the name given to a loose group of visual artists who first began to exhibit together in London, in 1988. Many of the artists graduated from the BA Fine Art course at Goldsmiths, in the late 1980s. The first use of the term "young British artists" was by Michael Corris in Art Forum, May 1992. It has become a historic term, as most of the YBAs were born in the mid-1960s.

5. **Walker Art Gallery**: The Walker Art Gallery is an art gallery in Liverpool, which houses one of the largest art collections in England, outside of London. It is part of the National Museums Liverpool group, and is promoted as "the National Gallery of the North" because it is not a local or regional gallery but is part of the national museums and galleries administered directly from central government funds.

6. **Lost Generation**: The "Lost Generation" was the generation that came of age during World War I. The term was popularized by Ernest Hemingway, who used it as one of two contrasting epigraphs for his novel, *The Sun Also Rises*.

7. **The Pulitzer Prize for Fiction**: The Pulitzer Prize for Fiction has been awarded for distinguished fiction by an American author, preferably dealing with American life. It originated as the Pulitzer Prize for the Novel, which was awarded between 1918 and 1947.

8. **The National Book Awards**: The National Book Awards are a set of annual U.S. literary awards. The National Book Awards were established in 1936 by the American Booksellers Association, abandoned during World War II, and re-established by three book industry organizations in 1950. Non-U.S. authors and publishers were eligible for the pre-war awards. Now they are presented to U.S. authors for books published in the U.S. roughly during the award year.

9. **The New Culture Movement**: The New Culture Movement of the mid 1910s and 1920s sprang from the disillusionment with traditional Chinese culture following the failure of the Chinese Republic, founded in 1912 to address China's problems. Scholars like Chen Duxiu, Cai Yuanpei, Li Dazhao, Lu Xun, Zhou Zuoren, and Hu Shi, had classical education but began to lead a revolt against Confucianism. They called for the creation of a new Chinese culture based on global and western standards, especially democracy and science.

10. **The Hugo Awards**: The Hugo Awards, first presented in 1953 and presented annually since 1955, are a set of literary awards given annually for the best science fiction or fantasy works and achievements of the previous year. The Hugo Awards are voted on by members of the World Science Fiction Convention, which is also responsible for administering them.

11. **Sanxingdui**: Sanxingdui is the name of an archaeological site and a major Bronze Age culture in modern Guanghan, Sichuan, China. Largely discovered in 1986, following a preliminary finding in 1929. The discovery at Sanxingdui, as well as other discoveries such as the Xingan tombs in Jiangxi, challenges the traditional narrative of Chinese civilization spreading from the central plain of the Yellow River. Since then Chinese archaeologists have begun to speak of "multiple centers of innovation jointly ancestral to Chinese civilization". Sanxingdui, along with the Jinsha site and the Tombs of boat-shaped coffins, is on UNESCO's list of tentative world heritage sites.

Glossary

allegory [ˈæliɡəri] *n.* 比喻；寓言；讽喻
pilgrimage [ˈpilɡrimidʒ] *n.* 朝圣，参拜圣地
fortitude [ˈfɔːtitjuːd] *n.* 坚强意志，坚忍，刚毅
vice [vais] *n.* 罪恶，恶习；瑕疵；不道德行为
expostulate [iksˈpɔstjuleit] *vi.* 规劝，忠告
extant [eksˈtænt] *adj.* 现(尚)存的

vernacular［vəˈnækjulə］*n.* 土语；方言；口语

stanza［ˈstænzə］*n.*（诗的）节

sonnet［ˈsɔnit］*n.* 十四行诗；短诗

flux［flʌks］*n.* 流，流出；涨潮；变迁，熔解

upheaval［ʌpˈhiːvəl］*n.* 举起；动乱；大变动

conviction［kənˈvikʃən］*n.* 确信，坚定的信仰

turbulence［ˈtəˈbjul(ə)ns］*n.*（喻）冲突；混乱

satire［ˈsætaiə］*n.* 讽刺文学；讽刺作品

couplet［kʌplit］*n.* 两行诗；对句；双韵

epigram［ˈepigræm］*n.* 警句；讽刺短诗

prologue［ˈprəulɔg］*n.* 序言，开场白；序幕

introspection［ˌintrəuˈspekʃən］*n.* 内省，反省

amour［əˈmuə］*n.* 恋情；不正当的男女关系

hypocrisy［hiˈpɔkrəsi］*n.* 伪善，虚伪

libertine［ˈlibə(ː)tain,-tiːn］*adj.* 自由思想的

deride［diˈraid］*vt.* 嘲笑，愚弄

impair［imˈpɛə］*vt.* 损害，伤害

expulsion［iksˈpʌlʃən］*n.* 驱逐，开除

agitator［ˈædʒiteitə］*n.* 煽动者，宣传者

ostracism［ˈɔstrəsizəm］*n.* 流放；放逐；排斥

pantheism［ˈpænθi(ː)izəm］*n.* 泛神论；多神教

playwright［ˈpleiˌrait］*n.* 剧作家

hark［hɑːk］*vi.*［主要用于祈使句］听

caricature［ˌkærikəˈtjuə］*n.* 漫画，讽刺画

nouveau［nuːˈvəu］*adj.* 现代的；新式的

wrangle［ˈræŋgl］*n.* 口角，争吵；争辩，争论

macabre［məˈkɑːbr(ə)］*adj.* 令人毛骨悚然的

novella［nəuˈvelə］*n.*（pl. novellas,-le[-le]）短中篇小说

absurdist［əbˈsəːdist］*n.* 荒诞主义者

lavishly［ˈlæviʃli］*adv.* 浪费地；极其丰富地

patronize［ˈpætrənaiz］*vt.* 庇护；照顾

deformity［diˈfɔːmiti］*n.* 畸形；瑕疵；缺陷

swagger［ˈswægə］*vi.* 大摇大摆地走路，昂首阔步（about；in；out）；摆架子；妄自尊大；傲慢；吹嘘，说大话（about）

minutely［maiˈnjuːtli］*adv.* 详细地

ossified［ˈɔsifaid］*adj.* 极端守旧的；不进步的

vilify［ˈvilifai］*vt.* 诽谤；辱骂；贬低

subversive［sʌbˈvəːsiv］*adj.* 颠覆（性）的

occult［ɔˈkʌlt］*adj.* 神秘的；超自然的；秘密的

repression [ri'preʃən] *n.* 镇压；抑制；约束

stark [stɑːk] *adj.* 明显的

seafaring ['siːfeəriŋ] *adj.* 以航海为业的，在航海中发生的　*n.* 航海业，海上航行

obsession [əb'seʃən] *n.* 分心，分神，着魔；执意；积念；迷念；(精神)强迫观念

memoir ['memwɑː] *n.*实录；[pl.]回忆录

evocative [i'vɔkətiv] *adj.* 唤(引)起……的(of)

irreverently [i'revərəntli] *adv.* 不敬地；无礼地

scrutinize ['skrutinaiz] *vt.*, *vi.* 细察，详审

expatriate [eks'pætriət] 被逐出国外的人

poignant ['pɔinənt] *adj.* 深切的，尖锐(刻)的；辛辣的；尖酸刻薄的；生动的，(记忆等)活鲜鲜的；强烈的，痛快的

carnage ['kɑːnidʒ] *n.* 大屠杀，残杀

protagonist [prəu'tægənist] *n.*(戏剧的)主角

hymnbook ['himbuk] *n.* 赞美诗集

magnum opus [mægnəm'əupəs] *n.*〈拉〉巨著，杰作，代表作，主要作品

genteel [dʒen'tiːl] *adj.* 有礼貌(教养)的；绅士风度的；[讽]假斯文的

wrought [rɔːt]形成的；精炼的；装饰的，刺绣的；激动的，兴奋的

laureate ['lɔːriət] *adj.* 戴桂冠的；卓越的

jaundiced ['dʒɔːndist] *adj.* 有偏见的，有猜忌心的，嫉妒心重的

temperance ['tempərəns] *n.* 节制，自我克制

pewter ['pjuːtə] *n.* 锡

figurehead ['figəhed] *n.* 船头雕饰

portraiture ['pɔːtritʃə] *n.* 肖像画法

fauve [fəuv] *n.* 野兽派

embellish [im'beliʃ] *vt.* 装(修)饰；润色(文章)

mural ['mjuərəl] *adj.* 墙壁上的；险峭的

eclecticism[e'klektisizəm] *n.* 折中主义

resurgence [ri'səːdʒəns] *n.* 复苏

sacrificial [sækri'fiʃəl] *adj.* 供奉的，献祭的

pastoral ['pɑːstərəl] *adj.* 有关田园生活的

lute [ljuːt] *n.* 古琵琶

germinate ['dʒəːmineit] *vi.* 发芽，发育

deity ['deiəti] *n.* 神；神性

fatuous ['fætjuəs] *adj.* 愚蠢的；昏庸的；荒唐的

sutra ['suːtrə] *n.*(＝Sutta)箴言(集)；经文

subversive [sʌb'vəːsiv] *adj.*颠覆(性)的

allure [ə'ljuə] *vt.* 引诱，诱惑

pigment ['pigmənt] *n.* 颜料，(着)色料

troupe [truːp] *n.* 戏班子；马戏团

derogatory［diˈrɔɡətəri］*adj.* 毁损的；贬义的

valor［ˈvælə］*n.*（尤指战斗中的）勇猛，英勇

enterprising［ˈentəpraiziŋ］*adj.* 有事业（进取）心的；有魄力的

Further Reading

1）**Canadian Literature and Art**

http://en.wikipedia.org/wiki/Canadian_literature

http://en.wikipedia.org/wiki/Canadian_art

2）**Australian Literature and Art**

http://en.wikipedia.org/wiki/Australian_Literature

http://en.wikipedia.org/wiki/Australian_art

3）**New Zealand Literature and Art**

http://en.wikipedia.org/wiki/New_Zealand_literature

http://en.wikipedia.org/wiki/New_Zealand_art

Group Tasks

The text you have read here has focused by design upon aspects of the major themes and majority cultures of the U.K.,U.S. and China. Of course, it would be impossible to represent all aspects of art and literature in even three major nations. However, it might be interesting to explore more generally the cross-fertilisation of ideas that affected the development of art and literature. You may choose a focus, and three alternative suggestions are as follows:

1）Take the issue of how the art and literature of the First Nations Peoples, the original and ancient inhabitants of the lands we now know as China, the U.S. and the U.K. was subsumed into or dominated by later cultures. Conduct research in libraries and on the Internet to see if you can discern how native peoples affected the artistic cultures in their own lands.

2）Go to websites related to U.K.,U.S. or Chinese official sources concerned with art and literature and discuss in groups how each country portrays its culture. Try to discern why they may wish to project certain appearances and perhaps avoid others? What does this say about the power of the arts in general to affect the human situation?

Such sites as:

http://www.cultural-china.com/chinaWH/features/chinaoverview/LiteratureandArt.html

http://www.britishcouncil.org/china-arts-literature-mg.htm

http://beijing.usembassy-china.org.cn/literature3.html

The above sites might be useful, but feel free to explore your sources.

3）Choose one Nobel Laureate for Art or Literature from each of the three countries.

Choose one that you would like to know more about, for instance, in literature, Mo Yan (http://www.bbc.co.uk/news/entertainment-arts-19907762 or http://www.telegraph.co.uk/culture/books/9602529/Mo-Yan-the-Nobel-prize-winner-his-writing-explained.html); Ernest Hemingway or Pearl Buck (see http://tomastranstromer.net/nobel-prize/american-nobel-laureates-in-literature); or George Bernard Shaw or maybe Rudyard Kipling (see http://classiclit.about.com/library/bl-bio/bl-nobel.htm). When you have selected one or more, research and consider their lives and works in the context of their countries of origin. Discuss your thoughts with others in a group setting to contextualise the learning from the book.

Chapter 7   Customs and Etiquette

Section A   Customs and Etiquette in the United Kingdom

Customs and etiquettes vary from country to country, and people from different regions within a country may also have their unique customs and etiquette. The ability to adapt to the customs and etiquette of each culture may determine the success of intercultural communication. The British people have their own particular customs and etiquette, and in this chapter some important ones will be introduced.

1. Customs

Customs are behaviors generally expected in specific situations and are long-established, socially acceptable ways of behaving in given circumstances, such as the customs of festivals and celebrations, daily-life customs, social customs, religion customs, etc.

◉ Marriage Customs

Most weddings take place on Saturday afternoons, and this is the "peak period" in any week for getting married. Besides, over half of the weddings in the U.K. take place in local register offices and the rest are religious ceremonies of one kind or another.

Traditionally the bride wears a white dress and the groom wears a suit. The bride may be attended by bridesmaids and pageboys. The groom and the bride say their vows, give each other rings, and sign a wedding register.

The Wedding Dress

After the wedding ceremony guests are invited to attend a meal and further celebrations, and this is known as the Wedding Reception. Guests leave presents for the bride and groom on a table in the room where the reception takes place. Usually, the best man, the bride's father and the groom will give a speech at the wedding reception. Besides, it is traditional to have a special wedding cake at the reception, often with two or more tiers, and each tier may be made of a different type of cake to satisfy the tastes of all the wedding guests. The couple go away on a holiday, called a honeymoon, after the wedding has taken place. Centuries ago it was customary for the bride and groom to drink mead made from honey, for a month after the wedding. A month was known as a moon, hence honeymoon.

There are also some wedding superstitions. Bride and groom must not meet on the day of the wedding except at the altar; the bride should never wear her complete wedding clothes before the day; for good luck the bride should wear "something old[1], something new[2], something borrowed[3] and something blue[4]"; placing a silver sixpence[5] in the bride's left shoe is said to be a symbol of wealth; the husband should carry his new wife over the threshold of their home, etc..

Most British people may attach great importance to their wedding anniversaries[6], and the most important ones are: Paper wedding anniversary, Tin wedding anniversary, China wedding anniversary, Silver wedding anniversary, Pearl wedding anniversary, Ruby wedding anniversary, Golden wedding anniversary, and Diamond wedding anniversary. Instead of a greeting card that the husband or wife will keep in a drawer, many British people may give some personalized keepsakes to celebrate their anniversaries.

▶ Funeral Customs

A funeral is a ceremony for celebrating, respecting, sanctifying, or remembering the life of a person who has died. Funerary customs comprise the complex of beliefs and practices used by a culture to remember the dead, from interment itself, to various monuments, prayers, and rituals undertaken in their honor. Customs vary widely between cultures, and between religious affiliations within cultures.

In the Church of England, a funeral is used to mark the end of a person's life here on earth. Family and friends come together to express grief, give thanks for the life lived and commend the person into God's keeping. These can be a small, quiet ceremony or a large occasion in a packed church.

Everyone is entitled to either a burial service or to have their ashes buried in their local parish churchyard by their local parish priest regardless of whether they attended church or not. If the churchyard has been closed, then the Local Authority will provide alternative places for burial and the minister can carry out the service there instead of the church or crematorium. The service will follow a clear plan. The focus moves from earth to heaven as the service moves from greeting the mourners, to remembering the one who has died all the while asking for God's comfort and then committing your loved one into God's care.

In Christian tradition the funeral ends with a burial of either the coffin or ashes. If you have chosen a cremation you may bury the ashes in the churchyard, or use the crematorium's Garden of Remembrance. The ashes may be buried a few days after the funeral with a very brief service.

Some churches have annual memorial services (sometimes held around the beginning of

November) to remember those who have passed away and you may find it helpful to attend.

▶ Clothing Customs

The most prominent England national dress is the English gentleman's bowler hat. The bowler hat, also known as a coke hat, is a hard felt hat with a rounded crown originally created in 1849 for the British soldier and politician Edward Coke, the younger brother of the 2nd Earl of Leicester. The bowler hat was popular with the working class during the Victorian era, and later on with the middle and upper classes in the U.K.. Today, in the streets of major cities, such hats have been rare, but not disappeared.

During the Victorian period, from 1837 to 1901, women's clothing was characterized by extensive use of the lace, spinning, lotus leaf, ribbons, bows, multi-layered cake cutting, wrinkle, and other elements, and the collar, high waist, princess sleeves, leg of mutton sleeves and other court style. Women with high social status would wear corsets, and wearing this tight-fitting suit might make them look elegant. By the 1830s, English women had adopted the poke bonnet which was in the shape of a hood, featuring a projecting rim on the front side.

A tailcoat is a coat with the front of the skirt cut away, so as to leave only the rear section of the skirt, known as the tails. Tailcoats originated in the U.K. in the 18th century, evolved from the cavalry service. The historical reason that coats were cut this way was to make it easier for the wearer to ride a horse. Gradually, the other branches followed suit, and cavalry clothing became fashion among civilians and officials and popular in Britain and its colonies. Over the years tailcoats of varying types have evolved into forms of formal dress for both day and evening wear.

Victorian Costume Styles

The kilt is a knee-length garment with pleats at the rear, originating in the traditional dress of men and boys in the Scottish Highlands of the 16th century. Since the 19th century, it has become associated with the wider culture of Scotland in general, or with Celtic (and more specifically Gaelic) heritage even more broadly. It is most often made of woolen cloth in a tartan pattern. Although the kilt is most often worn on formal occasions and at Highland games and

Scottish Kilt

sports events, it has also been adapted as an item of fashionable informal male clothing in recent years, returning to its roots as an everyday garment.

London Fashion Week is an apparel trade show held in London twice each year, in February and September. Organized by the British Fashion Council (BFC), it first took place in 1984 and currently ranks alongside New York, Paris and Milan as one of the "Big Four" fashion weeks. It is primarily a trade event and attracts significant press attention.

▶ British Superstitions

Superstition is a belief in supernatural causality. We cannot quite say that superstitions in Britain are dead because of their long history, and indeed many relics of them can be found in modern Britain, but they are only relics connected chiefly with vague notions of luck.

There are many superstitions in Britain which are more properly based on folklore than on religion. The custom of saying "bless you" when someone sneezes, is based on the proven link between sneezing and the spreading of infections.

There are also many superstitions surrounding good luck and bad luck. A clover plant with four leaves rather than three is lucky as well. Hanging a horseshoe over the front door brings good luck, but the horseshoe needs to be the right way up. The luck runs out of the horseshoe if it is upside down. If you catch falling leaves in autumn, you will have good luck, and every leaf means a lucky month next year. Cut your hair when the moon is waxing and you will have good luck. Putting money in the pocket of new clothes brings good luck. On the other hand, it is unlucky to walk under a

A Clover Plant with Four Leaves

ladder. Seven years of bad luck will ensue if you break a mirror, because mirrors are considered to be tools of the gods. It is unlucky to spill salt, and if you do so, you must throw it over your shoulder to counteract the bad luck. It is also unlucky to open an umbrella indoors. The number thirteen is unlucky, and Friday the thirteenth is a very unlucky day, because Jesus was crucified on a Friday. It's unlucky to put new shoes on the table, and unlucky to pass someone on the stairs.

In addition, animals feature strongly in superstition. It is considered lucky if a black cat crosses your path and black cats are featured on many good luck greeting cards and birthday cards in England. In some parts of the U.K., meeting two or three ravens together is considered really bad. Also, it is said to bring bad luck if you see bats flying and hear their cries. If a sparrow enters a house, it is an omen of death to one who lives there. It is thought very unlucky to have the feathers of a peacock within the home or handle anything made with them, and this is because the eye shape on these feathers (the evil eye) is associated with wickedness.

2. Etiquette

Etiquette refers to a set of rules that allow people to interact with others in a civilized manner. The most important principle in all etiquette is "to treat others the way you would like to be treated", i.e., treating other people with courtesy and respect and making them feel comfortable with you. Some etiquette in the daily communication of the British people are as follows.

Greetings

Greeting could be formal or informal depending on different occasions. British people are quite reserved when greeting one another. Greeting can be a bright "Hello", "Hi" or "Good morning", when they arrive at work or at school. A handshake is the most common form of greeting among the British and it is customary when they are introduced to somebody new. Kiss might be another way of greeting, but not all British do it in greeting. It is only when they meet friends whom they haven't seen for a long time that they would kiss the cheek of their friends, and one kiss is generally enough. When people meet in a small town or community, they also smile and greet each other even though they do not know each other. In addition, the British often start to converse on the subject of weather. When you meet a British and do not know how to start your conversation, the weather is a constant topic which is quite safe to talk about. When leaving, people say "Goodbye" in a formal situation, and "Goodbye", "Bye", "Bye-bye" and "See you" in an informal situation.

Introduction

An introduction is necessary, and people would feel uncomfortable without it. For example, when you are with one friend and meet another, you must immediately introduce them if they do not know each other. In a house it is the duty of the host or the hostess to introduce any who do not know one another. The general rule of introducing two people is to introduce other people to the person one wishes to honor, so one should introduce a man to a woman, a younger person to an older person of the same gender, an unimportant person to an important person of the same gender, and children to adults. When a newcomer enters the room, all that are seated should stand up to be greeted or introduced. It is proper to shake hands with everyone to whom you are introduced, both men and women. Sometimes at the meeting or gathering, it is all right to introduce oneself to another of the same gender and position.

Invitations

"Drop in anytime" and "come see me soon" are idioms often used in social settings but seldom meant to be taken literally. Invitations may be in the form of a written note, a printed card, or a telephone call. The choice of form may depend on the size and formality of the event and the time available for organizing it. For instance, you might use the telephone to invite a few friends to dinner. But for a wedding, you might use printed or engraved invitations and mail them a few weeks before the event.

Most formal invitations are engraved or handwritten. If you receive a written invitation to an event that says "RSVP" (Reply, if you please.), you should respond to let the person who sent the invitation know whether or not you plan to attend. Never accept an invitation unless you really plan to go. If after accepting, you are unable to attend, be sure to tell those expecting you as early as possible that you will not be there. If the invitation is given in person or by telephone, you can either say "Yes" or "No" at once or should call back with your answer within a day or two at most. In addition, when you accept a dinner invitation, tell your host if you have any dietary restrictions, so that he or she can plan a meal that you can enjoy.

British people place considerable value on punctuality, and they make great effort to arrive on time. If you are unable to keep an appointment, it is expected that you call the person you are meeting. You should arrive at the exact time specified for dinner, lunch, or appointments with professors, doctors, and other professionals; any time during the hours specified for teas, receptions, and cocktail parties; a few minutes early for public meetings, plays, concerts, movies, sporting events, classes, church services, and weddings.

However, if you are invited to someone's house for dinner, you may arrive a few minutes later, and they will not expect you to be there on the dot. It is considered good manners to arrive ten or fifteen minutes "late". You should not be early, because your host or hostess will probably be busy doing other things and not prepared to meet you. But if an invitation says "sharp", you should arrive in plenty of time. Besides, everyday dress is appropriate for most visits to people's homes. However, you need to dress more formally when attending a holiday dinner or cultural event, such as a concert or theatre performance. Although it is not necessarily expected that you give a gift to your host, it is considered polite to do so, especially if you have been invited for a meal. A bottle of wine, a bouquet of flowers, a box of candy or other small gifts are all appropriate. A thank-you note or telephone call after the visit is also considered polite and is an appropriate means to express your appreciation for the invitation.

▶ Table Manners

The British generally pay a lot of attention to good table manners. While people are dining, food may be served in several ways: "family style" by passing the serving plates from one to another around the dining table; "buffet style" with guests serving themselves at the buffet; and "serving style" with the host filling each plate and passing it to each person. Guests usually wait until everyone at their table has been served before they begin to eat.

The British eat most of the food with cutlery, and even young children are expected to eat properly with knife and fork. The fork is held in the left hand and the knife in the right. Hold your knife with the handle in your palm and your fork in the other hand with the prongs pointing downwards. When eating in formal situations, rest the fork and knife on the plate between mouthfuls, or for a break for conversation. Unless a knife stand is provided, the knife should be placed on the edge of your plate when not in use and should face inward. If you put your knife down, you can turn your fork over. It's correct to change hands when you do this, too, so if you are right-handed you would switch and eat with the fork in your right hand. If you are having difficulty getting food onto your fork, use a small piece of bread or your knife to assist, but never use your fingers. You may eat chicken and pizza with your fingers if you are at a barbecue, finger buffet or other informal settings. Otherwise always use a knife and fork.

When having soup, put the spoon into the bowl closest to you, moving it across, catching in it a little drip and have it.

When eating dessert, break the dessert with the spoon, one bite at a time. Push the food with the fork into the spoon (fork in the left hand; spoon in right), and eat from the spoon.

When you have finished your meal, place your knife and fork together, with the prongs (tines) on the fork facing upwards and any knives blade-side-in, on your plate.

● Polite Behaviors towards Ladies

"Ladies First" is also popular in Britain, though it is less observed today than it used to be. It is still considered polite to let a woman go first, to protect her from traffic, to help her to be seated, and to do many other things for her. The main reason for this is the feeling that women need protection as well as respect.

It is polite for a man to allow a lady to go before him in places where one has to go before the other. When going through a doorway, the man should open the door and hold it so that the lady may go first. When getting on a train or bus, men should always allow women to get on first. A man should not get into a car until the lady with him is in it and the door on her side is closed. When sitting down to eat at a table, men do not sit down until women are seated. On a bus or other public places, it is not polite for a man to remain seated while a woman is standing, unless the woman asks him to. When a woman enters a room, every man in the room should stand up and remain standing until she sits down or asks them to sit down. When a man walks down the street with a woman he should walk on the outside.

A man should go first in the following cases: when getting off a train or bus, or getting out of a car; when finding a table in a restaurant; when it is difficult or dangerous to go forward.

Section B　Customs and Etiquette in the United States of America

All countries have their own customs and courtesies, and the U.S. is no exception.

1. Customs

Today the U. S. is an ethnically and racially diverse country as a result of large-scale immigration from many different countries throughout its history. However, the strongest influences on American culture came from northern European cultures, most prominently from Britain and Ireland. Therefore, there are many similarities between the U.S. customs and those of the U.K..

▶ Wedding Ceremony

Wedding is a momentous day in a couple's life. Weddings across the world are shaped by culture. In the U.S., many weddings, no matter where or how they are performed, include certain traditional customs. Before marriage, the couple should become engaged, and then invitations are sent to those who live nearby, their close friends and their relatives who live far away. Next, they will select a wedding party. Often, a handful of their close friends and family are selected to form the "wedding party" as bridesmaids and groomsmen. The wedding party often helps plan the wedding, as well as different events such as the bridal shower or bachelor party before the big day. When everything is ready, then comes the most exciting moment. The wedding itself usually lasts between 20 and 40 minutes. Wedding ceremonies may vary because of religious require-ments or the size of the wedding party, and many traditional weddings take place within a couple's religious institutions, such as churches or temples.

The ceremony usually begins with the seating of special family members. As music is played, grandmothers are escorted in by ushers and seated. Next, mothers are escorted and seated. After the mothers are seated, the groom in tuxedos, the best man and other male wedding party members walk to their places, and the officiant also enters at this moment. After the males are in place, the music often changes, and the junior bridesmaids enter, followed by the bridal attendants and then the maid of honor. The last attendants to process before the bride are the flower girl and ring bearer. The bride in an elaborate white wedding gown carrying a bouquet enters last with her father. It is customary for guests to rise during this procession, and the bride should walk to the right of her escort. When the bride arrives at the end of the aisle, the officiant welcomes guests and may pray to offer a blessing over the marriage. A friend or family member may be appointed to read passages from the Bible or a favorite quotation. After this, vows are ex-changed. The bride and groom may choose to write their own vows, offering their personal promises of love and devotion. Some religions may not allow the writing of personal vows, in which case the bride and groom will use the vows the officiant recites for them to repeat. The best man and/or maid of honor typically hold the rings prior to the exchange. During the ex-change of rings, the bride and groom recite additional vows and exchange rings. Wearing the wedding ring on the fourth finger of the left hand is an old custom. Once the rings are ex-changed, the officiant declares, "I now pronounce you husband and wife". Some may choose to seal this declaration with a kiss, and the bride and groom's first kiss as a married couple is one of the highlights of a traditional American wedding. Then a prayer may be offered, or music may be cued to begin the recessional. The bride and groom leave first, followed by the flower girl and ring bearer, and then the attendants. Mothers and grandmothers should be escorted following the attendants. The car in which the couple leaves the church is decorated with balloons, streamers and other things. The words "Just Married" are painted on the trunk or back window. The bride and groom run to the car under a shower of rice thrown by the wedding guests. When the couple drives away from the church, friends often chase them in cars.

After the ceremony there is often a party, called a "reception" which helps the couple celebrate their new marriage with close family and friends. At the reception, the couple cut their layered and decorated wedding cake together, feed each other a piece of cake before serving the guests, and share their first dance. There is food, dancing and merriment. Other traditions, such as the bride tossing her bouquet, are frequently found in American weddings. The bride stands in the center of the room, often on a chair, and throws her flowers to the unmarried women at the party. Tradition says that whoever catches the flowers will be the next bride. Some women eagerly try to catch the flower; others shy away.

Tossing the Bouquet

And then it is time for the bride and groom to set off the tradition of a honeymoon, a trip after the wedding. The trip nowadays varies greatly by wealth, time and preference.

Traditional Funerals

In most cultural groups and regions of the U.S., the funeral rituals can be divided into three parts: visitation, funeral, and the burial service.

At the visitation (the viewing), in Christian or secular Western custom, the body of the decedent is placed on display in the casket (a coffin). The viewing often takes place on one or two evenings before the funeral. In the past, it was common practice to place the casket in the decedent's home for viewing. The body is traditionally dressed in the decedent's best clothes; while in recent times, there has been more variation in what the decedent is dressed in. The body will often be adorned with common jewelry, such as watches, necklaces, brooches, etc.. The jewelry may be taken off and given to the family of the deceased or remain in the casket after burial. Jewelry will most likely be removed before cremation. Whether the body will be embalmed or not depends upon such factors as the amount of time since the death has occurred, religious practices, or requirements of the place of burial, but in general embalming is preferable.

The most commonly prescribed aspect of this gathering is that the attendees sign a book kept by the deceased's family to record who attend. In addition, a family may choose to display photographs taken of the deceased person during his or her life, prized possessions and other items representing his or her hobbies or accomplishments. A more recent trend is to create a DVD with pictures and video of the deceased, accompanied by music, and play this DVD continuously during the visitation. However, Jewish funerals are held soon after death (preferably within a day or two, unless more time is needed for relatives to come), and the corpse is never displayed. As well, Jewish law forbids anyone to embalm the body of the deceased. Traditionally, flowers (and music) are not sent to a grieving Jewish family since it is a reminder of the life that is now lost. The viewing typically takes place at a funeral home or at a church.

A funeral may be held a few days after the time of death, allowing family members to attend the service. This type of memorial service is most common for Christians, and Roman Catholics call it a mass when Eucharist is offered, the casket is closed and a priest says prayers and blessings.

The common open-casket service allows mourners to have one last opportunity to view the deceased and say good-bye. There is an order of precedence when mourners are approaching the casket at this stage. It usually starts with the immediate family (siblings, parents, spouse, and children), followed by other mourners, after which the immediate family may file past again, so they are the last to view their loved one before the coffin is closed.

The deceased is usually transported from the funeral home to a church in a hearse, a specialized vehicle designed to carry casketed remains. The deceased is often transported in a procession (also called a funeral cortege), with the hearse, funeral service vehicles, and private automobiles traveling in a procession to the church or other location where the services will be held. After the funeral service, if the deceased is to be buried, the funeral procession will proceed to a cemetery. If the deceased is to be cremated, the funeral procession may then proceed to the crematorium.

During the funeral services, a relative or close friend will be frequently asked to give a eulogy, which details happy memories and accomplishments. Sometimes the delivering of the eulogy is done by the clergy. Clergy are often asked to deliver eulogies for people they have never met. Church bells may also be tolled both before and after the service. In the U.S., any type of noise other than quiet whispering or mourning is considered disrespectful.

A burial service, conducted at the side of the grave, tomb, mausoleum or cremation, at which the body of the decedent is buried or cremated at the conclusion.

According to most religions, coffins are kept closed during the burial ceremony. In Eastern Orthodox funerals, the coffins are reopened just before burial to allow loved ones to look at the deceased one last time and give their final farewells.

The morticians will typically ensure that the jewelry that was displayed at the wake is in the casket before it is buried or entombed. Custom requires that everything go into the ground; however this is not true for Jewish services. Jewish tradition is that nothing of value is buried with the deceased.

▶ Clothing

The Cowboy Style

Apart from professional business attire, clothing in the U.S.

is eclectic and predominantly informal. While Americans' diverse cultural roots are reflected in their clothing, particularly those of recent immigrants, cowboy hats and boots and leather motorcycle jackets are emblematic of specifically American styles.

Blue jeans were popularized as work clothes in the 1850s by merchant Levi Strauss, a Jewish-German immigrant in San Francisco, and adopted by many American teenagers a century later. They are now widely worn on every continent by people of all ages and social classes. Along with mass-marketed informal wear in general, blue jeans are arguably U.S. culture's primary contribution to global fashion. The country is also home to the headquarters of many leading designer labels such as Ralph Lauren and Calvin Klein. Labels such as Abercrombie & Fitch and Eckō cater to various niche markets.

Superstitions in the U.S.

Like the superstitions in other cultures, American superstitions often involve the things important in daily life, such as health, numbers, and marriage. For example, have you ever had a cough that would not go away? According to one American superstition, you should take a piece of your hair and put it between two slices of buttered bread. Next, feed this hair sandwich to a dog and say, "Eat well, you hound, may you be sick and I be sound." This will trick the evil spirits and help you get rid of the cough.

In American superstitions, the number three is very important. Often, Americans will say, "All things come in threes". Three is lucky because it represents the traditional family: mother, father and child. Therefore, gifts, letters, and guests will often arrive at your home in groups of three. However, it is also possible for bad events, like accidents and funerals, to come in threes as well. Keep your fingers crossed, and stay lucky!

2. Etiquette

Etiquette rules are not uniform in America. However, the U.S. shares cultural and linguistic heritage originating in Europe, and quite a few points of etiquette in the U.S. are nearly the same as those in Europe. The following etiquette topics pertain to basic interactions in the American society.

Table Manners

Table manners are the way you behave when you are dinning. To have good table manners, there are some general rules to follow.

Table setting should be paid attention to. Bread or salad plates are to the left of the main plate, beverage glasses are to the right. Modern etiquette provides the smallest numbers and types of utensils necessary for dining. Only utensils which are to be used for the planned meal should be set. Even if needed, hosts should not have more than three utensils on either side of the plate before a meal. If extra utensils are needed, they may be brought to the table along with later courses. If a salad course is served early in the meal, the salad fork should be further from the main course fork, both set on the left. The fork is used in the "American" style: use the fork in your left hand while cutting, and switch to right hand to pick up and eat a piece, which is different from the European "Continental" style (fork always in left hand). If a soup is served, the spoon is set on the right, further from the plate than the knife. Glasses designed for certain types of wine may be set if available. If only one type of glass is available, it is considered correct regardless of the type of wine provided. If a wine glass and a water glass are set, the wine glass is on the right directly above the knife. The water glass is to the left of the wine glass at a 45° angle, closer to the diner. Hosts should always provide cloth napkins to guests. When paper napkins are provided, they should be treated the same as cloth napkins, and therefore should not be balled up or torn. Coffee or tea cups are placed to the right of the table setting, or above the setting to the right if space is limited. The cup's handle should be pointing right.

Before dining, put a napkin on the lap, but never tuck into any part of the clothing. A prayer may be customary in some household, and guests may join in or be respectfully silent. Most prayers are made by the host before the meal. You should not begin to eat until your host or hostess has begun.

While dining, you should neither lean on the back of the chair nor bend forward to place the elbows on the table. You may rest forearms or hands on the table, but not elbows. When a dish is offered from a serving dish, the food may be passed around or served by a host or staff. If passed, you should pass on the serving dish to the next person in the same direction as other dishes are being passed. Place the serving dish on your left, take some, and pass to the person next to you. You should consider how much is on the serving dish and not take more than a proportional amount so that everyone may have some. If you do not care for any of the dish, pass it to the next person without comment. If being served by a single person, the server should request if the guest would like any of the dish. The guest may say "Yes, please", or "No, thanks". Do not make any noise with your mouth while eating; eat slowly, with your mouth closed; do not put too much food in your mouth at a time. Before asking for additional helpings, always finish the serving on your plate first. Burping, coughing, yawning, sneezing, or flatulence at the table should be avoided. If you do so, say "Excuse me". Do not talk on your phone at the table. If an urgent matter arises, apologize, excuse yourself, and step away from the table so your conversation does not disturb the others. Say "Excuse me" before leaving the table. Gentlemen should stand when a lady leaves or rejoins the table in formal social settings.

At the end of the meal, place any forks or spoons pointed face up and any knives blade-side-in, to show that you have finished eating. You should not clean your teeth at the table with a toothpick, or your finger, or even your tongue. When you leave the table at the end of the meal, loosely place the used napkin on the table to the left of your plate. Wait for your host or hostess to rise before getting up from a dinner party table, and thank them when leaving.

◉ Other American Etiquette Rules

People greet by shaking hands, and hugs and kisses are not considered proper except among very close friends and relatives. If gloves are being worn indoors, they should be removed before shaking hands. This is especially applicable to men. Besides, it is impolite for men to wear hats or other head coverings indoors. Men should always remove hats in places of worship, when sitting at a table for a formal meal, and when a national anthem is played. These rules do not apply to head coverings used due to religious beliefs, such as those worn by Sikhs and many orthodox Jewish men. Traditionally (until the mid-1960s), most women considered it mandatory to wear a hat when outside of one's home, such as when in public, while visiting others, and especially in houses of worship. Nowadays, however, wearing hats is not as popular as it used to be.

It is considered impolite in a social or professional setting, especially when first meeting someone, to ask if they are married or dating, their political or religious affiliations or beliefs, their age, weight, or other personal physical matters. It is also considered impolite to comment negatively on a person's physical condition, such as telling someone they "look tired" or to ask "Are you okay? You don't look well".

One should attempt to suppress yawning in polite company, concealing the mouth with the hand, to avoid appearing bored. Blowing one's nose should be done into a tissue or handkerchief, and never while eating. It is preferable to do so, along with habits which should not be done around others, such as nose and ear picking, by excusing oneself and doing so in private.

Though etiquette rules may seem arbitrary at times, these are the situations in which a common set of accepted customs help to eliminate awkwardness.

Section C   Customs and Etiquette in China

China is a country with a splendid history of civilization. Variety of customs and etiquette is one part of its civilization, and they all show the brilliant civilization of China.

1. Customs

◉ Wedding Customs

China is a large country with 56 nationalities. Different nationalities have different marriage customs, but whatever the nationality is, the wedding ceremony is usually very complicated. In China, marriage is regarded as a lifelong matter and thus given special attention to. Personally, it is a sign of establishing a family and getting settled; while for the whole family, it is an expansion and continuation. Marriage is of great significance in one's life.

Unlike western tradition, the color red dominates traditional Chinese weddings. Red signifies love, joy and prosperity and is used in a variety of ways in Chinese wedding traditions, such as wedding gown, shoes, quilt, pillow, etc..

The traditional Chinese marriage usually involves "Six Etiquette[7]", indicating the six important parts and corresponding rituals during the process from the proposal to the consummation. "Six Etiquette" includes "Nacai" (proposal), "Wenming" (name-asking), "Naji" (to present the lucky sign), "Nazheng" (to present betrothal gifts), "Qingqi" (to decide the right time of wedding), and "Qinying" (to welcome the bride).

According to the old wedding custom of China, parents and matchmakers arranged the marriage. First, the matchmaker would go between the two families to communicate the conditions of both. When a young man's parents identified a likely bride-to-be, they would send the matchmaker to present gifts to the woman's parents and express their hope for the match, which was called "Nacai".

If the woman's parents permitted, then the next step was "Wenming". The young man's family would send gifts to the betrothed's family to ask about the woman's age or year of birth (Chinese zodiac). Then the eight characters about both parties' birthday were taken to the fortune-teller to predict whether the marriage was auspicious. If it was auspicious, the young man's family would inform the good news and make certain of the marriage, which was so-called "Naji".

If both parties were satisfied with each other, the "betrothal gifts" might be given, "Nazheng" by name. The matchmaker wrote out the betrothal card and negotiated with the bride's family to decide the items. Then the bridegroom's side gave the betrothal gifts according to the betrothal card. The betrothal gifts consisted of gift list, gifts and monetary gifts, and they might vary widely depending on local customs and family wealth.

After giving the betrothal gifts, the wedding day could be finally fixed. The bridegroom's side would select a lucky day for the wedding and ask the permission of the bride's family with gifts, which was the so-called "Qingqi".

The following step was the most grand and complicated, "Qinying", when the bridegroom went in person to fetch the bride from her home to his home. The richer the family was, the more complicated these rituals were.

On the day before the wedding, the "good luck woman" would be selected to arrange the bridal bed. In order to bless the couple with fertility, the bed was scattered with red dates, lotus seeds, peanuts and other fresh or dried fruits. Then nobody was allowed to touch the bed until the couple entered the bridal chamber after the wedding ceremony. In addition, usually the bride's dowry should be sent to the bridegroom's family the day before the wedding day. Apart from jewelry, embroidered beddings, kitchen utensils and furniture, the traditional dowry normally consisted of such symbolic items as scissors, a pair of pillows, shoes, clothes, chopsticks tied in red ribbon and bowls.

On the way of welcoming the bride, red color was used to fit the joyful occasion, firecrackers were set off, red lanterns were lit, and musical troops were hired to perform all along the way. The bridegroom rode to the bride's home on a horse or by sedan chair. The bride was dressed in red silk, and wore red flower, red lipstick and rouge. Before the bride left for the bridegroom's home, the "good luck woman" would lead her to the sedan chair. On her way to the chair, one of her sister would shield her with a red parasol, while another sister would throw the rice at the sedan chair. Before she got on the sedan chair, the bride would cry over the love and care her parents had given to her for so many years. At that moment, the bride's mother would pass on to her daughter the secrets of how to be an adequate wife and daughter-in-law.

The Bride Getting on the Sedan Chair

When everything was all right, the bridegroom could take leave. The bride was still unseen to the bridegroom with a piece of red silk veil covering her head and face. Usually the joyful tunes would be played during the whole trip. Dancing lions, if any, preceded the procession.

When the wedding procession reached the bridegroom's home, an elder woman who had many offsprings would help the bride come out of the sedan chair, and then fed boiled rice

Three Bows

dumplings to the new couple because the round shape of the dumplings signifies harmony and union. Then the new couple would hold the two ends of a red ribbon respectively, and were led to the family altar, where the couple bowed to Heaven and Earth, to the family ancestors and parents, and finally bowed to each other. The ceremony proceeded under a director's prompts and applauses of the audience. After the wedding ceremony, the new couple would be led to the bridal chamber. On the wedding night, the wedding guests would tease the new couple in the nuptial chamber.

The wedding ceremony often ended with a very extravagant banquet known as Xijiu (literally joyful wine), and there were ceremonies such as the bride presenting wines or tea to parents and guests. Relatives and friends usually gave the new couple gifts as well as their blessings.

Traditionally, the newlyweds were to return to visit the bride's parents three days after the wedding. It was an indispensable etiquette. A month after the wedding the bride would visit her parents' home again accompanied by her husband and bringing many kinds of gifts. The bridegroom went home on the same day after the escort mission, leaving his wife staying at her parents' home for several days.

Nowadays, weddings in China, especially the weddings in the cities, become much simpler. When a new couple is engaged, what follows is a choice of the date of their marriage. The date often coincides with the bank holidays or some special Chinese festivals, so that it is more convenient for relatives and friends to attend the wedding. On the wedding day, the newlyweds give banquets in the restaurants, where they propose toasts and receive congratulations from their guests. After the banquet, wedding candies are distributed as a conclusion of the wedding. Besides, due to cultural exchanges between China and western countries, more western elements are taken into the Chinese weddings, such as exchanging rings, a white wedding gown for the bride and suit for the bridegroom, honeymoon and so on. The young couples have discarded the religious meaning of the western weddings but maintained its modern form and spirit, which makes the marriage more personal and romantic.

▶ Funeral Customs

"Funeral" is a ritual for lamenting the deceased and the way to treat the remains. In China, there are different customs in different regions, among which inhumation is very common. Other than inhumation, cremation, "water burial", "open burial" and "hanging-coffin burial" were also practiced in ancient China. The funeral rites in China originated from the concept of undying spirit and the worship for ancestors. The Confucian School regards funeral rites as embodiment of ethics. Buddhism, which is popular in China, even takes death as the start of reincarnation.

To a certain degree, Chinese funeral rites and burial customs are determined by the age of the deceased, cause of death, position in society, and marital status. According to Chinese customs, an elder should never show respect to someone younger. If an infant or child dies, no funeral rites are performed since respect cannot be shown to a younger person. The child is thus buried in silence. However, funeral rites for an elder must follow a prescribed form. Rites befitting a person's status, age, etc., must be performed even if this means the family of the deceased will go into debt.

When a death occurs in a family, the family members of the dead shall wear mourning dresses. A funeral hall shall be arranged in the house, with scrolls of cloth hung up and elegiac couplets pasted.

Before being placed in the coffin, the corpse is cleaned with a damp towel dusted with talcum powder, and dressed in his or her best clothes before being placed on a mat while all other clothing of the deceased will be burned. The body is completely dressed, including the footwear, and even cosmetics. Usually, the corpse is not dressed in red clothing (this will turn the corpse into a ghost), and white, black, brown and blue are the usual colors.

The coffin is placed in the hall of the house, and it is placed with the head of the deceased facing the inside of the house, resting at about one foot from the ground on two stools. Wreaths, gifts and a portrait or photograph of the deceased are placed at the head of the coffin. The coffin is not sealed during the wake. Food is placed in front of the coffin as an offering to the deceased. The deceased's comb is broken into two—one part is placed in the coffin and the other is kept by the family.

During the wake, the family members of the deceased gather around the coffin positioned according to their rank in the family. The children and daughters-in-law wear a hood of sackcloth over their heads, and it is customary for blood relatives and daughters-in-law to wail and cry during mourning as a sign of respect and loyalty to the deceased.

An altar where burning incense and a lit white candle are placed is positioned at the foot of the coffin. Joss paper and prayer money are burned continuously throughout the wake. Funeral guests are required to light incense for the deceased and bow as a sign of respect to the family. There will also be a donation box since money is always offered as a sign of respect to the family of the deceased. This money will also help the family defray the costs of the funeral.

The length of the wake depends on the financial resources of the family, although it should be at least one day long to allow for the offering of prayers. While the coffin is in the house, a monk will chant verses from Buddhist or Taoist scriptures at night. It is believed that the souls of the dead face many obstacles and even torment and torture for the sins they have committed in life before they enter the afterlife. Prayers, chanting and rituals offered by the monks help ease the passage of the deceased's soul into heaven. These prayers are accompanied by music played on the gong, flute and trumpet.

When the prayer ceremonies are over, the wailing of the mourners reaches a crescendo and the coffin is nailed, which represents the separation of the dead from the living. Then yellow and white "holy" paper is pasted on the coffin to protect the body from malignant spirits. During the sealing of the coffin, all present must turn away since watching a coffin being sealed is considered very unlucky. The coffin is then carried away from the house using a piece of wood tied over the coffin, with the head of the deceased facing forward. It is believed that blessings from the deceased are bestowed upon the pallbearer, so there are usually many volunteers.

The coffin is not carried directly to the cemetery but is first placed on the side of the road outside the house where more prayers are offered and paper is scattered. The coffin is then placed into a hearse that moves very slowly for a mile. The order of the funeral procession follows the status of the family members. A white piece of cloth is tied to vehicles accompanying the hearse, or a white piece of paper can be pasted on their windshields. The eldest son usually sits next to the coffin. A long, lit joss stick is held throughout the journey, symbolizing the soul of the deceased; it is relit immediately if it goes out. If the procession must cross a body of water, the deceased must be informed of this since it is believed that an uninformed soul will not be able to cross water.

Chinese cemeteries are generally located on hillsides since this is thought to improve "Feng-shui" (geomantic omen). The higher a grave is located, the better Fengshui is. At the graveside, when the coffin is taken down from the hearse and lowered into the ground, all present must turn away. Family members and other relatives throw a handful of earth into the grave before it is filled. After the funeral, all of clothes worn by the mourners are burned to avoid bad luck associated with death. After the coffin is buried, the keeper of the cemetery will also offer prayers to the deceased.

The eldest son of the deceased will retrieve some earth from the grave to put into an incense holder, and the deceased will be worshipped by the family at home using an ancestral tablet. Although the funeral rites are over, the period of mourning by the family continues for another 100 days. However, a period of mourning is not required if the deceased is a child or a wife.

◉ Traditional Clothing

Chinese clothing often transformed dramatically following dynastic changes, and each dynasty had special clothing of its own. The progress of nation can be seen through its changes in clothing styles. In ancient feudal society, people's rank and position could easily be distinguished from their daily dress.

China's complete code of costume and trappings was established in the Han Dynasty. The yarn-dyeing, embroidering and metal-processing technologies developed rapidly

The Dresses of the Tang Dynasty

in the period, spurring changes in costume and adornments. The Tang Dynasty wrote the most brilliant page in the history of Chinese clothing. The dresses of the Tang Dynasty were mainly made of silk, so they were famous for softness and lightness. The clothing materials were exquisite, the structure was natural, graceful and elegant, and adornments were splendid. Though the forms of garments were still the continuation of the Han Dynasty, they boldly adopted the features of foreign garments in terms of forms and adornments, and thus a special open and romantic style of dress and personal adornments for women was formed. The garments in the Tang Dynasty also greatly affected the garments of neighboring countries. For instance, Japanese kimono adopted the elites of the dresses of the Tang Dynasty in terms of colors and the Hanbok (traditional Korean clothing) also adopted the advantages of the dresses of the Tang Dynasty.

Chinese Cheongsams

The cheongsam or Qipao in Chinese, which evolved from ancient clothing of the Manchu ethnic minority, is one of the most popular Chinese clothings, because it fits the Chinese female figure well, has simple lines and looks elegant; it is suitable for wearing in all seasons by young or old and can either be long or short, unlined or interlined, woolen or made of silk floss. With different materials, cheongsams present different styles. Cheongsams made of silk demonstrate charm of femininity and staidness; those made of brocade are eye-catching and magnificent and suitable for occasions of greeting guests and attending banquets. From the 1930s, cheongsam almost became the uniform for women, which even became a formal suit for occasions of social intercourses or diplomatic activities. When Chinese cheongsams were exhibited for sales in countries like Japan and France, they received warm welcome from local women, who did not hesitate to buy Chinese cheongsams especially those top-notch ones made of black velour interlined with or carved with golden flowers. It is recognized around the world and has inspired many foreign adaptations because of its simple yet exotic lines. Cheongsam features strong national flavor and embodies beauty of Chinese traditional costume. It not only represents Chinese female costume but also becomes a symbol of the oriental traditional costume.

Clothes of Chinese ethnic minorities are flowery, colorful, extremely exquisite, and highly distinctive. They play an important role of the rich history and culture of the ethnic groups. There are numerous clothing designs and forms in Chinese ethnic minorities. Generally speaking, they can be classified into two types: long gowns and short clothes. People usually wear a hat and boots to match long gowns, and headcloth and shoes to match short clothes. The gowns take various forms: the high-collar and big-front type worn by the Mongolian, the Manchu, the Tu and so on; the collarless tilted-front type worn by the Tibetan, the Moinba and so on; the tilted-front type worn by the Uygur and other ethnic minorities and so on. As for short clothes, they fall into two types: trousers and skirts.

Costumes of ethnic minorities vary greatly not only with different nationalities, but also with different branches and different regions within the same ethnic group. Difference can be seen from province to province, from county to county, and even from village to village. Costume is the most obvious symbol of an ethnic group, and in the history, many ethnic groups were named just according to their garments.

In such a vast country, with so many ethnic groups, styles of clothes vary a lot. This is one of the characteristics of folk garments.

2. Etiquette

China is a country that has long been known for its ceremonies and etiquette through the ages, and it has often been referred to as the Nation of Etiquette. The following is a brief introduction to the daily manners and courtesies of social life in China.

▶ Greetings

In China, a handshake or a simple and kind salutation is common. Handshaking is a kind of silent language, which is considered formal greeting behavior in China. It is the common propriety on most social occasions as an expression of courtesy and greeting when people meet or say goodbye to each other.

As for the question as to who should offer his hand first, there are some basic principles you should follow. Generally speaking, the elder, the senior, the teacher (compared with the students), the female, the married (compared with the unmarried), the superior should reach out their hands first. If you have to shake hands with more than one person, you should shake hands in succession with the senior and superior to the junior and inferior, from the nearest to the furthest. Specially, when the host meets the guest, the host should shake hands first to show his welcome; however, when they say goodbye with each other, it is the guest who should offer his hand first. There are also some exceptions. If someone, whether he is superior or not, offers his hand before you, it is courteous to give an unreserved response. It is inappropriate to shake hands too long or too short, three to five seconds is the best, not exceed 30 seconds at most. Handshaking should be simple and light, without over exertion.

There are also some things that are unacceptable when shaking hands: shaking hands absent-mindedly; shaking hands with left hand; shaking hands while wearing gloves or sunglasses; having your other hand in your pocket; shaking hands while seated unless disabled, etc..

A form of address is to some extent a reflection of social climate. In China, various forms of address are used according to circumstances. Choosing the appropriate and correct form shows your wit and high respect to others. Generally, for Chinese people it should be in accord with convention and care much about the personal favor of the people being addressed. You can call someone directly by his job title or put it before his surname or full name, which is often used in the workplace and on more formal occasions, such as Manager Wang, Director Zhang, etc.. An address may also be based on professional qualifications, which expresses respect to those being addressed, such as Professor Li, Engineer Zhao, etc.. Besides, an address based on educational qualifications is helpful to emphasize the academic authority of the people being addressed, such as Dr. Yang. You can call others by their family name or full name by putting the Mr. or Ms. in front. This is the general address most widely used in company, hotels, and other places.

When you meet someone for the first time, the most commonly-used words are "Hello", "Hi", "Nice to meet you", "How do you do", etc.. For greeting acquaintances, the words will be more informal and friendly, such as "Long time no see", "You look very well today", "Have you had your meal", "How are you doing recently", "How is your family", "Where are you going", etc.. This phatic communion is a salutation without expectation of a response, the question being rhetorical. However, it should be compact, friendly and respectful. It is improper to ask about the personal affairs of other people for delving into another's privacy is considered to be discourteous. Remember always to be active, passionate, natural and attentive when greeting others.

▶ Family Visiting

Chinese people are hospitable. There are common rules for inviting guests over. When the guest of honor enters into the room, the hosts stand until the guest of honor is seated. The host then orders the dishes, and the guest should be silent. When the dishes arrive, the meal begins with a toast from the host, and the guests then make a toast in turn in the honor of the host. The guest of honor should be the first one to start the meal.

If you are invited by or wish to pay a visit to a Chinese family, there are some formalities that you should follow: make an appointment in advance, and then you should always be punctual for the appointment; choose an appropriate time to have the family visiting, and avoid visiting at other's dining or resting time; bring some gifts; hand your hat, overcoat, raingear, etc. to the host for placement; greet all people in the family no matter they are acquaintances or not; be seated only when invited to do so by your host; usually you will be offered tea, beverage, cigarette, fruits, candies and dim-sum, and just express your thankfulness, then you can help yourself to them; generally do not stay more than an hour unless being asked by the host to stay longer; always express your thanks to the host when you leave.

The gift giving to Chinese people should be appropriate for the condition or occasion. If you pay a visit to a Chinese family, it is smart to bring gift for the hostess like bouquet, cosmetic, or scarves. Toys, candies, and books are good for the children. If you attend a wedding party, the artistic adornment, bouquet, or some practical items are the best choices. During the traditional Chinese festivals, you can bring wines, cigarettes, tea, candies, fruits, or some of your local products. However, there are some tips for you to note, which is considered to be unpropitious: clocks should never be presented as gift to others, especially to elders; pears cannot be sent to couples; people who are unwell may not be given medicine as gift; intimate items of clothing may not be gifts for friends of the opposite gender.

● Table Manners

Many eating manners date from the time of ancient China, such as how to sit in a banquet or the layout of the place settings, and some of them are still followed in modern Chinese life. Eating is a dominant aspect of Chinese culture, and in China, eating out is one of the most common ways to honor guests.

Table etiquette is very important to Chinese people. Compliance with these rules sometimes signals a person's status, culture, and family education to others. In casual settings, and sometimes with the youth, many of these table manners go by the wayside. In formal settings, however, these table manners become more apparent.

Usually, both square and rectangular tables are used for small groups of people. When large groups are dining, particularly in restaurants, round tables are common. A basic place setting consists of a small teacup, a large plate with a small, empty rice bowl in the centre, a set of chopsticks on the right hand side of the table, and a spoon. More elaborate place settings may include a chopstick holder, a water or red wine style glass, and a small "distilled spirit" glass. At each place setting, a cloth napkin may be present. Un-

A Basic Place Setting

like formal Western dinners, a cloth napkin is not placed on the lap. Instead, whether provided by the hosts or waitress, or already present, folded at the place setting, it is to be placed with one corner under the large plate of the place setting, and the rest hanging down diagonally over the edge of the table, and partially onto the lap of the diner. Also present on the table, for communal usage, are toothpicks, and paper napkins. It is polite, when taking a napkin for oneself, to provide one to guests seated next to you.

Seating arrangement is an important part of Chinese dining etiquette. The respect structure in modern dining etiquette has been simplified. The seat of honor, reserved for the master of the banquet or the guest with highest status, is the one in the center facing east or facing the entrance. Those of higher position sit closer to the master of the banquet. The guests of lowest position sit furthest from the seat of honor. When a family holds a banquet, the seat of honor is for the guest with the highest status and the head of the house takes the least prominent seat. If round tables are used, the seat facing the entrance is the seat of honor. The seats on the left hand side of the seat of honor are second, fourth, sixth, etc. in importance, while those on the right are third, fifth, seventh and so on in importance, until they join together. During the dinner, with some exceptions, hands should never be used to handle food.

A formal Chinese dinning is always accompanied by tea, beer or distilled spirit. The one who sit closest to the teapot or wine bottle should pour them for others from the senior and superior to the junior and inferior. And when other people fill your cup or glass, you should express your thanks. Guests cannot pour tea or wine themselves. Water and other non-alcoholic beverages may be consumed anytime. However, alcohol must be consumed only during toasts. If that beverage is beer, then an ordinary amount is consumed, such as a few swallows. In the case of grape wine, a single sip is common. If the toast is being made with a small glass of "distilled spirit", then the toast may call for "gan bei" in Chinese, literally "dry glass", and the equivalent of "bottoms up". After that, the empty glass is sometimes shown to prove that all has been consumed. If the guests are few in number, or are seated at a small table, touching glasses is common. But, at a large table, or when the toastees are too great in number or too far away, this is impossible. Then, simply raising a glass is acceptable. A variant is to tap the bottom of the glass on the table, whereafter the toastee will do the same, which acts as a substitute for touching glasses.

A Lazy Susan is a rotating tray at the center of the table. Many Chinese tables are circular, and the Lazy Susan is also circular. It is put there so that everyone has equal access to the food. It is customary to start with the dishes at the guest of honor first, and then rotate clockwise after, but not starting with the host. If there is only one table and there is no obvious guest of honor, then start with the person to the left of the host and continue clockwise. This shows that the host is taking care of all of his guests, by waiting and being willing to be last in line for the food.

A Table with a Lazy Susan

Since chopsticks are often used in many dishes in Chinese cuisine, knowing correct chopsticks usage is essential. It does not matter whether you hold the chopsticks in the middle or at the end, but you should make sure that the ends are even. When not in use, chopsticks must always be placed neatly on the table with the two sticks lying tidily next to each other at both ends. Treat chopsticks as extension of your fingers. It is impolite to use them to point at other people or to wave chopsticks around. Do not impale food with chopsticks. Do not leave chopsticks sticking out of a bowl of rice with the tips down and the back ends up. Do not bang your chopsticks as though you were playing a drum.

A hand must be placed over the mouth while using a toothpick, and not doing so is considered extremely rude. Throwing toothpicks on the floor or on the tablecloth is rude.

In Chinese culture, using correct table manners is believed to bring "luck" while incorrect use will bring shame. One should pay attention to manners at the table and especially to the Chinese eating taboos.

Notes

1. **something old**: Wearing something old refers to wearing something that represents a link with the bride's family and her old life. Usually, the bride wears a piece of family jewelry or maybe her mother's or grandmother's wedding dress.

2. **something new**: Wearing something new represents good fortune and success in the bride's new life. The bride's wedding dress is usually chosen, if purchased new, but it can be any other new item of the bride's wedding attire.

3. **something borrowed**: Wearing something borrowed, which has already been worn by another happy bride at her wedding, is meant to bring good luck to the marriage. Something borrowed could be an item of bridal clothing, a handkerchief or an item of jewelry.

4. **something blue**: Wearing something blue dates back to biblical times when the color blue was considered to represent purity and fidelity. Over time this has evolved from wearing the blue clothing to wearing a blue band around the bottom of the bride's dress and to today's wearing a blue or blue-trimmed garter.

5. **silver sixpence**: This not only refers to financial wealth, but also a wealth of happiness and joy throughout her married life. This part of the tradition is not used very often in modern times. However, if a bride would like to include it in her wedding, she can purchase a silver sixpence from many companies that sell bridal supplies.

6. **wedding anniversaries**: Paper Wedding, Cotton Wedding, Leather Wedding, Silk Wedding, Wood Wedding, Iron Wedding, Copper Wedding, Appliance Wedding, Pottery Wedding, Tin Wedding, Steel Wedding, Linen Wedding, Lace Wedding, Ivory Wedding, Crystal Wedding, China Wedding, Silver Wedding, Pearl Wedding, Coral Wedding, Ruby Wedding, Sapphiye Wedding, Golden Wedding, Emerald Wedding, Diamond Wedding.

7. **Six Etiquette**: "Nacai"(纳采), "Wenming"(问名), "Naji"(纳吉), "Nazheng"(纳征), "Qingqi"(请期), and "Qinying"(亲迎).

Glossary

bridesmaid [ˈbraidzmeid] *n.* 女傧相,伴娘

pageboy [ˈpeidʒbɔi] *n.* 男小傧相

mead [miːd] *n.* 蜂蜜酒,草地

keepsake [ˈkiːpseik] *n.* 纪念品,赠品

sanctify [ˈsæŋktifai] *vt.* 使净化；把……奉献给神；洗清……的罪孽；使纯洁

crematorium [ˌkreməˈtɔːriəm] *n.* 火葬场

Garden of Remembrance 纪念花园

bowler [ˈbəulə] hat 圆顶硬礼帽

lace [ˈleis] *n.* 蕾丝

spinning [ˈspiniŋ] *n.* 细纱

lotus leaf 荷叶边

ribbon [ˈribən] *n.* 缎带

multi-layered cake cutting 多层次蛋糕裁剪

wrinkle [ˈriŋkl] *n.* 褶皱

princess sleeves 公主袖

leg of mutton sleeves 羊腿袖

corset [ˈkɔːsit] *n.* [常用复]妇女紧身胸衣

poke bonnet 帽边朝前撑起的阔边女帽

kilt [kilt] *n.*(苏格兰高地男子穿的)褶叠短裙(通常用格子呢制作)

pleat [pliːt] *n.*(衣服上的)褶

tartan [ˈtɑːtən] *n.* 格子花呢(服)；格子织物

British Fashion Council 英国时装协会

causality [kɔːˈzæliti] *n.* 因果关系,因果性

clover [ˈkləuvə] *n.* 三叶草

ensue [inˈsjuː] *vi.* 接着发生；因而发生

crucify [ˈkruːsifai] *vt.* 把……钉[绑]在十字架上

buffet [ˈbʌfit] *n.* 自助餐

cutlery [ˈkʌtləri] *n.* [总称]刀具,餐具

momentous [məuˈmentəs] *adj.* 重大的,重要的

usher [ˈʌʃə] *n.* [美] 婚礼中的迎宾招待员

ring bearer 在西式婚礼中,负责拿戒指的人(通常是小男孩)

recessional [riˈseʃənl] *n.*(礼拜结束时唱的)赞美歌

streamer [ˈstriːmə] *n.*(作装饰用的)彩色纸带

embalm [imˈbɑːm] *vt.* 涂敷防腐药物保存

Eucharist [ˈjuːkərist] *n.*[宗] 圣餐

hearse [həːs] *n.*灵车

cortege [kɔː'teiʒ] n. 送葬等的行列

cemetery ['semitri] n. (非教堂的)墓地,公墓

eulogy ['juːlədʒi] n. 颂词;赞美词

mausoleum [ˌmɔːsə'liəm] n. 陵墓

mortician [mɔː'tiʃən] n. [美] 承办殡葬者

eclectic [ek'lektik] adj. (思想观点、风格或品味)兼收并蓄的;不拘一格的

Six Etiquettes 六礼

consummation [ˌkɔnsʌ'meiʃən] n. 成婚

betrothed [bi'trəuðd] n. 未婚夫,未婚妻

Chinese zodiac ['zəudiæk] 生肖

auspicious [ɔːs'piʃəs] adj. 幸运的;吉祥如意的

betrothal [bi'trəuðl] n. 许婚;订婚

dowry ['dauəri] n. 嫁妆

sedan [si'dæn] n. 轿子

rouge [ruːʒ] n. 胭脂,口红

parasol [ˌpærə'sɔl, 'pærəsɔl] n. (女用)阳伞

prompt [prɔmpt] n. 提示;(给演员的)提词

nuptial ['nʌpʃəl] adj. 婚姻的,婚礼的

newlywed ['njuːliˌwed] n. 新婚的人

inhumation [ˌinhjuː'meiʃən] n. 埋葬,土葬

reincarnation [ˌriːinkɑː'neiʃən] n. 再生,转世

elegiac [ˌeli'dʒaiək] adj. 挽歌的;哀悼的

talcum ['tælkəm] n. (=talcum powder)滑石粉

the wake 守灵

joss paper [dʒɔs 'peipə] n. (中国)祭祀所用的纸,纸钱

defray [di'frei] vt. 支付,付给

gong [gɔŋ] n. (铜)锣

crescendo [kri'ʃendəu] adj.,adv. [音] 渐强的

malignant [mə'lignənt] adj. 恶毒的

geomantic [ˌdʒiːəu'mæntik] adj. 风水的

unlined [ʌn'laind] adj. (指衣服等)无衬里的

interline [ˌintə(ː)'lain] vt. 给(衣服)装内衬

floss [flɔs] n. 丝棉,绣花丝线,绒毛

brocade [brə'keid] n. 锦缎,织锦

top-notch ['tɔpnɔtʃ] adj. 拔尖的

velour [və'luə] n. 丝绒;天鹅绒;棉绒

propriety [prə'praiəti] n. 礼节;[the -ties]礼仪

exertion [ig'zəːʃən] n. 努力,尽力;运用

phatic ['fætik] adj. 交流感情的

delve［delv］*vt.*,*vi.* 深入探究,钻研

dim-sum 点心

unpropitious［ˈʌnprəˈpiʃəs］*adj.* 不祥的

distilled spirit 烈酒;白酒

impale［imˈpeil］*vt.* 刺穿,钉住

Further Reading

1) **Customs and Etiquettes in Canada:**

http://www.thecanadaguide.com/manners

http://www.kwintessential.co.uk/resources/global-etiquette/canada.html

2) **Customs and Etiquettes in Australia**

http://en.wikipedia.org/wiki/Etiquette_in_Australia_and_New_Zealand

http://nomadsworld.com/news/blog/australian-etiquette-a-guide-to-australian-etiquette

3) **Customs and Etiquettes in New Zealand**

http://en.wikipedia.org/wiki/Etiquette_in_Australia_and_New_Zealand

http://www.vayama.com/etiquette/new-zealand/

Group Tasks

You may have read through the variety of customs and courtesies that may be found in the U.K.,China and the U.S.. Of course,it is not possible to cover all variations and the huge number of minority cultures and ethnicities in each case,but you will have some idea of the dominant expectations. To further your understanding two tasks are suggested.

1) Individually,review the three sections and analyse the content seeking a) the major points of similarity and b) major distinguishing differences. Don't just list the things you find, but analyse them to form a view as to what those similarities and differences mean in terms of the historical,political and cultural perspectives of the three countries. When each of you have responded individually to this task,meet together to debate your views and see if it's possible to form any group consensus as to the over-arching meaning of "customs and courtesies" as aspects of human behaviour.

2) All three countries under our consideration have very diverse populations and histories, but an aspect that you might find interesting to consider is that of ex-patriot communities. This refers to the phenomenon of how people from one country who have emigrates to another tend to form communities of their own within the host country,to some extent resisting assimilation and sticking to "their own" customs, traditions and ceremonies. There are several famous "China

Towns" in the U.K. and the U.S. for example. The development of these diaspora communities is notable often for the way in which they tend to "freeze" the traditions of the homeland in time. Ex-patriot communities can appear much more "traditional" and "old-fashioned" than those of their original lands, which tend to become "modernised" over time, with cultural progression in the "homeland".

Working in groups, research three examples of "ex-patriot" communities and compare your consideration of customs and courtesies from these groups. What do you conclude from your comparisons?

Chapter 8   Food Culture

Section A   Food Culture in the United Kingdom

British cuisine has specific set of cooking traditions and practices associated with the U.K.. It has been described as dishes made with high-quality local ingredients and matched with simple sauces to accentuate flavor. However, British cuisine has absorbed the cultural influence of those that have settled in Britain, producing hybrid dishes.

1. History

Britain has always been a rich and fertile land, supporting diverse agriculture even before the Roman invasion. Many of the basic vegetables and herbs were introduced to Britain by the ancient Romans such as onions, celery, rosemary, parsnips, turnips and peas. Early cooking techniques included stewing with herbs, which has persevered as the principle cooking method of ordinary people to this century, or roasting meat over a fire for more celebratory occasions.

Wheat, oats and rye have been the staple grains in Britain. Rough breads would accompany most meals. The potato which became the favored British staple only arrived on the shores from the New World in 1586 and was treated with great suspicion for a while, considered difficult to digest and poisonous when undercooked.

As a sea-faring nation, Britain traded in spices from afar which were expensive and sought after. The tables of the rich in the Middle Ages through to the Renaissance were graced with elaborate dishes spiced with saffron, cinnamon, nutmeg, cloves and pepper.

It was only with the influence of the Puritans that plain food, served as simply as possible, became the sign of a virtuous British household and spices faded from the staple dishes of the middle classes, holding a place only at the tables of the Royal court and nobles.

The decline of British cuisine came with the two World Wars in the last century. Food rationing and the loss of servants meant that many middle class women were struggling with learning to cook for their families at a time when there were very few ingredients available. Food rationing endured into the 1950s, but by the end of the decade, cookery writers like Elizabeth David, brought a new interest in cooking and European food to the British palate. It took a while for this influence to penetrate throughout Britain, but gradually Modern British cuisine grew up, taking inspiration from Europe but basing itself on the best of British ingredients and restoring Britain's reputation for good food.

Modern British (or New British) cuisine is a style of British cooking which fully emerged in the late 1970s, and has become increasingly popular. It uses high-quality local ingredients, preparing them in ways which combine traditional British recipes with modern innovations, and has an affinity with the Slow Food movement[1].

Much Modern British cooking also draws heavily on influence from Mediterranean cuisines, and more recently, Middle Eastern, South Asian, East Asian and Southeast Asian cuisines. The traditional influence of northern and central European cuisines is significant but fading.

The later half of the 20th century saw an increase in the availability of a greater range of good quality fresh products and greater willingness by many sections of the British population to vary their diets and select dishes from other cultures such as those of Italy and India.

2. Daily Meals

In many European countries it is normal to have a long break in the middle of the day when all members of the family return to their houses to eat together. This is not very common in Britain because normally it is a long way from the place of work or school to the home. Consequently the British people tend to have a big breakfast before they go to work and the meal at midday is not spent with the members of the family but with workmates or schoolmates.

▶ Breakfast

Breakfast is the first meal of the day. A traditional full English breakfast includes bacon, poached, fried or scrambled eggs, fried or grilled tomatoes, fried mushrooms, fried bread or toast with butter, sausages and black pudding, usually served with a mug of tea. It can even be a multi-course meal, with lighter breakfast ingredients such as fruit or cereal being eaten as a starter to the fry-up. As nearly everything is fried in this meal, it is commonly called a "fry-up". When an English breakfast is ordered to contain everything available, it is often referred to as a Full English or a Full

A Full English Breakfast

Monty. Full English breakfasts are usually consumed in the home on non-working days, when there is enough time to prepare them, or at a hotel or café.

Generally speaking, the British breakfast is much bigger than in most other countries. Many people like to have a fried breakfast which can consist of fried bacon and eggs with fried bread and possibly fried tomatoes or black pudding. Of course, not everybody wants to eat a lot early in the morning and many people prefer to just eat toast and marmalade with tea or coffee. Cereals are also very popular. The most common is cornflakes. They are made with different grains such as corn, wheat, oats, etc.. If you go to a British supermarket, you will see that there are many types of cereals available. In Scotland many people eat "porridge" or boiled oats. Porridge is very heavy, but in the winter it will keep you warm.

▶ Lunch

A Packed Lunch

Many children at school and adults at work will have a "packed lunch". A packed lunch normally consists of some sandwiches, a packet of crisps, a piece of fruit and a can of something to drink, for example, coca-cola. The "packed lunch" is kept in a plastic container. The quality of the packed lunch can vary from terrible to very good, and it all depends on who makes it. Some factories and schools have canteens where you can eat, but the packed lunch is the most common thing to eat.

Sunday Roast

On Sundays people don't have to work, so they take the opportunity to eat with their family, and the main meal of the day is often eaten at midday instead of in the evening. Sunday lunch is usually the best meal of the week. It is a typical time to eat the traditional Sunday Roast. It consists of roast meat (cooked in the oven for about two hours), two different kinds of vegetables and potatoes with a Yorkshire pudding. The most common joints are beef, lamb or pork; chicken is also popular. Beef is eaten with hot white horseradish sauce, pork with sweet apple sauce and lamb with green mint sauce. Gravy is poured over the meat.

▶ Afternoon Tea

A Cream Tea

Afternoon tea time is a small meal time. A cream tea, comprising tea taken with scones, clotted cream and raspberry jam. It is a widespread stereotype that the English "drop everything" for a teatime meal in the mid-afternoon. This is no longer the case in the workplace, and is rarer in the home than it once was. A formal teatime meal is now often an accompaniment to tourism, particularly in Devon and

Cornwall, where comestibles may include scones with jam and clotted cream. There are also fairy cakes and simple small sponge cakes which can be iced or eaten plain. Nationwide, assorted biscuits and sandwiches are usually eaten. Nowadays the teatime meal has been replaced by snacking, or simply dispensed with.

● Dinner

A typical British meal for dinner is "meat and two veg". This is covered with "gravy" which is a sauce made with the juice that was obtained when the meat was cooked. One of the vegetables is always potatoes. The British eat a lot of potatoes. Things are changing and in fact you could even say that the British don't eat much British food. Most people in Britain eat curry, and rice or pasta are now favored as the "British Dinner". However, vegetables growing in England, like potatoes, carrots, peas, cabbages and onions are still very popular.

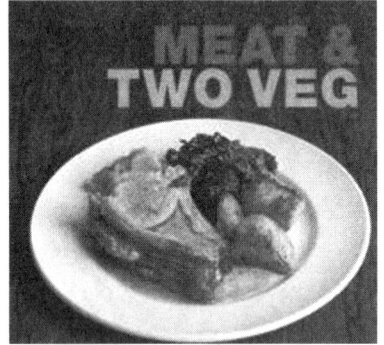

Meat and Two Veg

3. Typical Food

British food has traditionally been based on beef, lamb, pork, chicken, fish and generally served with potatoes and one other vegetable. The most common and typical foods eaten in Britain include bread, fish and chips, pies and so on.

Fish and Chips

There is a wide variety of traditional bread in Britain, often baked in a rectangular tin. Round loaves are also produced, such as the North East England specialty called a stottie cake[2]. Mass-produced bread was developed in England in the 1960s. The sliced white bread brands, such as Wonder loaf, have been criticized on grounds of poor nutritional value and taste of the loaves. Brown bread is seen as healthier by many, with popular brands including Allinson and Hovis. Rye bread is mostly eaten in the form of Scandinavian-style crisp bread, such as that produced by Ryvita in Birmingham.

A wide variety of fish are caught in British waters; the English tend to eat only a few species. Cod, haddock, plaice, huss, and skate are the fish-and-chip shop favorites. Salmon and trout are the most popular freshwater fish.

Different types of pastry can be found in Britain. Meat pies generally contain standard fillings such as chicken-and-mushroom,

A Cornish Pasty

steak and ale, minced beef and onion, lamb, mixed game or meat-and-potato. The Cornish pasty is oval or crescent shaped with a stiff, crimped rim, traditionally filled with beef and swede, although many variations are possible. In recent years, more exotic fillings, such as balti curry have appeared. Other pasties may be rectangular and filled with beef, cheese or vegetables.

4. Regional Cuisines

British cuisine has many regional varieties, and each has developed its own regional dishes.

English cuisine encompasses the cooking styles, traditions and recipes associated with England. It often involves use of coconut, yogurt, and almonds. Roasts and curries, rice dishes, and breads all have a distinctive flavor. Fish and meat are often cooked in curry with Indian vegetables and Indian-style spices, such as cloves and red chilies.

The cuisine of Northern Ireland is similar to that of the rest of the island of Ireland. In this region, the Ulster Fry is particularly popular. This dish is a full breakfast which consists of items like fried or over-easy eggs, bacon, sausage, vegetable roll, soda bread, potato bread, and even things like beans, fried tomatoes, or mushrooms. As you might expect, nearly all the side dishes are also to be fried, hence the name "Ulster fry". Tea is the usual accompaniment.

Ulster Fry

Scottish cuisine is the specific set of cooking traditions and practices associated with Scotland. It shares much with English cuisine, but has distinctive attributes and recipes of its own. Traditional Scottish dishes such as haggis (sheep's intestine stuffed with meat and vegetables) and shortbread exist alongside international foodstuffs brought about by migration. Scotland is known for the high quality of its beef, lamb, potatoes, oats, and sea foods. In addition to foodstuffs, Scotland produces a variety of whiskies.

Welsh cuisine has influenced and been influenced by other British cuisine. Although both beef and dairy cattle are raised widely, especially in Carmarthenshire and Pembrokeshire, Wales is best known for its sheep, and thus lamb is the meat traditionally associated with Welsh cooking.

All in all, British cuisine has traditionally been limited in its international recognition to the full breakfast, fish and chips, and the Christmas dinner. Other famous British dishes include the Sunday roast, steak and kidney pudding, and shepherd's pie. British cuisine has many regional varieties within the broader categories of English, Scottish and Welsh cuisine, and each has developed its own regional or local dishes.

Section B   Food Culture in the United States of America

Many meals in America are arranged in popular television shows. People like to eat in front of the TV, sitting in a chair or on a sofa. Cooking in the U.S. is not just hamburgers, pizza and fast food. However, the American fast food restaurant chains have been very successful in introducing American style fast food around the world.

Most traditional American foods were introduced by the early European immigrants but modified to take advantage of the locally available ingredients. Fried chicken, meatloaf, baked potato, corn, baked beans and apple pie would be considered traditional American dishes.

Regional cooking varies from state to state and is highly influenced by the types of ingredients locally available, as well as the cultural background of the people that settled in the area. New England cooking, native to the northeastern states, was heavily influenced by the cuisine of the original English settlers. Southern cooking has definite African influences. Cajun cooking, from the New Orleans area, is a spicy mixture of Spanish, French and African styles. California cooking is known for the use of fresh fruits and vegetables in combinations with Asian, Mexican and Spanish flavorings.

1. History

Seafood in the U.S. originated with the Native Americans, who often ate cod, lemon sole, flounder, herring, halibut, sturgeon, smelt, drum on the East Coast, and salmon on the West Coast. Whale was hunted by Native Americans off the Northwest coast, especially by the Makah, and used for their meat and oil.

Early Native Americans utilized a number of cooking methods in early American cuisine that have been blended with early European cooking methods to form the basis of American cuisine. Grilling meat was common. Spit roasting over a pit fire was common as well. Vegetables, especially root vegetables, were often cooked directly in the ashes of the fire. As early Native Americans lacked the proper pottery that could be used directly over a fire, they developed a technique. They would heat rocks directly in a fire and then add the bricks to a pot filled with water until it came to a boil so that it would cook the meat or vegetables in the boiling water. Native Americans in other parts often made ovens out of dug pits. These pits were also used to steam foods by adding heated rocks or embers and then seaweed or corn husks placed on top to steam fish and shellfish as well as vegetables; potatoes would be added while still in-skin and corn while in-husk, this would later be referred to as a clambake by the colonists.

When the colonists came to America, their cuisine was similar to their previous British cuisine. So the manner of cooking for the American colonists followed along the line of British cookery up until the Revolution.

The American colonial diet varied depending on the settled region in which someone lived. The New England colonies were extremely similar in their dietary habits to those that many of them had brought from England. In addition, colonists' close proximity to the ocean gave them a bounty of fresh fish to their diets, especially in the northern colonies. Wheat, however, the grain used to bake bread back in England, was almost impossible to grow, and imports of wheat were far from cost productive. Substitutes in cases such as this included cornmeal. The Johnnycake[3] was such a substitute for wheaten bread.

During the 18th and 19th centuries, many new foods were developed by Americans. Some stayed regional in nature, such as Rocky Mountain oysters; some spread throughout the nation but with little international appeal, such as George Washington Carver's crowning achievement, peanut butter (a core ingredient of the famous peanut butter and jelly sandwich); and some spread throughout the world, such as the cookie, popcorn, Coca-Cola and its competitors, fried chicken, cornbread, unleavened muffins such as the poppyseed muffin and brownies.

One characteristic of American cooking is the fusion of multiple ethnic or regional approaches into completely new cooking styles. Asian cooking has played a particularly large role in American fusion cuisine.

Similarly, some dishes that are typically considered American have their origins in other countries. American cooks and chefs have substantially altered these dishes over the years, to the degree that the dishes now enjoyed around the world are considered to be American. Hot dogs and hamburgers are both based on traditional German dishes, but in their modern popular form they can be reasonably considered American dishes. Pizza is based on the traditional Italian dish, brought by Italian immigrants to the U.S..

Many companies in the American food industry develop new products requiring minimal preparation, such as frozen entrees. Many of these recipes have become very popular.

A wave of celebrity chefs began perhaps with Julia Child and Graham Kerr in the 1970s, with many more following after the rise of cable channels like Food Network. Trendy food items in the 2000s and 2010s include doughnuts, cupcakes, macaroons, and meatballs.

2. Daily Meals

▶ Breakfast

A typical American breakfast menu includes scrambled or fried eggs or an egg omelet, juice, bacon or sausage, toast, biscuits or bagels. An alternative American breakfast could be cereal with milk, juice, and toast or pancakes or waffles with syrup and butter, juice, and white milk. Drinks include orange juice, milk, tea or coffee.

There is a difference of eating habits in the people of South and North Americans. An authentic North American will have eggs, meat in the form of ham, sausages, scrapple, bacon or steak along with toast. Along with this it may have some baked food like bangles or muffins. Potato in some form like fries, potato salad or hash brown is also included. Fruits or fruit juices also features in their breakfast along with coffee. The South American Breakfast is much lighter in comparison to the breakfast served up north.

Sunday Breakfast

Breakfast generally comprises of sandwiches with fruit juices or a streaming cup of coffee. There is also a tradition of having heavy breakfast on Sundays or special occasions and so is named "Sunday breakfast". Such breakfast offers a wide spread of cinnamon rolls, pastries, biscuits, pancakes and grits.

Lunch

A typical American lunch menu normally involves sandwiches, rolls, hamburgers, hot dogs, pizza, tacos, chicken, salad, fruit, milk, soft drink, tea or coffee.

The normal practice in America is to eat the salad before the main course. There are many different salads, such as "Grilled Chicken Salad", "Chicken Tender Salad" and "Steak Salad". Sandwiches are also served in many different ways, such as Cheeseburger, Zone Burger and Turkey Burger.

Dinner

Dinner is normally the largest meal of the day. It involves pizza, meat (steak, chicken, fish, pork, turkey) with potatoes and a vegetable (corn, green beans, beans, carrots, spinach, peas, greens, asparagus, cauliflower, broccoli), spaghetti with either tomato or meat sauce, lasagna, tacos and dessert (cake, cookies, pies, ice cream, and candy). Dessert is served after the main meal, and the typical desserts are Triple Chocolate Cake, All-American Apple Pie, Rum Carrot Cake, Chocolate Chip Cookie Sundae, and Berries and Sorbet.

Berries and Sorbet

The U.S. is a large country and is a culmination of different cultures, and the food customs differ in various parts of the country. The menu is often the reflection of the culture and tradition of that particular region.

3. Regional Cuisines

Given the large size of the U.S., it has numerous regional variations. The regional cuisines are characterized by its extreme diversity with each region having its own distinctive cuisine.

▶ Cuisine of New England

New England is a northeastern region of the U.S., including the six states of Connecticut, Maine, Massachusetts, New Hampshire, Rhode Island and Vermont. The Native American cuisine became part of the cookery style that the early colonists brought with them. Much of the cuisine started with one-pot cookery, which resulted in such dishes as succotash, chowder, baked beans, etc..

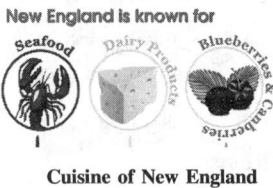

New England is known for

Seafood　Dairy Products　Blueberries & Cranberries

Cuisine of New England

Lobster is an integral ingredient to the cuisine, indigenous to the coastal waters of the region. Other shellfish of the coastal regions include little neck clams, sea scallops, blue mussels, oysters, soft shell clams and razor shell clams. Much of this shellfish contributes to New England tradition, the clambake, which is a colonial interpretation of an American Indian tradition.

▶ Cuisine of Hawaii

The Cuisine of Hawaii is a fusion of many foods brought by immigrants to the Hawaiian Islands, including plant and animal food sources imported from around the world for agricultural use in Hawaii. Many local restaurants serve the ubiquitous plate lunch featuring the Asian staple, two scoops of rice, a simplified version of American macaroni salad (consisting of macaroni and mayonnaise), and a variety of different toppings—the hamburger patty, a fried egg, gravy of a Loco Moco, etc..

Loco Moco

Hawaiian regional cuisine covers everything from wok-charred ahi tuna, opakapaka (snapper) with passionfruit, to Hawaiian island-raised lamb, beef and aquaculture products such as Molokai shrimp. Some cuisine also incorporates a broad variety of produce and locally grown agricultural products, including tomatoes, strawberries, mushrooms, sweet maui onions and tropical fruits such as papayas, mangoes, lilikoi (passionfruit) and lychee.

▶ Cuisine of the Midwestern United States

Midwestern cuisine is a regional cuisine of the American Midwest. It draws its culinary roots most significantly from the cuisines of Central, Northern and Eastern Europe, and is influenced by regionally and locally grown foodstuffs and cultural diversity.

Everyday Midwestern home cooking generally showcases simple and hearty dishes that make use of the abundance of locally grown foods. Its culinary profiles may seem synonymous with "American food". Midwestern cuisine covers everything from barbecue to the Chicago-style hot dog.

Beef and pork processing have always been important in Midwestern industries, with a strong role in regional diets. Chicago and Kansas City were historically stockyard and processing centers of the beef trade, while Iowa remains the center of pork production in the U.S..

Far from the oceans, Midwesterners traditionally ate little seafood, relying on local freshwater fish, such as perch and trout, supplemented by canned tuna and canned or cured salmon and herring, although modern air shipping of ocean seafood has been increasing Midwesterners' taste for ocean fish.

Dairy products, especially cheese, form an important group of regional ingredients, with Wisconsin known as "America's Dairyland", although other Midwest states make cheese as well.

The upper Midwest, a prime fruit-growing region, sees the extensive use of apples, blueberries, cranberries, cherries, peaches and other cold-climate fruit in its cuisine.

As with many American regional cuisines, Midwestern cooking has been heavily influenced by immigrant groups. Traditionally, Midwestern cooks used a light hand with seasonings, preferring sage, dill, caraway, mustard and parsley to hot, bold and spicy flavors. However, with new waves of immigrants from Latin America and Asia moving into the region, these tastes are changing.

In its urban centers, however, the Midwest's restaurants offer a diverse mix of ethnic cuisines as well as sophisticated, contemporary techniques.

● Cuisine of the Southern United States

The cuisine of the American South has been influenced by many diverse inhabitants of the region, including Americans of European descent, Native Americans and African Americans. The cuisine of the American South, along with the rest of its culture, is one of the most distinct in all of the country.

Many items such as squash, tomatoes, corn as well as the practice of deep pit barbecuing were inherited from the southeastern American Indian tribes. Foods associated with sugar, flour, milk, eggs (many kinds of baking or dairy products such as breads and cheeses) are more associated with Europe.

The South's propensity for a full breakfast is derived from the English fry-up, although it was altered substantially. Much of Cajun or Creole cuisine is based on France, and on Spain to a lesser extent. Floribbean is more Spanish-based with obvious Caribbean influences, while

Tex-Mex has considerable Mexican and Native American influences.

◑ Cuisine of the Western United States

Cooking in the American West gets its influence from Native American and Mexican cultures, and other European settlers into the part of the country.

In the Northwest, Oregon and Washington, various specialties involving salmon, perhaps grilled over a wood fire, and such naturally occurring foodstuffs as blackberries and mushrooms may often be served in forms close to those in which they naturally occur as regional cuisine. The bounty of the land and those things the hunter-gatherers and fisherpeople found in abundance are major influences.

In the Plains or Mountain States, cowboy or ranch culture is a factor, and variations on the beef theme, outdoor cooking, and such events as chuckwagon dinners abound on dude ranches and at other tourist locations. Hunting is still important in the West, and wild game is part of the cuisine. Rocky Mountain oysters are certainly a part of Western regional food served up for the delight of squeamish tourists.

Rocky Mountain Oysters

A growing wine industry is of great importance along the West Coast and increasingly important inland and to the north, not only in California. Along the coast, seafood is important. The evolution of California Cuisine and the influence of Alice Waters are major factors in what could be called regional cuisine of the West. The slow food and local food movements are parts of this phenomenon. The influence of the Pacific Rim is huge along the coast, and fusion cuisine, along with interesting Asian-influenced and Mexican-influenced drinks, has become extremely popular.

Near Mexico, the influence of that country is important in food, with the culture of Mexico spreading as workers move farther from the border. The food of other South American countries can also be found and is increasingly an influence, with the food described as Nuevo Latino more and more often seen.

Throughout the West in areas where sheep ranching/sheep herding is important (Idaho, Montana, Wyoming, Nevada, eastern Washington, eastern California, and other nearby states) restaurants featuring Basque cuisine can be found. They are usually family-style, featuring large tables where diners sit with other parties and share serving dishes which are passed around the table.

The variety of foods enjoyed in the U.S. reflects the diversity of personal tastes. The food may be international or regional. It might be junk food, or maybe natural food. In any case, the style is American.

Section C   Food Culture in China

China's long history, vast territory and extensive contact with other nations and cultures have given birth to the distinctive Chinese culinary art. Like any cultural food, it has developed through great care over the centuries, and is known for a fine selection of ingredients, and a balancing of preparation, nourishment and how much cooking is relied on. The nearly endless variety of natural ingredients and cooking methods employed in Chinese cuisine stand out unequaled in the world, which may very well account for the universal popularity of Chinese restaurants and Chinese cuisine overseas. Chinese cuisine originated from different regions of China and has become widespread in many other parts of the world— from East Asia to North America, Australasia and Western Europe. Chinese Cuisine is one of the three world cuisines(Chinese Cuisine, French Cuisine and Turkish Cuisine), and modern China enjoys a worldwide reputation as the "kingdom of cuisine".

1. History

The history of Chinese cuisine in China stretches back for thousands of years and has changed from period to period and in each region according to climate, imperial fashions and local preferences. Much like in France, Chinese society has been valuing gastronomy and Chinese people are willing to eat virtually anything edible, plant or animal.

During the early part of recorded Chinese history in the Shang Dynasty and Zhou Dynasty, pork, beef, and mutton were eaten and various wild game hunted. Plants such as thistle, royal fern and smartweed were collected wild. Meat was preserved with salt, vinegar, curing and fermenting. Flavor of meat dishes was enhanced by cooking it in the fat of a different animal.

During the Han Dynasty, Chinese cuisine developed rapidly, and many famous cuisines appeared. On the unearthed bamboo slips from the No. 1 Tomb of Mawangdu Ruins, there were recorded over hundreds cuisines. In the "Qi Ming Yao Shu" written by Jia Sixie during North Wei Dynasty, there were over 200 kinds of cuisines recorded. Because of the introduction and influence of Buddhism, vegetarian dishes gradually had impact on people's daily life. During Sui, Tang and the Five Dynasties periods, the designed and colorful cuisines and diet dishes also had new development.

Song Dynasty is one of the climaxes of the development of Chinese cuisine. In the restaurants of Bianjing and Linan, there were numerous cold dishes, hot dishes, soups and colorful dishes. The dishes were marked with South, North, Chuan flavors and vegetarian dishes, which represented that the schools of cuisines began to form.

During Yuan, Ming and Qing Dynasties, Chinese cuisine has great development. Thousands of cuisines appeared. During this period, ethnic groups believing in Islamism moved to all the areas of China, and Halal Food as a new kind of Chinese food occupied a position in China. The schools of Chinese cuisine had been established in this period. From late Qing Dynasty, along with foreigners coming to China, Chinese cuisine absorbed some features of western cuisines.

Now, Chinese cuisine is very famous in the world for its color, aroma, favor and well design.

2. Daily Meals

▶ Breakfast

In northern China, people in towns and villages are particularly fond of a crisp fried form of food known as "You Tiao" (fried bread sticks, surprisingly similar to Native American Indian fry bread). Thick noodles soup is often eaten as well. In the North, soy bean milk is drunk while in the south, people drink a sort of clear soup made from rice (congee), which takes a long time to cook. Breakfast is substantial and entirely Chinese in composition. Except in those southern coastal cities like Guangzhou and Shenzhen, where foreign influence is strong, not many people would have tea or coffee at breakfast.

▶ Lunch and Dinner

Either lunch or dinner can be the largest meal of the day. People usually have rice and all kinds of cuisines for their lunch and dinner, and sometimes they also have a noodle variation.

A meal in Chinese culture is typically seen as consisting of two or more general components. A carbohydrate source or starch, known as "main food" or staple— typically rice, noodles, or steamed buns (mantou), and accompanying dishes of vegetables, meat, fish, or other items.

Staple Foods

Rice is a major staple food for people from rice farming areas in southern China. Steamed rice, usually white rice, is the most commonly eaten. Rice is also used to produce beers, wines and vinegars. Rice is one of the most popular foods in China and is used in many dishes. Glutinous rice (sticky rice) is a kind of rice used in many specialty Chinese dishes.

In wheat farming areas in Northern China, people largely rely on flour-based food, such as noodles, breads, dumplings and steamed buns. Chinese noodles come dry or fresh in a variety of sizes, shapes and textures and are often served in soups or fried as toppings. Some varieties, such as noodles of longevity (Shou Mian), are symbolic of long life and good health according to Chinese tradition. Noodles can be served hot or cold with different toppings, with broth, and occasionally dry. Noodles are commonly made with rice flour or wheat flour, but other flours such as soybean are also used.

Tofu is made of soybeans and is another popular product that supplies protein. Other products such as soy milk, soy paste, soy oil and fermented soy sauce are also important in Chinese cooking. Stinky tofu is a type of fermented tofu that has a strong odor. Like blue cheese or durian, it has a very distinct, potent smell, and is somewhat of an acquired taste. Its smell is as expected from the name; like spoiling tofu, and can be smelt from a block away when vendors are frying it or stewing it. It is often paired with soy sauce or something salty and spicy. Doufulu is another type of fermented tofu which has a red skin and salty taste. This is more of a pickled type of tofu and is not as strongly scented as the stinky tofu. Doufulu is frequently pickled together with soy beans and chili, and paired with rice congee.

Some common vegetables used in Chinese cuisine include Chinese leaves, bok choy (Chinese cabbage), bitter melon and Chinese broccoli. Other vegetables include bean sprouts, pea vine tips, watercress, celery, carrots, fresh mustard greens and (Western) broccoli.

A variety of dried or pickled vegetables are also eaten, especially in drier or colder regions where fresh vegetables traditionally were hard to get out of season. Chinese pickles or Chinese preserved vegetables consist of various vegetables or fruits, which have been fermented by pickling with salt and brine or marinated in mixtures based on soy sauce or savory bean pastes. The former is usually done using vegetables from Chinese mustard or Chinese cabbage, while the latter marinated group is

Chinese Pickles

made using a wide variety of vegetables, ranging from mustards and cucumbers to winter melon and radishes.

There are different types of Chinese sausages depending upon the region in which it is produced. Chinese sausage is darker and thinner than western sausages. The most common sausage is made of pork and pork fat. Flavor varies on the ingredients used, but it generally has a salty-sweet taste. Chinese sausage can be prepared in many different ways, including oven-roasted, stir-fried, and steamed.

Spices and seasonings such as fresh ginger root, garlic, scallion, white pepper and sesame oil are widely used in many regional cuisines. Sichuan peppercorns, star anise, cinnamon, fennel, cilantro, parsley and cloves are also used.

To add extra flavors to dishes, many Chinese cuisines also contain dried Chinese mushrooms, dried baby shrimps, dried tangerine peel and dried Sichuan chilies as well.

When it comes to sauces, China is home to soy sauce, which is made from fermented soy beans and wheat. Oyster sauce, clear rice vinegar, chili, Chinkiang black rice vinegar, fish sauce and fermented tofu are also widely used. A number of sauces are based on fermented soybeans, including Hoisin sauce, ground bean sauce and yellow bean sauce.

Soup

There are five basic traditional soup stocks in Chinese cuisine.

Superior broth or stock is the dark tan broth made from Jin-hua ham and chicken. This rich and umami broth is used in the creation of many expensive soups such as shark fin soup.

Chicken soup is the basic broth used in creating most Chinese soups. The basic broth is sometimes fortified with liquorice root, wolfberry and other Chinese herbs.

Lean pork is used most often as the soup base for long-simmered Chinese soups, and this soup base is often simmered over low heat for several hours with other roots, dried herbs,

Chicken Soup

vegetables, and edible fungi like shiitake mushroom, white fungus or wood ear. The Cantonese are especially known for their long-simmered Chinese soups, as they often pair ingredients under Chinese Medicine concepts to enhance health-benefiting functions of the soup.

White broth is made from lightly blanched pork bones that have been vigorously boiled for several hours, creating a white milky broth, and this broth has a rich mouthfeel.

Fish broth is made from fish that have been fried and boiled for several hours, creating a white milky broth. This broth has a rich feel, and sweet umami taste.

Desserts

Generally, seasonal fruits serve as the most common form of dessert consumed after dinner.

Chinese desserts are sweet foods and dishes that are served with tea, along with meals, or at the end of meals in Chinese cuisine.

In larger cities, a wide variety of Chinese bakery products are available, including baked, steamed, boiled, or deep-fried sweet or savory snacks. Bings are baked wheat flour based confections, and include moon cake, red bean paste pancake and sun cakes. Chinese candies and sweets are usually made with cane sugar, malt sugar, honey, nuts and fruits. Gao are rice-based snacks that are typically steamed and may be made from glutinous or normal rice.

Ice cream is commonly available throughout China. Another cold dessert is called baobing, which is shaved ice with sweet syrup. Chinese jellies are known collectively in the language as ices. Many jelly desserts are traditionally set with agar and are flavored with fruits, though gelatin based jellies are also common in contemporary desserts.

Chinese dessert soups typically consist of sweet and usually hot soups and custards. Chinese desserts are frequently less sugary and milder in taste than western style desserts. Some restaurants do not serve dessert at all.

Drinks

China was the earliest country to cultivate and drink tea which is enjoyed by people from all social classes. Tea processing began after the Qin and Han Dynasties. Many Chinese drink their tea with snacks such as nuts, plums, dried fruit (in particular jujube), small sweets, melon seeds and waxberry.

Chinese tea is often classified into several different categories according to the species of plant from which it is sourced, the region in which it is grown, and the method of production used. Some of these types are green tea, oolong tea, black tea, scented tea, white tea and compressed tea. China is the world's largest exporter of green tea.

Yellow wine has a long history in China, where the unique beverage is produced from rice and ranges between 10-15% alcohol content. The most popular brands include Shaoxing Lao Jiu, Shaoxing Hua Diao and Te Jia Fan. Wheat, corn and rice are also used to produce strong Chinese liquor which is clear and aromatic, containing approximately 60% alcohol. Some popular brands of liquor include Er guo tou, Du Kang, Mao Tai, Lu Zhou Te Qu and Wu Liang Ye.

Shaoxing Lao Jiu

Chinese in earlier dynasties evidently drank milk and ate dairy products, although not necessarily from cows, but perhaps koumiss (fermented mare's milk) or goat's milk. After the Tang Dynasty, there emerged a line dividing Asia into two groups, those who depend on milk products (India, Tibet, Central Asians) and those who reject those foods. Chinese depend on soy, as more efficient way of supporting density, and to differentiate themselves from border nomads. Most Chinese until recently have avoided milk, partly because pasturage for milk producers in a monsoon rice ecology is not economic, partly because milk products became negatively associated with horse riding, milk drinking nomadic tribes. But this non-dairy tradition has undergone some changes as a result of changing perceptions and global influences. For example, it has been suggested that, in the early 20th century Shanghai, "Western food, and in particular identifiably nourishing items like milk, became a symbol of a neo-traditional Chinese notion of family."

3. Regional Cuisines

China covers a large territory and has many nationalities, hence a variety of Chinese foods with different but fantastic and mouthwatering flavors came into being. Chinese food can be roughly divided into eight regional cuisines: Shandong cuisine, Sichuan cuisine, Cantonese cuisine, Fujian cuisine, Jiangsu cuisine, Zhejiang cuisine, Hunan cuisine and Anhui cuisine.

▶ Shandong cuisine

Shandong cuisine is commonly and simply known as Lu cuisine. Shandong is the birthplace of many famous ancient scholars such as Confucius and Mencius. And much of Shandong cuisine's history is as old as Confucius himself, making it the oldest existing major cuisine in China. With a long history, Shandong cuisine once formed an important part of the imperial cuisine and was widely promoted in North China.

Shandong cuisine is featured by a variety of cooking techniques and seafood. The dishes feature choice of materials, adept skill in slicing and perfect cooking techniques. Shandong cuisine is representative of northern China's cooking and its techniques have been widely absorbed by the imperial dishes of Ming and Qing Dynasties. Shandong is a large peninsula surrounded by the sea to the East and the Yellow River meandering through the center. As a result, seafood is a major component of Shandong cuisine.

The cuisine is generally salty, with a prevalence of light-color sauces. People in Shandong like to eat onions and scallion and to use them as a seasoning. The dishes include braised sea cucumber with onion, cartilage stewed with onions, and meat stewed with onions. Roast meats are also served with onions.

Shandong cuisine, clear, pure and not greasy, is characterized by its emphasis on aroma, freshness, crispness and tenderness. Shallot and garlic are usually used as seasonings, so Shandong dishes usually taste pungent. Soups are given much emphasis in Shandong dishes. Thin soup features clear and fresh while creamy soup looks thick and tastes strong. Jinan cuisine is adept at deep-frying, grilling, frying and stir-frying while Jiaodong division is famous for cooking seafood with fresh and light taste. The typical dishes on local menu are braised abalone, braised trepang, sweet and sour carp, Jiuzhuan Dachang and Dezhou Chicken.

Jiuzhuan Dachang

▶ Sichuan Cuisine

Sichuan cuisine is one of the most famous Chinese cuisines in the world. The cuisine features a wide range of materials, various seasonings and different cooking techniques. Statistics show that the number of Sichuan dishes has surpassed 5,000. With a rich variety of strong flavors, Sichuan food is famous for its countless delicacies, dominated by peppery, chili flavors, and best known for being spicy-hot. Chili peppers and prickly-ash are used in many dishes, giving it a distinctively spicy taste, called "Ma" in Chinese. It often leaves a slight numb sensation in the mouth. Besides, garlic, ginger and fermented soybean are also used in the cooking process. Wild vegetables and animals are usually chosen as ingredients, while frying, frying without oil, pickling and braising are applied as basic cooking techniques. It cannot be said that one who does not experience Sichuan food ever reaches China.

▶ Cantonese Cuisine

Cantonese cuisine originates from Guangdong (Canton), the southernmost province in China. Cantonese cuisine took shape in the Ming and Qing Dynasties. In the process of its development,

Dim Sum

it has borrowed the culinary essence of northern China and of the Western-style food, while maintaining its traditional local flavor. The majority of overseas Chinese people are from Guangdong, so Cantonese cuisine is perhaps the most widely available Chinese regional cuisine outside China.

Dim sum is a Cantonese term for small hearty dishes. These bite-sized portions are prepared using traditional cooking methods such as frying, steaming, stewing and baking. It is designed so that one person may taste a variety of different dishes. Some of these may include rice rolls, lotus leaf rice, turnip cakes, buns, style dumplings, stir-fried green vegetables, congee porridge, soups, etc.. The Cantonese style of dining, yum cha, combines the variety of dim sum dishes with the drinking of tea.

The most characteristic cooking methods are cooking in salt or wine, baking in a pan and soft frying. Cantonese cuisine emphasizes unique mixed flavorings. For example, one flavoring liquid is a mixture prepared from onion, garlic, sugar, salt, and spices. The gravy is prepared from a mixture of peanut oil, ginger, onion, Shaoxing rice wine, crystallized sugar, anise, cassia bark, licorice root, clove, ginger powder, dried tangerine peel and Momordica grosvenori. Spiced salt is prepared from refined salt, sugar, powdered spices and anise. These flavorings, along with other favorite condiments such as oyster sauce, fish sauce, clam oil and curry, give Cantonese cuisine a unique taste.

◉ Fujian Cuisine

Fujian cuisine was a latecomer in southeast China along the coast. Economy and culture of Fujian Province began to flourish after the Southern Song Dynasty. During the Qing Dynasty, Fujian cuisine gradually became famous in China. It emphasizes seafood and river fishes. The Fujian coastal area produces 167 varieties of fish and 90 kinds of turtles and shellfish. Woodland delicacies such as edible mushrooms and bamboo shoots are also utilized. It also produces edible bird's nest, cuttlefish, and sturgeon. These special products are widely used in Fujian dishes. The most characteristic aspect of Fujian cuisine is that the dishes are served in soup. The cooking methods are stewing, boiling, braising, quick-boiling and steaming. Slicing techniques are valued in the cuisine and utilized to enhance the flavor, aroma and texture of seafood and other foods. Most dishes are made of seafood, and if they are not cut in a right way, the dishes will fail to display their true flavor. Consisting of Fuzhou cuisine, Quanzhou cuisine and Xiamen cuisine, Fujian cuisine is distinguished for its choice of seafood, beautiful color and magic taste of sweet, sour, salty and savory. Fujian dishes are slightly sweet and sour, and less salty. When a dish is less salty, it tastes more delicious. Sweetness makes a dish tastier, while sourness helps remove the seafood smell. In the Fujian cuisine, an important flavoring and coloring material is red distiller's grain, which is made of rice fermented with red yeast. After being kept in a sealed vessel for a year, the grain acquires a sweet and sour flavor and a rose-red color. Chicken, duck, fish, and pork can be flavored with the red grain as well as spiral shells, clams, mussels, bamboo shoots and even vegetables. As many Fujian people have emigrated overseas, their cuisine has become popular abroad.

◉ Jiangsu Cuisine

Jiangsu cuisine, also called Huaiyang cuisine, consists of the styles of Yangzhou, Nanjing, Suzhou and Zhenjiang dishes. It is especially popular in the lower reaches of the Yangtze River. Aquatics as the main ingredients, it stresses the freshness of materials. Its carving techniques are delicate, of which the melon carving technique is especially well known. Cooking techniques consist of stewing, braising, roasting, simmering, etc..

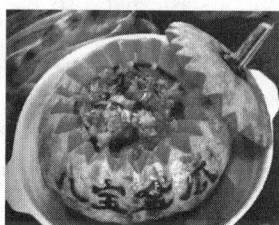
Melon Carving

While emphasizing the original flavors of well-chosen materials, it features carefully selected ingredients. In addition, the artistic shape and bright colors of the dishes add more ornamental value, and it is well known for its meticulous preparation methodology, and its not-too-spicy, not-too-bland taste. Since the seasons vary in climate considerably in Jiangsu, the cuisine also varies throughout the year. If the flavor is strong, it isn't too heavy; if light, not too bland.

Yangzhou cuisine is essentially a combination of the best elements of northern and southern cooking. Yangzhou was a military fort and a cultural center in ancient times, and was one of the most flourishing commercial cities in China. Extravagant consumption stimulated the thriving catering trade and the development of cookery. Every rich salt merchant employed a skilled cook who specialized in cooking a certain delicious dish. When a salt merchant treated his guests to a banquet, he often borrowed cooks from other salt merchants. In this way, the cooks exchanged their cooking skills and improved the cooking in Yangzhou.

Yangzhou Fried Rice

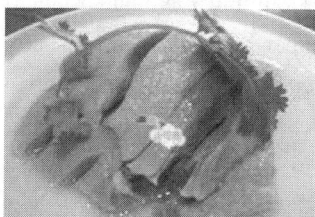
Salted Dried Duck

Typical courses of Jiangsu cuisine are Jinling salted dried duck (Nanjing's most famous dish), crystal meat (pork heels in a bright, brown sauce), clear crab shell meatballs (pork meatballs in crab shell powder, fatty, yet fresh), Yangzhou steamed Jerky strips (dried tofu, chicken, ham and pea leaves), triple combo duck, dried duck, and Farewell My Concubine (soft-shelled turtle stewed with many other ingredients such as chicken, mushrooms and wine).

Zhejiang Cuisine

Comprising local cuisines of Hangzhou, Ningbo and Shaoxing, Zhejiang cuisine, not greasy, wins its reputation for freshness, tenderness, softness, smoothness of its dishes with mellow fragrance. Each of the three sub-cuisine traditions is noted for its special flavor and taste, but they are all characterized by the careful selection of ingredients, emphasizing minute preparation, as well as unique, fresh and tender tastes. Zhejiang cuisine specializes in quick frying, stir-frying, deep-frying, simmering and steaming, by which the dishes obtaining the natural flavor and taste. Special care is taken in the cooking process to make the food fresh, crispy and tender. Thanks to exquisite preparation, the dishes are not only delicious in taste but also extremely elegant in appearance.

Hangzhou style is characterized by rich variations and the use of bamboo shoots, shaoxing style specializes in poultry and freshwater fish, and Ningbo style specializes in seafood. Hangzhou cuisine is the most famous one among the three, such as Hangzhou roast chicken (commonly known as Beggar's Chicken), Dongpo Pork and Westlake fish in vinegar sauce.

Dongpo Pork

Hunan Cuisine

The cooking skills employed in Hunan cuisine reached a high standard as early as the Western Han Dynasty, giving it a history of more than 2,100 years. Hunan is located in south-central China along the middle reaches of the Yangtze River. It contains rivers, lakes, mountains, rolling hills, plains and pools, which provide abundant delicacies, such as fish, shrimp, crab and turtle. Making full use of these rich resources, local people created a wide variety of delicacies. Hunan cuisine is well known for its hot spicy flavor, fresh aroma and deep color. Common cooking techniques include stewing, frying, pot-roasting, braising and smoking.

Hunan cuisine consists of local cuisines of Xiangjiang Region, Dongting Lake and Xiangxi coteau. It characterizes itself by thick and pungent flavor. Chili, pepper and shallot are usually necessaries in this division. The humid weather here makes it difficult for the human body to eliminate moisture, so the local people eat hot peppers to help remove dampness to keep health.

Anhui Cuisine

Anhui cuisine, comprising the specialties of Southern Anhui, Yanjiang and Huaibei, is derived from the native cooking styles of the Mount Huangshan region in China and is similar to Jiangsu cuisine, but with less emphasis on seafood and more on a wide variety of local herbs and vegetables. The highly distinctive characteristic of Anhui cuisine lies not only in the elaborate choices of cooking materials but also in the strict control of cooking process. Most ingredients in Anhui cuisine, such as pangolin, stone frog, mushroom, bayberry, tea leaves, bamboo shoot, and dates, come from mountain areas. Mount Huangshan has abundant raw materials for cooking. Anhui province is particularly endowed with fresh bamboo and mushroom crops. The white and tender bamboo shoots growing on Mount Huangshan can be made into very delicious food, and Xianggu, a kind of top-grade mushroom growing on old trees, is also very tasty.

Anhui cuisine chefs pay more attention to the taste, color of dishes and the temperature to cook, and they are good at braising and stewing, especially at cooking delicacies from mountains. Anhui dishes preserve most of the original taste and nutrition of the materials. Generally, the food is slightly spicy and salty. Some typical dishes stewed in brown sauce with stress on heavy oil and sauce. Ham is often added to improve the taste and sugar candy added to gain freshness.

◉ Other Cuisines

Apart from the Han, China also has 55 minority ethnic groups whose living habits vary greatly. Many ethnic groups with unique dishes and styles are represented in China.

Living on the grassland and engaging in herding and hunting, the Mongolians are called the "ethnic group on the horseback". Their typical food, like Roast Whole Lamb, Roast Lamb Leg, Mutton Eaten with Fingers and Milky Tea, is well known both inside and outside China. The Tibetan dwells on the roof of the world. Due to high altitude, water's boiling point is too low to cook highland barley. So they bake the barley and grind it into flour to make a special staple named Zanba. The minorities living in muggy zones in southwest China flavor

Zanba

sour, bitter and spicy food, such as Roast Fish Wrapped in Lemongrass created by the Dai people in Yunnan Province. Apart from adding ingredients like ginger and pepper, they wrap the fish with lemongrass and then grill it on a fire. Besides, Islamic Dishes have become more and more popular as Islam was introduced into China and absorbed the traditional cookery of nomadic peoples in Northwest and Northeast China. Visitors can find the Islamic Cuisine restaurants all over the country especially in the North and Northwest of China.

Chinese food is different from either British food or American food, but there is one thing in common: there are a lot of varieties which may be tempting to the foreign stomaches.

Notes

1. **Slow Food movement**：Slow Food is an international movement founded by Carlo Petrini in 1986. Promoted as an alternative to fast food, it strives to preserve traditional and regional cuisine and encourages farming of plants, seeds and livestock characteristic of the local ecosystem.

2. **a Stottie cake**：A Stottie cake or stotty is a type of bread that originated in North East England. It is a flat and round loaf, usually about 30 centimetres in diameter and 4 centimetres deep, with an indent in the middle produced by the baker.

3. **Johnnycake**：Johnnycake is a cornmeal flatbread that was an early American staple food and is prepared on the Atlantic coast from Newfoundland to Jamaica. The food probably originates from the native inhabitants of North America.

Glossary

accentuate [æk'sentjueit] *vt.* 使突出;强调

rosemary ['rəuzməri] *n.* 迷迭香；艾菊

parsnip ['pɑːsnip] *n.* 欧洲防风草

turnip ['təːnip] *n.* 芜菁，萝卜

rye [rai] *n.* 黑麦;黑麦粒

saffron ['sæfrən] *n.* 藏[番]红花

cinnamon ['sinəmən] *n.* 肉桂，桂皮;肉桂树

nutmeg ['nʌtmeg] *n.* 肉豆蔻(树)

palate ['pælit] *n.* 口味;香味

poach [pəutʃ] *vi.* 水煮(荷包蛋)

scrambled eggs ['skræmbəld] 炒鸡蛋，摊鸡蛋

grill [gril] *vt. & vi.* 烧烤

marmalade ['mɑːməleid] *n.* 果酱

horseradish ['hɔːsrædiʃ] *n.* 山葵，其根所制调味剂

scone [skɔn, skəun] *n.* 烤饼;烤小圆面包

clotted ['klɔtid] *adj.* 凝结的

raspberry ['rɑːzbəri] *n.* 覆盆子;木莓，山莓

comestibles [kə'mestiblz] *n.* 食物,食品

assorted [ə'sɔːtid] *adj.* 各种各样的

dispense [dis'pens] *vt.* 分配;(with) 摒弃

pasta ['pɑːstə] *n.* 意大利面食

haddock ['hædək] *n.* 黑线鳕

plaice［pleis］*n.*［sing., pl.］鲽（一种海鱼）

huss［hʌs］*n.*（作为食品的）鲨鱼肉

trout［traut］*n.* 鳟鱼

pastry［'peistri］*n.* 油酥面；油酥面馅饼

crimped［krimpt］*adj.* 起皱褶的，有波纹的

swede［swiːd］*n.* 蕉青甘蓝

haggis［'hægis］*n.*（把牛羊肉杂碎与麦片等放在羊肚中烹煮的食品）苏格兰布丁

meatloaf［miːt'ləuf］*n.* 烘肉卷

Cajun［'keidʒən］*n.* 移居美国路易斯安那州的法人后裔

lemon sole［'lemənsəul］*n.* 檬鲽

flounder［'flaundə］*n.* 鲆，鲽

herring［'heriŋ］*n.* 鲱鱼，青鱼

halibut［'hæləbət］*n.* 大比目鱼

sturgeon［'stəːdʒən］*n.* 鲟鱼

smelt［smelt］（复同单，或 smelts）*n.* 银白鱼；胡瓜鱼

drum［drʌm］*n.*（亦作 drumfish）（复同单）石首鱼

ember［'embə］*n.* 燃屑，余火，余烬

husk［hʌsk］*n.* 外皮，壳，荚

clambake［'klæmbeik］*n.*（北美）户外烤蛤野餐会（尤指海鲜野餐）

crowning［'krauniŋ］*adj.* 登峰造极的

unleavened［ʌn'levnd］*adj.* 未予发酵的

muffin［'mʌfin］*n.*（主北美）（用鸡蛋和发酵粉制成）美式拱顶小蛋糕

entree［'ɔntrei］*n.*（美）主菜

trendy［'trendiː］*adj.* 时髦的，赶时髦的

macaroon［ˌmækə'ruːn］*n.* 蛋白杏仁甜饼（干）

omelet［'ɔmәlit, 'ɔmlit］*n.* 煎蛋饼，煎蛋卷

bagel［'beigl］*n.* 硬面包圈

waffle［'wɔfəl］*n.* 蛋奶烘饼，华夫饼

syrup［'sirəp］*n.* 糖浆

scrapple［'skræpl］*n.* 玉米肉饼

hash［hæʃ］*n.* 切碎的食物（肉丁、土豆丁等）

grits［grits］*n.* 粗磨粉，粗面粉，粗燕麦粉，〈美〉粗玉米粉

taco［'tɑːkəu］*n.*（墨西哥）玉米面豆卷

broccoli［'brɔkəliː］*n.* 花椰菜，花茎甘蓝

lasagna［lə'zɑːnjə］*n.*（=lasagne）烤宽面条（上浇肉末番茄汁）

succotash［'sʌkətæʃ］*n.* 豆煮玉米（常加有腊肉）

chowder［'tʃaudə］*n.*（以鱼、蛤或玉米辅以土豆、洋葱煨成的）浓汤，羹

scallop［'skɔləp］*n.* 扇贝肉；干贝

mussel［'mʌsl］*n.* 贝类，蛤贝，贻贝

ubiquitous [juːˈbikwitəs] *adj.* 普遍存在的

macaroni [ˌmækəˈrəuni] *n.* (pl. macaronis, macaronies)(意大利)通心面条，通心粉

mayonnaise [ˌmeiəˈneiz] *n.* 用蛋黄油、柠檬汁等混合制成的调味汁

patty [ˈpæti] *n.* 小馅饼

snapper [ˈsnæpə] *n.* 麝香鳖；红鳍笛鲷

passionfruit 西番莲的果实

aquaculture [ˈækwəˌkʌltʃə] *n.* 水产养殖

perch [pəːtʃ] *n.* (pl. perch, perchs)河鲈鱼

dude ranch [djuːˈdrɑːntʃ] *n.* ［美西部］(供东部人休假时休息的）休养农场；仿西部农场造的休养处

squeamish [ˈskwiːmiʃ] *adj.* 苛求的；难于取悦的

gastronomy [gæsˈtrɔnəmi] *n.* 烹调法，美食学

thistle [ˈθisl] *n.* 蓟，蓟属植物

fern [fəːn] *n.* 蕨类；羊齿植物

smartweed [ˈsmɑːtwiːd] *n.* 荨麻

curing [ˈkjuəriŋ] *n.* (肉、鱼等的)腌制；熏制

halal [həˈlɑːl] *n.* (穆斯林教律)合法食物

congee [ˈkɔndʒiː] *n.* 粥

carbohydrate [ˈkɑːbəuˈhaidreit] *n.* 碳水化合物，糖类

glutinous [ˈgluːtinəs] *adj.* 胶质的；黏的

potent [ˈpəutənt] *adj.* 有力的；(药等)有效力的；(茶等)浓的

bok choy [ˈbɔkˈtʃɔi] 白菜

watercress [ˈwɔːtəkres] *n.* 水田芥；西洋菜

brine [brain] *n.* 卤水；盐水

marinate [ˈmærineit] *vt.* 用腌泡汁泡；醋渍；用腌泡汁来腌制(鱼或肉)

scallion [ˈskæljən] *n.* 青葱，冬葱，大葱，韭菜

peppercorn [ˈpepəkɔːn] *n.* 胡椒粒

anise [ˈænis] *n.* 大茴香，八角茴香

fennel [ˈfenl] *n.* 茴香

cilantro [siˈlɑːntrəu] *n.* 芫荽叶

hoisin sauce [ˈhɔisin, hɔiˈsin] (中国式烹饪中使用的由酱油、蒜泥等调制成的)海鲜沙司

umami [uːˈmaːmi] *n.* 鲜味

fortified [ˈfɔːtifaid] *adj.* 加强的

liquorice [ˈlikəris] *n.* 甘草属，甘草

wolfberry [ˈwulfbəri] *n.* 枸杞

simmer [ˈsimə] *vi.* 温火慢慢煮

fungus [ˈfʌŋgəs] (pl. fungi) *n.* 真菌

shiitake [ʃiːˈtɑːkiː] *n.* 香菇

blanch [blɑːntʃ] *vt.* 用沸水烫以便去皮

confection ［kən'fekʃən］ *n.* 甜食,糕点

agar ［'eigɑː］ *n.* 洋菜,琼脂,石花菜

gelatin ［'dʒelətin］ *n.* 凝胶,白明胶

custard ［'kʌstəd］ *n.* 乳蛋糕,牛奶蛋糊冻

waxberry ［'wæksbəri］ *n.* 杨梅

scented tea 花茶,有花香的茶

compressed tea 压缩茶

koumiss ［'kuːmis］ *n.* (＝kumiss)(中亚地区牧民用马乳或骆驼乳做的)乳酒

pasturage ［'pɑːstjuridʒ］ *n.* 畜牧,放牧;牧场

braise ［breiz］ *vt.* (＝braize)炖,焖,蒸

sea cucumber 海参

cartilage ［'kɑːtlidʒ］ *n.* 软骨

shallot ［ʃə'lɔt］ *n.* 青葱

pungent ［'pʌndʒənt］ *adj.* 辣的,(气味等的)刺激性的,刺鼻的

abalone ［ˌæbə'ləuni］ *n.* 鲍鱼

trepang ［tri'pæŋ］ *n.* 海参

carp ［kɑːp］ *n.* 鲤鱼

prickly-ash 花椒

yum cha (drink tea) 饮茶

cassia bark ［'kæsiəbɑːk］ *n.* 桂皮,肉桂

Momordica grosvenori 罗汉果

spiced salt 椒盐

condiment ［'kɔndimənt］ *n.* 佐料,调味品

cuttlefish ［'kʌtlfiʃ］ *n.* 乌贼(鱼)

distiller's ［dis'tilə］ grain 酒糟

yeast ［jiːst］ *n.* 酵母(菌)

jerky strips 肉干条

combo ［'kɔmbəu］ *n.* 套餐,组合食物

mellow ［'meləu］ *adj.* 甘美多汁的

coteau ［kəu'təu］ *n.* 高地,山区,分水岭

pangolin ［pæn'gəulin］ *n.* 鲮鲤;穿山甲

Zanba ［'zænbə］ *n.* 糌粑

Further Reading

1) **Canadian Food Culture**

http∶//www.tripadvisor.com/Travel-g153339-c11593/Canada∶Canadian.Cuisine.html

2) **Australian Food Culture**

http∶//www.list-directory.info/lists/australian-food.html

3) **New Zealand Food Culture**

http://www.newzealand.com/travel/media/features/food-&-wine/food&wine_nz-culinary-culture_feature.cfm

Group Tasks

While it is valuable to understand the apparent norms of national trends in cuisine, it is also important to know why certain peoples in certain places make the food choices that they do. In this way "food culture" is an expression of geography, history (especially migration) and cultural traditions, including religion and relative wealth. As a student of language and culture, it is important for you to understand these relationships. To do this, it might be useful to start with your immediate peer and family groups. Get together in teams of about five people and discuss how you will investigate your "food histories". A simple questionnaire that you can use between you and with friends and family might be appropriate, but some groups might wish to conduct short interviews and analyse the responses in detail.

When you have gathered your empirical data, re-form your groups to discuss the history and importance of food to the people you have researched. Compare this information with the data in the textbook. Note similarities and differences between the responses. If you have friends and family living overseas, why not seek their responses too and add their data into the mix?

Use your findings to construct a reference text of your own that you are able to use when meeting someone from another culture to help you find out their attitudes to food and what meaning it has for them. It would be very beneficial to develop this idea alongside the "customs and courtesies" chapter, since there are many areas of overlap in the subjects.

Chapter 9   Sports and Recreations

Section A   Sports and Recreations in the United Kingdom

People spend their free time enjoying various indoor and outdoor activities in Britain, such as doing sports, listening to the music, watching television, reading, gardening, eating out, and going to the cinema, etc..

1. Sports

The English people are great lovers of competitive sports. Many of the world's famous sports began in Britain, including football, cricket, lawn tennis, golf, rugby and horse-racing, etc.. There are also many other sports which attract great public interest, such as badminton, squash, hockey, boxing, snooker and billiards.

▶ Football

Association football[1] or soccer is the most popular sport in Britain, and has been played for hundreds of years. The football season is from mid August to early May. Football is played in most of the schools and there are thousands of amateur teams all over the U.K.. Every large town has at least one professional football club. Professional football is controlled by two organizations, the Football League and the Football Association. An important competition is the Football Association (FA) Cup, and over 20 million tickets are sold to FA games each season.

The FA Cup is the trophy title for a series of games played by major member teams of the Football Association. This is open to all amateur football teams that belong to the FA as well as the professional teams. The teams play against each other in a Knockout competition which starts in August and ends in May. The two teams left in the competition play in the FA Cup Final at Wembley Stadium in London. Some

Wembley Stadium, London

of England's football teams are world famous, the most famous being Manchester United, Arsenal and Liverpool, and Britain also produces many world-famous football stars, such as David Beckham and Wayne Rooney.

Football "pools" provide amusement for millions of people, who bet on the results of the matches. Filling in the pools takes place during the week. At the end of the week, the results of the matches are announced on TV and published in the newspapers, and the one with a correct forecast will win a fortune.

▶ Cricket

Cricket is a very popular sport in Britain, played on village greens and in towns or cities on Sundays from April to August. It is one of the first team sports in Britain to have organized rules and to be played according to the same rules nationally, but it has been seriously and extensively adopted only in Britain, in some parts of the British Commonwealth and in Denmark. The liking for it seems to reflect the British character. Its comparative slowness and quietness is associated with its gentlemanly sportsmanship. It is a quite distinctive

Cricket

sport in many ways. First, the players wear white trousers and appear quite formally dressed. Second, matches do not last just a few hours and they can go on for days, and has much influence on British people's life. Third, cricket is often believed to be associated with a set of English moral values such as "fair play".

The main competition is the county championship, in which the 18 county cricket clubs play against one another during the season. Each match takes 3 or 4 days to complete. Test cricket is the highest standard of first-class cricket. A test match is an international fixture between teams representing those countries that are Full Members of the International Cricket Council (ICC), such as Australia, England, India, New Zealand, Pakistan, South Africa, Sri Lanka, and the West Indies. Test matches between two teams are usually played in a group of matches called a "series". Matches last up to five days and a series normally consists of three to five matches.

▶ Tennis

The modern game of tennis originated in Birmingham, England in the late 19th century as "lawn tennis". Tennis is a more gentle sport played by people in early summer. There are clubs in every town and in all the parks there are public courts where tennis may be played for an

Wimbledon's Centre Court, London

hour on payment of about one pound.

Every year the world's best players gather in Wimbledon to compete in the annual international tennis championships. It is one of the major events of the British sporting calendar and probably the most famous tennis event in the world. The Championships, Wimbledon, is the oldest tennis tournament in the world, and it is one of the four Grand Slam[2] tennis tournaments, the other three majors being the Australian Open, French Open and U.S. Open. Wimbledon is the only Major still played on grass, the game's original surface, which gives the game its original name of "lawn tennis". It is normally held between the last week of June and the first week of July, at a time of finest weather.

◉ Golf

The modern game of golf originated in 15th century in Scotland. By the 16th century, golf had already been very popular in Scotland and royal members like Mary Queen of Scots took great interest in it. Scotland is traditionally regarded as the home of golf, and there are over 400 golf courses in Scotland alone. Located on Scotland's picturesque east coast, the seven courses at St. Andrews make it the largest golf complex in Europe. The most well-known of the courses is the Old Course, where golfing legends like Seve Ballesteros, Jack Nicklaus and Tiger Woods have

The Old Course, St. Andrews

played. Woods has even called it his favorite course in the world. Despite its lofty reputation, the Old Course, along with the six others at St. Andrews, is open to the public.

The oldest golf club in the world is the Honorable Company of Edinburgh Golfers in Scotland. The Walker Cup is for amateurs and the Ryder Cup for professionals. In the early 20th century, British golfers were the best in the world, winning nearly all of the U.S. Open championships before World War I. American golfers later became dominant, but Britain has continued to produce leading golfers.

◉ Rugby

The most popular winter sport, after football, is rugby football (or rugger). The game "Rugby" originated from Rugby School in Warwichshire in the early 19th century. It is similar to football, but played with an oval ball. The best rugby teams compete in the Super League final each September.

There are two forms of rugby football played in Britain: Rugby Union and Rugby League. In 1871, the Rugby Football Union (RFU) for England was formed and a standard set of rules were approved. By 1880, Scotland, Wales and Ireland had also formed national unions.

Generally, clubs in the south of England wanted players to remain unpaid and amateur, while clubs in the north of the country felt that players should be compensated for missing time at work to play. After much debate, the breakaway clubs formed the Northern Rugby Football Union in 1895, which later became known as the Rugby League. League players could earn money by playing rugby, while union players could not. In the 1980s, many of the union's best players became frustrated with their amateur, unpaid status. As a result, a number of high-profile union players switched to Rugby League. Now Rugby Union players can also make a professional career in the game, rather than playing in their spare time.

◉ Horse Racing

The true royal sport in Britain is horse racing. Organized national horse races have been held throughout Britain for hundreds of years. At the medieval age, horse racing was taken as the symbol of wealth and authority. Since ordinary family couldn't afford to buy a horse, horse racing was also called aristocratic sports. However, commoners could rent horses at affordable prices and bet on a horse race.

Horse Racing

There are two kinds of horse racing: flat racing and steeple chasing. Flat racing is a form of thoroughbred horse racing which is run over a level track at a predetermined distance. It differs from steeplechase racing which is run over hurdles. The race is a test of speed, stamina, and the skill of the jockey in determining when to restrain the horse or to impel it. The steeplechase is a term now used to refer to a distance horse race with diverse fence and ditch obstacles; the world's most famous steeplechase is the Grand National run annually at Aintree Racecourse, in Liverpool, since its inception in 1836.

There is also the biggest social event associated with horse racing: the Royal Ascot. The Royal Ascot is the biggest social event associated with horse racing. People dress up and go to show off their fashionable clothes as well to watch the races and place their bets. Women especially wear very elaborate and exotic hats. This event gets much attention from the media and the public.

The Royal Ascot Racecourse

There are many other sports popular with the British, and most British have some interest in at least some sports.

2. Recreations

Recreation refers to refreshment of one's mind or body after work through activity that amuses or stimulates, and it stresses leisure-time participation in athletics or other non-vocational activities that are relaxing and enjoyable. Recreational activities in Britain could be almost endless, but the typical ones are going to the local pubs, going shopping and going on their holidays.

● Going to Pubs

Pubs are popular social meeting places and are an important part of British life. People talk, eat, drink, meet their friends and relax there. Some pubs maintain the traditional division: a public bar and a saloon bar. In the saloon bar, the drinks cost a little more, but the atmosphere is quieter.

Most pubs offer a range of beers, wines, spirits and soft drinks. The favorite British drink is beer. Besides, nearly all pubs sell pub lunches, and one of these is the Ploughman's Lunch[3]. Some pubs even offer elaborate hot and cold snacks free to customers on Sunday lunchtimes to prevent them getting hungry and leaving for their lunch at home.

Various traditional games, such as the well-known darts, skittles, dominoes, cards and bar billiards, are common features of pubs. In the U.K. betting is legally limited to certain games such as cribbage or dominoes, played for small stakes. In recent decades the game of pool has increased in popularity as well as other table based games such as snooker or Table Football. Increasingly, more modern games such as video games and slot machines are provided.

● Shopping

Going shoping is the number one leisure activity of the British. Peak shopping days are Saturdays and Sundays. Saturday is traditionally the day for shopping as well as watching sports. Sundays used to be a very special day of the week for "worship and rest" in Britain. Until a few years ago, shops were not permitted to open on a Sunday. In recent years, Sunday shopping has become popular and most large shops in towns are open for business.

Harrod's in London

The main shopping street in many towns is called the High Street. A few small shops are owned by the local people, and most are owned by national "chains" of stores. Some towns also have street markets where fresh food and cheap goods can be bought. Away from the town center, small "corner" shops provide groceries to local customers. Harrod's in London is the famous department store, with an illustrious 150-year history and an enviable reputation for luxury goods.

Bluewater is the largest out of town shopping development in Europe, located in a disused chalk pit at Dartford in Kent. With more than 300 shops and parking for 13,000 cars, it attracts around 30 million visitors each year. Supermarkets tend to be open 7 days a week with longer opening hours, usually until 8 p.m. or 10 p.m. most evenings, with reduced hours of 10 a.m. to 4 p.m. (or 11a.m. to 5 p.m.) on a Sunday.

⊙ Going on Their Holidays

Two-thirds of all British have their holidays in July and August. The British enjoy the family outing, and most of them choose well-known beauty spots or seaside beaches, where there are often so crowded together that the sand can't be seen. Others choose a lonely place, where there are very few people. They may follow tracks between the mountains and lochs and watch seals and seabirds.

Nowadays a lot of British people go abroad to somewhere warm for their holidays. Spain, together with other places in southern Europe, has been the favorite British holiday destination since 1994.

Section B Sports and Recreations in the United States of America

Sports and recreations absorb a huge amount of Americans' emotion, as well as their time and, in some cases, money. To understand American culture, remember that Americans not only work hard, they also play hard and almost always just for enjoyment.

1. Sports

Sports are an important part of American culture. The four most popular team sports are: American football, baseball, basketball and ice hockey. Besides, Americans play a variety of other sports. In warm weather, people enjoy water sports. Lovers of surfing, sailing and diving flock to the ocean. Swimmers and water skiers also revel in the wet stuff. Fishermen try their luck in ponds, lakes and rivers. In winter, sportsmen delight in freezing fun. From the first snowfall, skiers hit the slopes. Frozen ponds and ice rinks become playgrounds for skating and hockey. Racquetball, weightlifting and bowling are year-round activities.

American Football

American football, known within the country simply as football, is the American national sport, and it is played in almost every college and university in the country. It is derived from the English game of rugby. Although it is played in no other country in the world except Canada, it excites tremendous enthusiasm. In American football, there are eleven players on each side, and they are dressed inpadded uniforms and helmets, because the game is rough and injuries are likely to occur. Each team has a name,

American Football

which usually includes the name of the town or city that the team is associated with, such as New York Jets, Washington Redskins and New England Patriots. Many people support a particular team and watch the game that their team plays.

In the U.S., high school football, college football and professional football are the major forms, and each is played under slightly different rules. Popular high school footballers are usually encouraged to come to a college or university by offers of scholarships. Most colleges and universities have a varsity football team, with additional personnel in a marching band and a squad of cheerleaders. Besides, there are professional football teams in nearly all of the major cities of the U.S.. Professional football games are organized by National Football League (NFL) which is divided into two conferences: National Football Conference and American Football Conference, and both of them have 14 teams and three divisions.

The season starts in early autumn and ends at the end of January with the Super Bowl, which is the NFL championship game. The two teams that play in the Super Bowl are determined by games within the divisions and conferences. The Super Bowl is only one game and at the end of the game, they have a sudden-death play-off, in which the first team to gain points wins the game. Super Bowl Sunday is the biggest annual sporting event held in the U.S.. One reason football is so popular in America may be that the game combines teamwork with individual prowess in a rough, contact competition.

Baseball

Baseball is the oldest of the major American team sports. Evolving from older bat-and-ball games, an early form of baseball was being played in England by the mid-18th century. This game was brought by immigrants to North America, where the modern version developed. By the late 19th century, baseball was widely recognized as the national sport of the U.S.. Professional baseball dates back to 1869 and had no close rivals in popularity until the 1960s. Baseball is now popular in North America, parts of Central and South America and the Caribbean, and parts of East Asia.

In the U.S. and Canada, professional Major League Baseball (MLB) teams are divided into the National League (NL) and the American League (AL), each with three divisions: East, West, and Central. Each league has teams in many cities across America. The teams play against each other in each league. The winners from each league play against each other in the World Series at the end of each year (sometimes in October). MLB teams play almost every day from April to October.

Known as America's "national pastime", baseball is not only played by high school and college teams and professionals, but also played by children in the spring. On the other hand, baseball is largely a spectator sport, and baseball players, especially professional base-ballers play a very important role in American everyday life.

American Baseball

▶ Basketball

Basketball is the main game played during the winter in America. Basketball was created in 1891 by a physical education teacher in Massachusetts, Canadian-born James Naismith, to provide an indoor sports activity during the snowy winter months when outdoor playing fields could not be used. Like American football, basketball at both the college and high school levels is quite popular throughout the country, and state-wide high school basketball tournaments are held in many states every year. Also like American football, many high school basketball teams have intense local followings, especially in the Midwest and Upper South. Indiana alone has 10 of the 12 largest high school gyms in the U.S. and is famous for its basketball passion.

Michael Jordan

Basketball had its first professional team in 1896, but it wasn't until 1946 that one league was established in New York City as Basketball Association of America (BAA), and the league adopted the name National Basketball Association (NBA) in 1949. With thirty franchised member clubs (29 in the U.S. and 1 in Canada), the NBA is widely considered to be the premier men's professional basketball league in the world. In 1984 Michael Jordan and five other members of the gold medal-winning U.S. Olympic team entered the NBA, and the NBA came to its most significant period with its brightest star, Michael Jordan who led the Chicago Bulls in winning consecutively three NBA champions from 1991 – 1993. In the past decade, an increasing number of players born outside the U.S. have signed with NBA teams, sparking league interest in different parts of the world.

Because basketball is such a fast game, the score can suddenly shift, and many games are won or lost in the final few seconds. This keeps spectators at the game until the very end, whereas in football and baseball many fans leave before the game is over when one team is so far ahead that the outcome seems certain. Today, professional basketball has become a billion-dollar sport, and many now believe basketball has replaced baseball as the national sport.

▶ Ice Hockey

Ice hockey is less popular than football, baseball and basketball, but it is still considered a major sport in the U.S.. Originating from North America, the sport is commonly referred to simply as "hockey". In the U.S. the game is most popular in regions of the country with a cold winter climate, namely New England, the northern half of the Mid-Atlantic and the Midwest. However, since the 1990s hockey has become increasingly popular in the Sun Belt due in large part to the expansion of the National Hockey League (NHL) to South and Southwest cities.

The NHL is an "unincorporated not-for-profit association", which operates a major professional ice hockey league of 30 franchised member clubs, of which seven are currently located in Canada and 23 in the U.S.. Headquartered in New York City, the NHL is widely considered to be the premier professional ice hockey league in the world, and one of the major professional sports leagues in the U.S. and Canada. The Stanley Cup, the oldest professional sports trophy in North America, is awarded annually to the league playoff champion at the end of each season. Other professional leagues in the U.S. include the American Hockey League and the East Coast Hockey League. Besides, USA Hockey is the official governing body for amateur hockey in the U.S..

The Stanley Cup

▶ Soccer

Association football, commonly known as "soccer" in the U.S. and "football" in other countries, is not as popular as the four sports traditionally considered major in the U.S., although it has gained an increasing number of followers recent years. It is extremely popular as a children's sport, although it has not yet reached the international popularity of the sport. The U.S. men's and women's senior national teams, as well as a number of age-grade teams for both sexes, represent the U.S. in

American Women's Soccer

international soccer competitions and are controlled by the U.S. Soccer Federation.

Due to factors such as the continuing presence of the U.S. men's and specially women's national teams in international soccer competitions, the impact of the global trend towards globalization, and the large number of immigrants, particularly Latin Americans, it is possible that soccer will continue to rise in popularity in the U.S. and reach the level of the top four professional team sports in the future. Soccer-specific stadiums continue to be built around the country, and many American sports fans, as compared with decades ago, now have a keen awareness of and even follow major competitions such as the World Cup and the Union of European Football Associations (UEFA) Champions League as well as the leading European leagues.

Not all Americans worship sports, but athletics are an important part of their culture. Many people enjoy non-competitive activities like hiking, biking, horseback riding or hunting.

2. Recreations

The word "recreation" brings to mind activities that are relaxing and enjoyable. However, many American recreational activities seem to be approached with a high degree of seriousness, planning, organization and expense, and many Americans have some regular scheduled recreations. Some are types of spectator recreation, such as watching TV or going to a musical concert. Many others are types of participatory recreation, and a hobby is one kind of recreations that you participate in. In their leisure time, many Americans like traveling, collecting, and reading, but today, the popularity of home computers and surfing the Net has brought a whole new world of leisure time activities to Americans.

▶ Traveling

Since the 1940s, almost every American employee has received an annual vacation with pay, and it has become customary to use this time off for travel. Some families just stay at home to enjoy the local recreational facilities, but most Americans like to travel both at home and abroad.

For travelers interested in beautiful scenery, natural wonders and wildlife, the U. S. has 58 national parks. These parks include Yellowstone, Grand Canyon, Glacier National Park and Yosemite in the West, of which Yellowstone is the first national park in the U.S.. In the East, there is the Florida Everglades, which makes up one of the largest swamplands in the world, and it is rich in birds and other animals.

Yellowstone National Park

However, most Americans have a desire to visit other

countries. Each year three million go to Europe and nearly two million or more travel to Bermuda, the West Indies and central and south America. Countries in Asia and Africa are also attracting many American tourists each year.

Traveling is an attractive opportunity for fun and relaxation, and it is also a good chance for family members to spend leisure time together and get to know each other better.

◉ Collecting

Perhaps the most common American recreation is collecting, finding as many things of one kind as possible. The hobby of collecting includes seeking, locating, acquiring, organizing, cataloging, displaying, storing and maintaining whatever items are of interest to the individual collector. Some Americans collect antiques, such as old furniture, old bicycles, old books, old clock and so on, and their houses look like museums. Others collect stamps or coins, bottles or bottle caps, postcards, matchboxes, pins, buttons and badges. Some women may collect certain kinds of dishes, like cups, bowls, or all sorts of salt and pepper shakers. Collecting can be a very expensive recreational activity, or it may cost almost nothing because collectors' friends may give them something they are collecting as gifts.

◉ Reading

Reading used to be the almost universal form of recreations, and in every city there are public libraries where books can be borrowed free of charge. However, nowadays many Americans do not read much, and libraries are now more than just a place for books. You can borrow video and audio cassettes, use computers to find information, listen to lectures, see an art exhibit, or send your children to a "story corner" where someone will read a story to them, and sometimes the children will then borrow the book to read and find out how the story ends.

◉ Surfing the Net

Nowadays, wireless technology allows Americans to access the Internet just anywhere. They can have discussions with others online, communicate with friends or family via email and instant messaging, and play the latest computer games. Computers and Internet are also extremely popular with children and teenagers, and parents have to worry about monitoring the computer, in addition to monitoring the TV. Many Americans are happy that technology has made it possible for them to communicate with anyone anywhere. However, this 24/7 access (24 hours a day, 7 days a week) has a huge impact on leisure time and Americans' ability to relax.

Section C   Sports and Recreations in China

Traditionally, the Chinese love sports as an essential method for keeping fit as well as for entertainment, including the dragon-boat races during the Dragon Boat Festival, swings on Tomb-sweeping Day, and climbing mountains during the Double-ninth Festival. As a country with diverse cultural traditions passed down from one generation to another over a long history, China has developed a variety of sports, such as archery, cuju (traditional football), sumo and other forms of wrestling, equestrianism, martial arts, acrobatics and so on. Since the 20th century, a large number of sports activities, both Western and traditionally Chinese, are popular in China.

1. Traditional Chinese Sports

With such a long history, China has developed many unique and traditional sports and pastimes, and Chinese people have their own special ways to express their vigor and enthusiasm.

◉ Martial Arts

Kung-fu and Wushu are terms that have been borrowed into English to refer to Chinese martial arts. Chinese martial arts are a number of fighting styles that have developed over centuries in China. These fighting styles are often classified according to common traits, identified as "families", "sects" or "schools" of martial arts. Martial arts were developed under the great influence of ancient Chinese culture and they have benefited a lot from ancient Chinese philosophy. Besides, under the influence of ancient Chinese aesthetics, Chinese martial arts have formed their own aesthetic standards that incorporate a stage of conceptual contentment, harmony, and nature, as well as beauty and elegance. With vigorous, graceful and somewhat laborious movements, Chinese martial arts provide the exercises with beauty and strength. The persistent exercises will build up their body and strength.

Being an important part of the Chinese traditional martial arts, Shaolin Kung-fu is considered to be authentic Chinese Kung-fu. Shaolin Kung-fu has developed a variety of forms over the long history, hence the attribution of "72 types of Shaolin martial arts". Long boxing, short boxing, knife and stick play and swordplay, each claims its own unique skills. When people talk of the martial arts, they may immediately think of Bruce Lee, and his great

Taiji

accomplishments in boxing, swordplay, and skills with knives and sticks. With his superb Kung-fu popularized throughout the world, he became the embodiment of Chinese martial arts. His dazzling three-section stick skills left a deep impression on audiences.

Taiji or Chinese shadow boxing is considered to be one of the internal styles of the Chinese martial arts. It is a kind of Chinese boxing, combining control of breath, mind and body. It emphasizes body movement following mind movements, tempering toughness with gentleness and graceful carriage. Since it aids both self-defense and health, it has become a main method of physical exercise, widely practiced in the world today.

A system of deep breathing exercises, qigong is a unique Chinese way of keeping fit. It aims at enhancing health, prolonging life, curing illnesses and improving physiological functions by concentrating the mind and regulating the breath.

Today, the military functions of Chinese martial arts have faded and their physical welfare and athletic functions become dominant. Many people practice them to pursue health, defense skills, mental discipline, entertainment and competition.

Cuju

Cuju is an ancient ball game with similarities to association football, and it originated in China. Some claim that the Yellow Emperor invented the game for military training purposes, while others place its emergence during China's Warring States Period. During the Han Dynasty, the popularity of cuju spread from the army to the royal courts and upper classes, and cuju games were standardized and rules were established. It was improved during the Tang Dynasty. The feather-stuffed ball was replaced by an air-filled ball with a two-layered hull. Cuju flourished during the Song Dynasty due to social and economic development, extending its popularity to every class in society. Many ancient Chinese paintings depict scenes of cuju. One painting, One Hundred Children in the Long Spring, by Chinese artist Su Hanchen[4], features a scene of a group of children playing cuju together. Cuju began to decline during the Ming Dynasty and the 2,000-year-old sport slowly faded away.

One Hundred Children in the Long Spring

Tug of War

Tug of war, also known as rope war or rope pulling, is a sport that directly pits two teams against each other in a test of strength. The origins of tug of war are uncertain, but according to a Tang Dynasty book, tug of war, under the name "hook pulling", was used by the military commander of the State of Chu during the Spring and

Tug of War

Autumn Period to train warriors. During the Tang Dynasty, Emperor Xuan-zong promoted large-scale tug of war games, using ropes of up to 167 meters with shorter ropes attached and more than 500 people on each end of the rope. Each side also had its own team of drummers to encourage the participants. Both participants and audience joyously shout to boost the pullers' morale, presenting a grand and liveliest scene. Later, it developed into a sport and popular folk custom.

Skipping Ropes

▶ Skipping Ropes

Skipping ropes has a long history in China. It is a fun sport for both children and adults. With simply a rope, people have invented many ways to play and to compete. The most common way, also the easiest way for exercise, is to skip once in a round. Varieties can be wonderful and diverse. A skilled person can turn the rope many times in quick succession while keeping his or her feet off the ground in a single jump. Couples can skip together; or with a long rope two people turn it, and a whole group of people join in. In view of its sport effect, now students are encouraged to play this game, and many skipping ropes meetings are held by their schools. Skipping ropes has also been adopted as part of keeping-fit programs by adults.

2. Other Sports Games

▶ Table Tennis

Ping pong is the official name for the sport of table tennis in China. Apart from the national representative team, the table tennis community in China continues to produce many world-class players, and this depth of skill allows the country to continue dominating recent world titles after a short break in the 1990s. The overwhelming dominance of China in the sport has triggered a series of rules changes in the International Table Tennis Federation and as part of the Olympics. The sport plays an important role in China's international

The Chinese Table Tennis Team

relations. For example, in April 1972, the U.S. table tennis teams were invited to visit China, an event later called "Ping Pong Diplomacy". Table tennis is the biggest amateur recreational sport in China today, with an estimated 300 million players.

▶ Badminton

China has the most successful badminton team in history, having won the Thomas Cup 9 times and the Uber Cup 12 times. China has also won more medals in badminton at the Olympics than any other country, and Chinese badminton players have gained international success and fame. Lin Dan is the only player in badminton history to have won three consecutive titles at the World Championships.

Because of its relative simplicity, inexpensive equipment, and accessibility to venues, badminton is a very popular sport in China. It's a popular recreational sport, and amateur leagues exist across the country.

Lin Dan

▶ Basketball

Basketball was introduced to China by American YMCA (The Young Men's Christian Association) workers in 1896, just five years after the Canadian, Dr. James Naismith, had invented the game. The Chinese Basketball Association (CBA) was established in June in 1956. It is a non-governmental organization in charge of basketball at national level. The administration center of basketball, a sub-division of CBA, takes the responsibility of promoting the sport in China. After the introduction of some reforms in 1994, the first CBA league was launched the following

Chinese CBA Players

year, with 12 teams participating. By 2000, there were 43 men's teams and 42 women's teams registered under CBA. The advent of the CBA league represented a giant step in the development of professional basketball in China. In 1989, the first basketball club, sponsored by Anshan Steel Company, was founded in Shenyang. By 2000, the members of professional basketball clubs registered under CBA had reached 29.

A few Chinese CBA players, such as Yao Ming, Wang Zhizhi, Yi Jianlian, Mengke Bateer, and Sun Yue have played in the NBA. Conversely, a limited number of notable foreign players are allowed for each CBA team, such as NBA All-Stars Stephon Marbury, Steve Francis and Kenyon Martin. Yao Ming and other NBA success stories have helped to popularize basketball in China. It is estimated that as many as 300 million of China's 1.3 billion population now play basketball.

▶ Volleyball

Volleyball arrived in Asia in 1908, and began to be practiced in China and Japan. The

Chinese Volleyball Association (CVA), founded in 1953, is a member of the All-China Sports Federation. The CVA is a national non-government, nonprofit organization. As an Olympic event organization recognized by the Chinese Olympic Committee, the CVA is the only legitimate organization that represents China in international volleyball organizations. The CVA is a formal member of the International Volleyball Federation and Asian Volleyball Federation.

The Chinese women's national volleyball team is one of the leading squads in women's international volleyball, having won the Olympic title thrice (1984, 2004 and 2016). China took five consecutive World titles in the 1980s. Although it experienced an unstable development in the 1990s, the team won the Grand Prix title in 2003 and captured the gold medal in the 2004 Summer Olympics.

The Chinese Women's National
Volleyball Team in the 1980s

▶ Football

Football is the most popular spectator sport in the country and has been one of the most well supported sports in China ever since it was introduced in the 1900s. The Chinese Football Association (CFA) was founded after 1949, and its headquarters is located in Beijing. From 1994 to 2004, CFA established first professional football league, which was "Jia A". The Chinese Super League (CSL) is the premier football league in China, which was changed from "Jia A" in 2004, as the top of a league hierarchy that extends to four leagues. Since its foundation the Super League has been relatively unstable, and has struggled to maintain popularity.

At the international level, Chinese football has enjoyed little success despite the amount of support it receives from fans. Conversely, the women's national team has finished second at both the World Championships and the Olympic Games. Despite the Chinese women team's success at international competitions, women's football in China does not receive nearly as much attention as their counterparts in Canada and the U.S..

Football has always been among the more popular amateur team sports for recreation in China. High schools often have football facilities, some of which are rented on weekends to local amateur teams to organize matches. It is also the most popular sports to watch on television, with large international tournaments such as the World Cup and the European Championships.

▶ Tennis

Tennis is a growing recreational sport in China, although access to tennis courts can be limited in densely populated urban areas. Recently, Chinese tennis players, especially women, have seen success

Li Na

internationally both at the amateur level and at the professional one, and Li Na is the first player from China and Asia to win a title. International tennis tournaments receive wide coverage on Chinese sporting channels.

3. Recreation

There are many traditional forms of recreations in China, such as practicing Guqin, Go, calligraphy and painting, mahjong games, shuttlecock kicking, kite flying, etc.. The other forms of recreations include shopping, relaxing in the various resorts, dining and so on.

▶ Practicing Guqin, Go (Weiqi), Calligraphy, and Painting

In ancient China, Guqin, Go, calligraphy and painting not only act as recreational activities, but also exert immeasurable influence on the character of traditional scholars and creation of the Chinese cultural heritage.

The Guqin (ancient stringed instrument) is a plucked seven-string Chinese musical instrument of the zither family. It has a history of about 5,000 years, and it is viewed as a symbol of Chinese high culture and the instrument most expressive of the essence of Chinese music. It is sometimes referred to by the Chinese as "the father of Chinese music" or "the instrument of the sages". Go (weiqi) is a board game for two players that originated in China more than 2,500 years ago. The game is noted for being rich in strategy despite its relatively simple rules. It is because of its highly complicated playing but yet played by simple rules that make this game both an entertaining and favorite pastime of most Chinese. Calligraphy refers to the writing in brush. It resorts to the change of lines to express the style of writing and the mood of the writer. Painting in the traditional style is known today as "national painting", and traditional painting involves essentially the same techniques as calligraphy and is done with a brush dipped in black or colored ink. In imperial China, a well-educated scholar was expected to be skilled in these four arts.

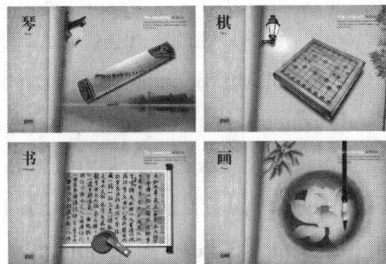
Guqin, Go, Calligraphy and Painting

▶ Mahjong

Mahjong is a game that originated in China, commonly played by four players. One of the myths of the origin of mahjong suggests that Confucius, the Chinese philosopher, developed the game in about 500 B.C.. Besides, many historians believe it was based on a Chinese card game calledmadiao in the early Ming Dynasty. In the Qing Dynasty, a new gambling art—mahjong, eventually took shape. Mahjong culture is deeply ingrained in China. For example, many gambling movies have been filmed in Hong Kong, and a recent sub-genre is the mahjong movie. Today mahjong becomes a social game, and it is a popular pastime in China.

Mahjong

▶ Shuttlecock Kicking

Shuttlecock Kicking is one of the traditional popular folk games in China, and it is suitable for people of all ages. Some records date its origin as far back as the Han Dynasty. It prevailed during the Tang Dynasty, and in the Ming Dynasty the game was so popular that there appeared formal Shuttlecock Kicking competitions. In the Qing Dynasty, shuttlecock kicking reached its climax in terms of both making techniques and kicking skills; while in the 1930s, the sport of shuttlecock kicking was in decline for a time. After the establishment of new China, it regained vitality and the first formal

Shuttlecock Kicking

National Shuttlecock Kicking Competition was held in Guangzhou City in 1956. Since the establishment of the China Shuttlecock Kicking Association in 1987, the national shuttlecock kicking tournament has been held annually.

Shuttlecock kicking is not only of great fun, but also provides vigorous physical exercise. Besides, it's very convenient for people to play, for only a very small area is needed to kick the shuttlecock, and it can be practiced just anywhere and anytime.

▶ Kite Flying

Nowadays, kite flying has become a popular recreation far and wide in China. Its history can be traced back to more than 2,000 years ago. Legend has it that the first Chinese kites were made of wood and called Muyuan (wooden kites) by the famous architect and carpenter Lu Ban during the Spring and Autumn Period; after the invention of paper, kites began to be made of this new material called Zhiyuan (paper kites). People today make colorful kites in the shapes of animals, birds, butterflies, fishes and centipedes, and some animal-shaped kites can even roll their eyes and flutter their wings. In modern China, kites are used not only as toys, but also as exquisite handicrafts worthy of collection, and it has been praised as the forerunner of modern aircrafts. In 1989, the International Kite Federation was established, headquartering Weifang in Shangdong Province. The well-known Weifang Kite Festival has become an annual feature in the country, drawing hundreds of

Kite Flying

participants each April from home and abroad.

▶ Playing Chinese Yo-Yo (**Kongzhu**)

The Chinese yo-yo is a toy from China consisting of two equal-ly-sized discs connected with a long axle. The Chinese yo-yo is kept spinning on a string tied to two sticks at its ends. Each stick is held in one hand. The oldest records of the Chinese yo-yo appeared in ancient Chinese literature written 1,700 years ago. It is considered to have been practiced for more than 2,000 years and to be one of the three major traditional folk games originated from China along with the shuttlecock and the kite. In modern times, it is used as a children's toy and as a performance tool in juggling and sometimes in

Playing Kongzhu

Chinese ethnic dance. It is possible to perform an enormous variety of tricks with the Chinese yo-yo, and it is widely popularized among common people throughout China.

Notes

1. **Association football**: Association football, commonly known as football or soccer, is a sport played between two teams of eleven players with a spherical ball. At the turn of the 21st century, the game was played by over 250 million players in over 200 countries, making it the world's most popular sport.

2. **Grand Slam**: The four Grand Slam tournaments, also called Majors, are the most important annual tennis events. The Grand Slam itinerary consists of the Australian Open in January, the French Open in May/June, Wimbledon in June/July, and the U.S. Open in August/September. Each tournament is played over a period of two weeks. The term "Grand Slam" also, and origi-nally, refers to the achievement of winning all four major championships in a single calendar year within one of the five disciplines: men's and women's singles; men's, women's, and mixed doubles. However, the term "Grand Slam" when used with an indefinite article is widely accepted as referring to any one of the Majors.

3. **Ploughman's Lunch**: A ploughman's lunch is a cold meal originating in the U.K., common-ly served in pubs. Its core components are cheese, chutney and bread. The dish can also include such items as boiled eggs, ham and pickled onions, and is traditionally accompanied with a drink of beer. As its name suggests, it is more commonly consumed as a midday snack.

4. **Su Hanchen**: Chinese painter. Su may originally have come from northern China, for the compiler Xia Wenyan claimed that Su was from Bianliang (modern Kaifeng), in Henan Prov-ince, the Northern Song (960 – 1127) capital, and that he served in Emperor Huizong's Hanlin Painting Academy from 1119 to 1125, learning figure painting from a court painter, Liu Zonggu.

Xia noted that subsequent to the Jin conquest in 1125 and the removal of the court to the south, sometime after 1131, Su was reinstated at Lin'an, the Southern Song (1127 – 1279) capital.

Glossary

lawn tennis 草地网球

squash [skwɔʃ] *n.* 软式墙网球,壁球

hockey ['hɔki] *n.* 曲棍球；冰球

snooker ['snuːkə] *n.* 一种落袋撞球戏(使用 15 个红球, 6 个其他颜色的球),彩色台球

billiards ['biljədz] *n.* 台球,桌球戏,弹子球

the Football League 足球联盟

the Football Association 足球协会

FA Cup 足总杯

knockout ['nɔ'kaut] *n.* (英)淘汰赛

Wembley Stadium 温布利球场

Manchester United 曼联

football "pools" 猜足球赛胜负的赌博

Full Members 完全会员

the International Cricket Council 国际板球理事会

the Championships 网球冠军赛

Grand Slam tennis tournaments 大满贯网球锦标赛

Mary Queen of Scots 苏格兰玛丽女王

picturesque [ˌpiktʃə'resk] *adj.* 风景如画的

golf complex 高尔夫球馆

the Walker Cup 沃克杯

the Ryder Cup 莱德杯

rugger ['rʌgə] *n.* 英式橄榄球(运动)

Rugby Union 联合会式橄榄球

Rugby League 联盟式橄榄球

high-profile 引人注目的

flat racing 平地赛马

steeple chasing 越野障碍赛马

thoroughbred ['θʌrəbred] *n.* 纯种的动物(尤指马)

level track 平路

stamina ['stæminə] *n.* 体力, 耐力, 持久力

jockey ['dʒɔki] *n.* 赛马骑师

the Grand National (英国一年一度的)全国越野障碍赛马

the Royal Ascot 皇家阿斯科特赛马会

a saloon bar 沙龙酒吧

Ploughman's Lunch 农夫午餐,简便午餐

skittle ['skitl] *n.* 九柱戏,撞柱戏

cribbage ['kribidʒ] *n.* 纸牌玩法之一

the High Street 商业大街

loch [lɔk] *n.* 湖；狭长的海湾

revel ['revl] *vi.* 作乐；狂欢

racquetball ['rækitbɔːl] *n.* 手球式墙球

padded ['pædid] *adj.* 有衬里的；带衬垫的

New York Jets 纽约喷气机队

Washington Redskins 华盛顿红人队

New England Patriots 新英格兰爱国者队

National Football League 国家美式橄榄球大联盟

National Football Conference 国家美式橄榄球联合会

American Football Conference 美国美式橄榄球联合会

the Super Bowl 美国橄榄球超级杯赛

sudden death 突然死亡法（足球加时赛先进球方为胜方）

play-off （平分后要决出胜负的）附加赛

prowess ['prauis] *n.* 高超的技艺；非凡的才能

Major League Baseball 美国职业棒球大联盟

the National League 国家联盟

the American League 美国联盟

the World Series 世界大赛（是大联盟的两个联盟,美联和国联的冠军最后决战决出总冠军的系列赛）

Upper South 上南方（美国南部偏北的地区,与其相对的是深南部 Lower South 或 Deep South）

Basketball Association of America 全美篮球协会

National Basketball Association （美国）全国篮球协会；美国篮球职业联赛

the Chicago Bulls 芝加哥公牛队

consecutively [kən'sekjutivli] *adv.* 连续地

the Sun Belt 阳光地带（从弗吉尼亚州至加利福尼亚州南部的美国南部地区）

National Hockey League 国家冰球联盟

the Union of European Football Associations 欧洲足球联盟

（UEFA）Champions League 欧洲冠军联赛

Yellowstone National Park 黄石国家公园

Grand Canyon National Park 大峡谷国家公园

Glacier National Park 冰川国家公园

Yosemite National Park 优胜美地国家公园

Florida Everglades National Park 佛罗里达国家大沼泽地野生公园

swing [swiŋ] *n.* 秋千

archery [ˈɑːtʃəri] *n.* 射艺,箭术

cuju 蹴鞠

sumo [ˈsuːməu] *n.* 相扑(=sumo wrestling)

equestrianism [iˈkwestriənizəm] *n.* 马术

martial arts 武术(指柔道、空手道、跆拳道等)

acrobatics [ˌækrəuˈbætiks] *n.* [pl.][用作单或复](=acrobatism)杂技

families 家

sects 派

schools 门

hull [hʌl] *n.* 壳,皮,荚,外部

One Hundred Children in the Long Spring 长春百子图

pit [pit] (使)与……竞争,与……较量

the International Table Tennis Federation 国际乒乓球联合会

the Thomas Cup 汤姆斯杯羽毛球赛

the Uber Cup 尤伯杯羽毛球赛

venue [ˈvenjuː] *n.* 聚集地点;会场;(尤指)体育比赛场所

The Chinese Basketball Association 中国篮球协会(也代指中国男子篮球职业联赛)

squad [skwɔd] *n.* 小组,小队,一小群人

The Chinese Football Association 中国足球协会

The Chinese Super League 中国足球超级联赛

Guqin, Go, calligraphy and painting 琴棋书画

pluck [plʌk] *vt.* 弹,拨(乐器)

zither [ˈziθə] *n.* 筝,齐特琴,扁琴

mahjong [ˈmɑːdʒɔŋ] *n.* 麻将牌,麻雀牌

Shuttlecock [ˈʃʌtlkɔk] Kicking 踢毽子

the China Shuttlecock Kicking Association 中国毽球协会

Muyuan 木鸢

Zhiyuan 纸鸢

centipede [ˈsentipiːd] *n.* 蜈蚣

the International Kite Federation 国际风筝联合会

Chinese yo-yo 空竹

Further Reading

1) **Sports and Recreations in Canada：**
http://en.wikipedia.org/wiki/Sport_in_Canada
http://en.wikipedia.org/wiki/Whitewater_recreation_in_Canada

http://www.britishcolumbia.com/recreation/? id=8

2) **Sports and Recreations in Australia**

http://en.wikipedia.org/wiki/Sport_in_Australia

http://www.dsr.wa.gov.au/recreation

3) **Sports and Recreations in New Zealand**

http://en.wikipedia.org/wiki/Sports_in_New_Zealand

http://en.wikipedia.org/wiki/Soccer_in_New_Zealand

http://en.wikipedia.org/wiki/Outdoor_Recreation_New_Zealand

Group Tasks

In your reading you will see that there is an element in "sports and recreation" that expresses something of the "national character" of people from the three nations we are studying. As we have seen, in terms of understanding people from English-speaking countries, we need to understand first of all ourselves as individuals within our own cultures; but to do that we need to recognise just how much of "our own culture" we actually own, in reality.

Exercise 1

For reflection upon this chapter, first consider how you as a person in your own right see "sport and recreations". Think about how much it means to you, what sort of things you do, what you like and what you avoid, and why. What is meaningful to you? What are your family traditions and expectations? To aid this process, write a paragraph in English, describing your real sport and recreation interests in the third person, as if you had inside knowledge of a stranger. Next, meet up with colleagues in a larger group than usual, but with people you do know; groups of 10-12 might be ideal. Bring with you the "third party description" of yourself and all of you place them into a container and mix them up. Take it in turns to pick a paper from the container and read the description out loud (in English!) to the others. Their task will be to listen and see if they can guess who wrote the description—see if they recognise you from your reflection upon your real interests and history. It does not matter if you happen to select your own paper, just read it anyway. Discuss together how you identify yourself as a person through your sport and recreation choices— how you pursue and shape your interests and how you, your family and your peers shape them. Try to form some sort of consensus about the relative importance of these aspects of your life to the whole of your life and how "well" you meet the norms and expectations of your perceived culture.

Exercise 2

Review the broad messages that the book imparts about the nature of sport and recreation in the three countries we are studying. Conduct some research on the Internet and in books or magazines to see how publications from each of the countries see and report the importance of sport and recreation within their own countries and globally. For instance, you might feel that the section on British sport references the importance of team games and how the game is played; the Americans, you may feel, get a great deal of their sport from spectating at huge events as mass entertainment and that the Chinese value sport and recreation as reflections of philosophies of life.

When you have formed a view summarising your understanding, deliberately seek evidence that challenges the information you have been given. For instance, in both America and Britain there are a huge number of "folk culture" games played with simple equipment and tools, as are emphasised in the Chinese section—and China is beginning to embrace massive spectator sports led by a growing leisure industry.

Don't overlook the important effects of video gaming and the Internet upon traditional sport and recreation activities and consider whether this too follows natural cultural patterns, or if it has a globalising effect, making the cultures less distinct in this respect. Ensure that you have a group discussion to share your thoughts and hear those of others. You might wish to have a debate on a proposal, such as:

Sport and recreation activities are/are not necessary for the advancement/betterment of human culture. (Modify or choose another interesting subject related to the topic to debate).

Chapter 10　Holidays and Festivals

Section A　Holidays and Festivals in the United Kingdom

Throughout the year the British celebrates many holidays and festivals which reflect the religious, historical, social and cultural diversity of the country. Some holidays and festivals are celebrated throughout the country and mark important events of the Christian calendar. Others are based on local customs and traditions in different regions. Among all these holidays and festivals, some of the typical ones are introduced here, such as New Year's Day, Epiphany, Burns Night, Valentine's Day, Mothering Sunday, Queen's Birthday and Boxing Day.

1. New Year's Day

New Year's Day is a public holiday in the U.K. on January 1 each year. It marks the start of the New Year in the Gregorian calendar.

December 31 is known as Hogmanay in Scotland and New Year's Eve in England, Wales and Northern Ireland. Many people spend most of December 31 quietly. They may spend time outdoors, reading the reviews of the last year in newspapers or resting in preparation for the New Year's Eve parties that begin in the late afternoon or evening. People who host parties may spend a large part of the day preparing food and arranging drinks. In the evening, New Year's Eve parties usually go on for many hours, well beyond midnight. Some, particularly young people, may choose to spend the evening in pubs, clubs or discos.

On New Year's Eve, just before midnight, people turn on a radio or television to see the countdown of the last few seconds of the old year and the display of fireworks just after midnight. People can see pictures of one of the four clocks on the Clock Tower on the Palace of Westminster or Houses of Parliament in London, counting down the last minute of the old year. At midnight, as the New Year begins, the chimes of Big Ben, the bell inside

New Year's Eve Celebration in London

the Clock Tower, are broadcast to mark the start of the New Year. At this point, people often hug and kiss each other, even strangers, and many start singing Auld Lang Syne, a poem written by Scottish poet Robert Burns.

In Scotland, the Hogmanay celebrations may last for one or two more days, as both January 1 and 2 are bank holidays. In the rest of the U.K., only January 1 is a bank holiday. Nearly all schools, large businesses and organizations are closed. In some areas stores may be open, although this varies a lot. Public transport systems do not usually run on their normal timetables. In general, public life shuts down completely on New Year's Day.

For many people, New Year's Day is time for recovering from the excesses of the night before. For others, it is the last day of the Christmas holiday before they return to work. Some take the opportunity to carry out home improvements or to go for a walk in the country. In many places around the coast, groups of people dress up in fancy costumes and run into the cold sea.

Usually, many people make New Year's resolutions. These are promises to themselves that they will lead a better life in some way in the coming year. Common New Year's resolutions include stopping smoking, losing weight, eating more healthily, getting more exercise or spending less money. Some types of resolution that would lead to a healthier lifestyle are supported by government advertising campaigns.

2. Epiphany

Epiphany or Twelfth Night marks the end of the Christmas and New Year season for most people in the U.K.. Many Christians around the world annually celebrate it on January 6. It is also an occasion for Christians to celebrate the three wise men's visit to Jesus shortly after his birth and Jesus' baptism.

People in the U.K. remove their Christmas decorations from their homes, schools and workplaces on or before Twelfth Night, and they believe that it is bad luck to display Christmas decorations after January 6. Decorations in town centers and shopping malls may stay on display for longer, as it can take many days or weeks to remove them all. The lights in these decorations are not generally turned on after January 6.

Three Wise Men's Visit to Infant Jesus

Some people hold Twelfth Night parties. They may serve a hot spicy punch called wassail or a Twelfth Night cake. A Twelfth Night cake usually contains one whole dried pea and one whole dried bean. The people who get the pea and the bean in their portion of cake are crowned king and queen for the evening. The first portion is always the "poor man's share", and is marked out by the youngest child of the family. There were also portions for those who were absent— the son in the army, or the fisherman who had been unable to return. The portion was stored until they came back. This was a way of saying "we were thinking about you". If it kept for a long time without crumbling or going mouldy, it was seen as a good omen.

3. Burns Night

Burns Night is annually celebrated in Scotland on or around January 25. It commemorates the life of the poet Robert Burns. The day also celebrates Burns' contribution to Scottish culture.

Robert Burns was born in Alloway, Scotland, in 1759, and he died in Dumfries, Scotland, in 1796. He was a poet and wrote many poems, lyrics and other pieces that addressed political and civil issues. Perhaps his best known work is "Auld Lang Syne", which is sung at New Year's Eve celebrations in Scotland, parts of the U.K. and other places around the world. Burns is one of Scotland's important cultural icons.

Burns and the Scottish Flag

The Tartan

Robert Burns' acquaintances held the first Burns' supper on July 21, the anniversary of his death, in Ayrshire, Scotland, in the late 1700s. The date was later changed to January 25, which marks his birthday. Burns' suppers are now held by people and organizations with Scottish origins worldwide, particularly in Australia, Canada, England and the U.S.. Formal events on this day include toasts and readings of pieces written by Robert Burns.

The Scottish flag is often displayed at Burns' Night celebrations. It is known as the Saltire and consists of a rectangular blue background with thick white bars on the diagonals.

At Burns' Night events, many men wear kilts and women may wear shawls, skirts or dresses made from their family tartan. A tartan was originally a woolen cloth with a distinctive pattern made by using colors of weft and warp when weaving. Particular patterns and combinations of colors were associated with different areas, clans and families. Tartan patterns are now printed on various materials.

The evening centers on the entrance of the haggis (a type of sausage prepared in a sheep's stomach) on a large platter to the sound of a piper playing bagpipes. When the haggis is on the table, the host reads the "Address to a Haggis" which is an ode that Robert Burns wrote to the Scottish dish. At the end of the reading, the haggis is ceremonially sliced into two pieces and the meal begins. Whisky is the traditional drink.

Burns' Night is an observance but it is not a bank holiday in the U.K..

4. Valentine's Day

Valentine's Day is a lovers' festival which is celebrated on February 14. Many people send Valentine's Day cards, gifts or text messages to their partner or somebody for whom they have romantic feelings. Cards and gifts are traditionally sent anonymously in the U.K. even if they are from a partner or spouse.

Valentine's Day has been celebrated in the U.K. for thousands of years. It probably originates from a pagan fertility festival in pre-Roman times. There was a Roman festival called Lupercalia in the middle of February to mark the start of spring. There were a range of fertility and marriage rites associated with Lupercalia. As Christianity spread across the Roman Empire, including much of the U.K., this festival became a day of remembrance for St Valentine.

The Catholic Church recognizes at least three different saints named Valentine, all of whom were martyred. One legend contends that Valentine was a priest who served during the 3rd century in Rome. When Emperor Claudius II decided that single men made better soldiers than those with wives and families, he outlawed marriage for young men. Valentine, realizing the injustice of the decree, defied Claudius and continued to perform marriages for young lovers in secret. When Valentine's actions were discovered, Claudius ordered that he be put to death.

Other stories suggest that Valentine may have been killed for attempting to help Christians escape harsh Roman prisons, where they were often beaten and tortured. According to one legend, an imprisoned Valentine actually sent the first "valentine" greeting himself after he fell in love with a young girl. Before his death, it is alleged that he wrote her a letter signed "From your Valentine", an expression that is still in use today. Although the truth behind the Valentine legends is murky, all stories emphasize his appeal as a sympathetic, heroic and romantic figure.

Popular Valentine's Day gifts include chocolates and other types of candy, red roses or bunches of flowers, Champagne or other sparkling wines, lingerie or other clothing, electronic gadgets or accessories (including USB sticks and skins for laptops, net books and mobile phones), a surprise meal in a restaurant or night in a hotel, a short break in the U.K. or abroad. Many couples try to eat a special meal with each other, and they may do this in a restaurant, hotel room or at home. Some opt for food and drink with a romantic feel, such as oysters, chocolate fondue, strawberries and champagne. Others choose less formal, but easily prepared dishes.

Valentine's Day symbols include red or pink hearts, red roses, teddy bears with roses or hearts and couples kissing or holding each other. These symbols are printed on cards, wrapping paper, lingerie

Valentine's Day Gifts

and clothing and made of chocolate or other types of food.

Pictures or models of Cupid are also often displayed on Valentine's Day in the U.K.. Cupid is usually portrayed as a small winged figure with a bow and arrow. According to mythology, he uses his bow and arrow to strike romantic love into people's hearts.

February 14 is not a public holiday in the U.K..

Picture of Cupid in the Card

5. Mothering Sunday

Mothering Sunday is held on the fourth Sunday of Lent in the U.K.. It is exactly three weeks before Easter Sunday and usually falls in the second half of March or the beginning of April.

In most countries, Mother's Day is a recent observance derived from the holiday as it has evolved in the U.S.. As adopted by other countries and cultures, the holiday has different meanings, is associated with different events (religious, historical or legendary), and is celebrated on different dates. In Britain, Mothering Sunday and Mother's Day have now been mixed up, and many people think that they are the same thing, even though they are celebrated on different dates.

Mothering Sunday was originally a time when people returned to the church in which they were baptized or where they attended services when they were children. This meant that families were reunited as adults returned to the towns and villages where they grew up. In time, it became customary for young people who were working as servants in large houses, to be given a holiday on Mothering Sunday. They could use this day to visit their own mother and often took a gift of food or hand-me-down clothing from their employers to her.

A Simnel Cake

Mothering Sunday or Mother's Day is now a day to honor mothers and other mother figures, such as grandmothers, stepmothers and mother-in-laws. Many people make a special effort to visit their mother. They take cards and gifts to her and may treat her to a meal.

Traditionally, many people prepared a Simnel cake to eat with their family on Mothering Sunday. A Simnel cake is a light fruit cake covered with a layer of marzipan and with a layer of marzipan baked in the middle of the cake. Traditionally, Simnel cakes are decorated with 11 or 12 balls of marzipan, representing the 11 disciples and, sometimes, Jesus Christ. One legend says that the cake was named after Lambert Simnel who worked in the kitchens of Henry VII of England sometime around the year 1500.

Mothering Sunday is not a bank holiday in the U.K..

6. Queen's Birthday

One of Britain's most impressive and colorful festivals is the Queen's birthday celebrations. The Queen has two birthdays, one in April (the Queen's actual birthday is on April 21) and one in June (the Queen's Official birthday or Trooping the Color ceremony).

No particular ceremony is held on the Queen's actual birthday, although the Union Flag is flown on public buildings. The Queen usually spends her actual birthday at Windsor Castle, where Prince Charles will host a family dinner.

The Queen's Official Birthday is the selected day on which the birthday of the monarch of the Commonwealth realms (currently Queen Elizabeth II) is officially celebrated in those countries. The date varies as adopted by each Commonwealth country, but is generally around the end of May to the start of June, to coincide with a high probability of fine weather in the Northern Hemisphere for outdoor ceremonies.

The day is marked in London by the ceremony of Trooping the Color, which is also known as the Queen's Birthday Parade. The list of Birthday Honors is also announced at the time of the Official Birthday celebrations. In British diplomatic missions, the day is treated as the National Day of the U.K.. Although it is not celebrated as a specific public holiday in the U.K., some civil servants are given a "privilege day" at this time of year, which is often merged with the Spring Bank Holiday (last Monday in May) to create a long weekend, which was partly created to celebrate the monarch's birthday.

Queen's Birthday Parade

Since 1748, Trooping the Color has marked the official birthday of the British sovereign. It is held in London annually on a Saturday in June on Horse Guards Parade by St. James's Park. Among the audience are the Royal Family, invited guests, ticketholders and the general public. The colorful ceremony, also known as "The Queen's Birthday Parade", is broadcast live by the BBC.

The Queen travels down The Mall from Buckingham Palace in a royal procession with a sovereign's escort of Household Cavalry (mounted troops or horse guards). After receiving a royal salute, she inspects her troops of the Household Division, both foot guards and horse guards, and the King's Troop, Royal Horse Artillery. Each year, one of the foot guards regiments is selected to troop its color through the ranks of guards. Then the entire Household Division assembly conducts a march past the Queen, who receives a salute from the saluting base.

The music is provided by the massed bands of the foot guards and the mounted bands of the Household Cavalry, together with a Corps of Drums, and occasionally pipers, totaling approximately 400 musicians.

Returning to Buckingham Palace, the Queen watches a further march-past from outside the gates. Following a 41-gun salute by the King's Troop in Green Park, she leads the Royal Family on to the palace balcony for a Royal Air Force flypast.

The Queen's 80th birthday in 2006 was marked by a large flypast of 40 planes led by the Battle of Britain Memorial Flight and culminating with the Red Arrows. It was followed by the first

The Queen at Trooping the Color

feu de joie ("fire of joy") fired in her presence during her reign, a second being fired at her Diamond Jubilee celebrations in 2012.

7. Boxing Day

Boxing Day in the U.K. is the day after Christmas Day and falls on December 26. Traditionally, it was a day when employers distributed money, food, cloth or other valuable goods to their employees. In modern times, it is an important day for sporting events and the start of the post-Christmas sales.

There are a number of stories behind the origin of the term "Boxing Day". It used to be customary for employers to give their employees or servants a gift of money or food in a small box on this day. This is still customary for people who deliver letters or newspapers, although the gift may be given before Christmas Day. In feudal times, the lord of the manor would gather all those who worked on his land together on this day and distribute boxes of practical goods, such as agricultural

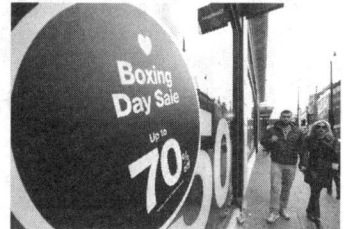

Boxing Day Sale

tools, food and cloth. This was payment for the work that they had done throughout the passed year.

For many people, Boxing Day is a time to recover from the excesses of Christmas day and an opportunity to spend time with family, friends and neighbors. Some people choose to go for a

Boxing Day Hunt

walk in the countryside, while others flock to the post-Christmas sales in large stores that often begin on Boxing Day. Some people even spend part of the night and early morning queuing to get into the stores when the best bargains are still available.

Boxing Day is also an important day for sports events. Traditionally, using dogs to hunt for foxes was a popular sport amongst the upper classes. Pictures of hunters on horseback dressed in red coats and surrounded by hunting

223

dogs are often seen as symbolic of Boxing Day. Nowadays, fox hunting is outlawed; horse racing and football (soccer) are now popular sports.

Boxing Day is a bank holiday. Many people travel to visit family or friends in this period, so bus, plane and train services can be very busy.

Whether they are local, regional or national, all these holidays or festivals have something in common, that is, they provide an opportunity for families and friends to get together to visit, eat, and exchange good wishes.

Section B Holidays and Festivals in the United States of America

Holidays in the U.S. usually occur at least once a month. Most months have a national holiday that has been arranged to be celebrated on a Monday. The holidays have all been decided to be celebrated on a Monday so that the workers may have 3-day weekends in order to rest or travel or do things with their families. Some major holidays and festivals in the U.S. are introduced in this part, such as New Year's Day, Easter Sunday, Mother's Day, Father's Day, Halloween, Thanksgiving Day and Christmas Day.

1. New Year's Day

New Year's Day is the first day of the new year. On the modern Gregorian calendar, it falls on January 1st. It marks the end of New Year's Eve celebrations and gives many Americans a chance to remember the previous year.

Like many people all over the world, Americans enjoy celebrating the arrival of each New Year. Almost everyone makes an occasion of New Year's Eve in order to see the old year out and welcome the new one. New Year's Eve is a major social holiday for many people in the U.S., and people hold parties at home or attend special celebrations, where alcohol, such as wine and champagne, may be consumed to celebrate the upcoming New Year. A particularly striking aspect of the New Year's Eve festivities is the ball drop in Times Square in Manhattan, New York City. The ball is made of crystal and elec-

Ball Drop in Times Square

tric lights and is placed on top of a pole, which is 77 feet high. At one minute before midnight on December 31, the ball is lowered slowly down the pole. It comes to rest at the bottom of the pole at exactly midnight. When the moment arrives, bedlam breaks forth. Bells ring, whistles blow, people cheer with their happy excitement.

The cheerful scene goes one after another in public squares throughout the country, but not at the same moment. Because of the four time zones in the U.S., the New Year comes to the Central States one hour later, to the Mountain States two hours later, and finally to the Western States three hours after the Eastern States have said goodbye to another year.

Some people prefer to see the old year out at a church service, although the holiday does not have religious origin. Many churches hold "Watch Night" services[1] on New Year's Eve, and those who go to churches can solemnly renew their dedication to God for the coming year.

The custom of visiting friends, relatives and neighbors is one of the popular activities on New Year's Day. This activity is called Open House. This custom was brought by the Dutch when they first came to New York. An Open House is just what the name implies: the front door is left open. Inside the door there is a spirit of relaxed cordiality, and guests are free to arrive and leave as they like. Invitations are very simple, like "Drop in after the game" or "Come to drink a New Year's toast with us". On January 1, now, families hold "Open House" so that their friends can visit them throughout the day to express good wishes for the New Year.

The Rose Parade

Many championship football games are scheduled for New Year's Day, and there is usually an elaborate parade before each football game. Often, much of the day is spent watching these games on television. Most Americans begin their New Year's Day watching at least part of the Rose Parade. In 1890, some people living in sunny and warm Pasadena picked flowers from their gardens and put them on their horses and buggies and on New Year's Day drove through their small town of Pasadena. Now because of TV, this flower-filled, two-or-three-hour parade has become part of New Year's Day, especially welcomed in the cold and snowy parts of north America.

Government offices, organizations, schools and many businesses are closed in the U.S. on New Year's Day. Public transit systems do not run on their regular schedules. Where large public celebrations have been held, traffic may be disrupted by the clean-up operation. In general, public life is completely closed down.

2. Easter Sunday

Many Christians celebrate Jesus Christ's resurrection on Easter Sunday. The Easter date depends on the ecclesiastical approximation of the March equinox, and it falls on the first Sunday after the full moon that occurs on or after March 21st.

Many churches hold special services on Easter Sunday to celebrate the Jesus Christ's resurrection after his crucifixion. In Christian times, the crucifixion is remembered on Good Friday and the resurrection is remembered on Easter Sunday. The idea of the resurrection joined with the ideas of re-birth in Pagan beliefs. In Pagan times, many groups of people organized spring festivals. Many of these celebrated the re-birth of nature, the return of the land to fertility and the birth of many young animals.

Many people celebrate Easter Sunday by decorating, exchanging or searching for eggs. The eggs may be fresh or boiled eggs laid by chickens or other birds, chocolate eggs or eggs made of other materials. Many children believe that the Easter bunny or rabbit comes to their house or garden to hide eggs, and they may search for these eggs. Some businesses and attractions hold Easter egg hunts. These can be competitions to see who can collect the most eggs. People roll hard boiled eggs down slopes or a-

Easter Egg Hunts

gainst other people's eggs. The winner is the person whose egg remains whole. After the game, the eggs are eaten. Eggs, rabbits, hares and young animals are thought to represent the re-birth and return to fertility of nature in the spring.

Easter Parades

Easter is celebrated in U.S. with traditional fervor and gaiety. Sunday church services and festive celebrations blend together during the Easter weekend. On Easter Sunday in New York and other cities, large Easter parades are held where people turn out in their fashionable outfits and trendy Easter bonnets. The person leading the parade holds Easter candle or cross in his hand. Easter festivity can be observed here in the well decorated markets and beautifully adorned homes across the city.

Easter Sunday is not a federal holiday, but a number of stores are closed in many parts of the U.S., and if they are open, they may have limited trading hours. In some cities, public transit systems usually run their regular Sunday schedules, but it is best to check with the local transport authorities if any changes will be implemented during Easter Sunday.

3. Mother's Day

Mother's Day in the U.S. is annually held on the second Sunday of May. It celebrates motherhood and it is a time to appreciate mothers and mother figures. Many people give gifts, cards, flowers, candy, a meal in a restaurant or other treats to their mothers and mother figures.

Although many Mother's Day celebrations world-wide have

Anna Jarvis

quite different origins and traditions, most have now been influenced by the more recent American tradition established by Anna Jarvis. In 1907, Anna Jarvis held a private Mother's Day celebration in memory of her mother, Ann Jarvis, and then she campaigned to establish Mother's Day first as a U.S. national holiday and later as an international holiday. The holiday was declared officially by the state of West Virginia in 1910, and the rest of the states followed quickly. On May 10, 1913, the U.S. House of Representatives passed a resolution calling on all federal government officials to wear a white carnation the following day in observance of Mother's Day. On May 8, 1914, the U.S. Congress passed a law designating the second Sunday in May as Mother's Day and requesting a proclamation. The next day, President Woodrow Wilson issued the first proclamation making Mother's Day an official national holiday. The Grafton church, where the first celebration was held, is now the International Mother's Day Shrine.

Carnations have come to represent Mother's Day since Anna Jarvis delivered 500 of them at the first celebration. Anna Jarvis chose the carnation because it was the favorite flower of her mother, and white carnations also represented the sweetness, purity and endurance of mother love. In part due to the shortage of white carnations, and in part due to the efforts to expand the sales of more types of flowers in Mother's Day, florists invented the idea of wearing a red carnation if one's mother was living, or a white one if she was dead.

Common Mother's Day gifts are flowers, chocolate, candy, clothing, jewelry and treats, such as a beauty treatment or a trip to a spa. Some families organize an outing for all of their members or hold a special meal at home or in a restaurant. In the days and weeks before Mother's Day, many schools help their pupils to prepare handmade cards or small gifts for their mothers. All people have the same purpose, to express the love, gratitude and reverence for their mothers.

Mother's Day is not a federal holiday. Organizations, businesses and stores are open or closed, just as they are on any other Sunday in the year. Public transit systems run to their normal Sunday schedules. Restaurants may be busier than usual, as some people take their mothers out for a treat.

4. Father's Day

Father's Day in the U.S. is on the third Sunday of June. Observing the day, people reflect on the invaluable role played by fathers in building the character of children and in the development of the nation. On Father's Day, people honor their father and express gratitude for his love and affection. As a Father's Day tradition, people in U.S. also pay tribute to other father figures.

A woman called Sonora Smart Dodd, a loving daughter from Spokane, was an influential figure in the establishment of Father's Day. Sonora attended a Mother's Day Sermon in 1909 and she was inspired by the work of Anna Jarvis. Sonora was struck with the noble idea that society must observe a day to honor the important contribution made by father in the raising of children.

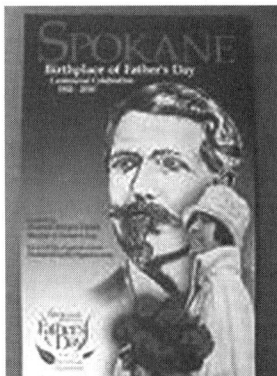

Sonora Smart Dodd

Encouraged by the love of her father who was a civil war veteran and single-handedly raised her along with her five siblings after the death of her mother, Sonora worked hard to make her concept a reality. The noble idea of celebrating Father's Day soon spread across the nation. Father's Day was recognized by a Joint Resolution of Congress in 1956. Finally, Father's Day was officially recognized as a holiday in 1972 by President Nixon.

Common Father's Day gifts include sports items or clothing, electronic gadgets, outdoor cooking supplies and tools for household maintenance. Besides, the red and white rose is recognized as the official Father's Day flower. Father's Day is a relatively modern holiday, so different families have a range of traditions. These can range from simple phone calls or greeting cards to large parties honoring all of the "father" figures in a particular extended family.

Father's Day is not a federal holiday. Organizations, businesses and stores are open or closed, just as they are on any other Sunday in the year. Public transit systems also run to their normal Sunday schedules.

5. Halloween

Many Americans celebrate Halloween on October 31. Halloween is a big deal in the U.S. for kids and adults alike. Halloween originated as a pagan festival in parts of Northern Europe, particularly around what is now the U.K.. Many European cultural traditions hold that Halloween is a time when magic is most potent and spirits can make contact with the physical world. In Christian times, it became a celebration of the evening before All Saints' Day [2]. Immigrants from Scotland and Ireland brought the holiday to the U.S..

Halloween is usually celebrated amongst family, friends and, sometimes, co-workers. However, some areas hold large community events. Parties and other events may be planned on October 31 or in the weekends before and after this date. Adults may celebrate by watching horror films, holding costume parties or creating haunted houses or graveyards.

Trick or Treat

For Children, dressing up and trick or treat door to door is still the main event. Many children dress up in fancy costumes and visit other homes in the neighborhood. At each house, they demand sweets, snacks or a small gift. If they do not get this, they threaten to do some harm to the inhabitants of the house. This is known as playing "trick-or-treat" and is supposed to happen in a friendly spirit, with no nasty or mean tricks being carried out.

Some families carve lanterns with "scary" faces out of pumpkins or other vegetables and decorate their homes and gardens in Halloween style. These were traditionally intended to ward off evil spirits. If you are at home on Halloween, it is a good idea to have a bowl of small presents or sweets to offer to anyone who knocks on your door. This will help you to please the little spirits in your neighborhood.

One cause that ties with Halloween is collecting donations for the United Nations International Children's Emergency Fund (UNICEF). As children trick-or-treat on Halloween night, some of them might carry small cardboard boxes with the UNICEF logo on them and collect coins instead of the usual candy. The money collected is then given to UNICEF and used to help needy children worldwide.

There are various symbols associated with Halloween. These include the spooks, ghosts and walking skeletons that represent the contact between the spiritual and physical world, and between the living and the dead. Human figures that are often represented on Halloween are witches and wizards, who are believed to have the power to contact with the spirit world. Bats, black cats and spiders are often connected with this holiday. These animals are associated with the night and darkness and often accompany witches and wizards. There are also a range of objects associated with Halloween. These include blood, fire, gravestones, pumpkins, bones and skulls. They all have connections with death, the spirit world or protecting property from evil spirits. Many of these objects are now available in stores as decorations for the Halloween season.

Halloween is not an official holiday. Government offices and businesses are open as usual and public transit services run on regular schedules.

6. Thanksgiving Day

Thanksgiving Day is a harvest festival, and is America's preeminent day. It is celebrated on the fourth Thursday of November. Many people trace the origins of the modern Thanksgiving Day to the harvest celebration that the Pilgrims held in Plymouth, Massachusetts in 1621. Because of the religious persecution by the established church in England, the pilgrims left their land with the purpose of enjoying religious freedom. They crossed the Atlantic in the year 1620 on a ship called the Mayflower. About 102 people traveled for nearly two months with extreme difficulty, and when they arrived at

First Thanksgiving Day Feast

Plymouth, Massachusetts, it was November. The first winter was very difficult for them and over half of them died because of hunger and illness, hard work and severely cold weather. In the following spring, the Indians taught them how to grow corn, showed them to grow other crops in the unfamiliar soil and how to hunt and fish. In the summer of 1621, owing to severe drought, pilgrims called for a day of fasting and prayer to please God and ask for a bountiful harvest in the coming season. God answered their prayers and it rained at the end of the day. It saved the corn crops, and the pilgrims had a bumper harvest that year. The pilgrims thought that the harvest was a kind of deliverance by God, so they decided to have a day of celebration after their harvest to express their thanks to God, and they also invited the Indians in gratitude.

From the time of the Founding Fathers[3] to the time of Lincoln, the date of Thanksgiving varied from state to state. The final Thursday in November had become the customary date in most U.S. states by the beginning of the 19th century. Thanksgiving was first celebrated on the same date by all states in 1863 by a presidential proclamation of Abraham Lincoln. In 1941, President Franklin D. Roosevelt signed a joint resolution of Congress changing the national Thanksgiving Day from the last Thursday in November to the fourth Thursday.

Thanksgiving Day is a time for many people to give thanks for what they have, and it is traditionally a day for families and friends to get together for a special meal. The meal often includes a turkey, stuffing, potatoes, cranberry sauce, gravy, pumpkin pie, and vegetables.

Thanksgiving Day parades are held in some cities and towns on or around Thanksgiving Day. Some parades or festivities also mark the opening of the Christmas shopping season.

Most government offices, businesses, schools and other organizations are closed on Thanksgiving Day. Some people have a four-day weekend so it is a popular time for trips and to visit family and friends. Public transit systems do not usually operate on their regular timetables. It is one of the busiest periods for travel in the U.S., which can cause congestion and overcrowding.

7. Christmas Day

Christmas Day, which is the most festive time in the U.S., falls on December 25. The name Christmas is short for "Christ's Mass". A Mass is a kind of Church service. The original meaning of Christmas is a special church service, or mass, to celebrate the birth of Jesus Christ.

According to the Bible, God decided to allow his only son, Jesus Christ, to be born to a human mother and live on earth so that people could understand God better and learn to love God and each other more. "Christmas" meaning "celebration of Christ" honors the time when Jesus was born to a young Jewish woman Mary. Mary was engaged to be married to Joseph, a carpenter, but before they came together, she was found to be with child. Because Joseph, her husband, was a righteous man and did not want to expose her to public disgrace, he had in mind to divorce her quietly. An angel of the Lord appeared to him in a dream and said, "Do not be afraid to take Mary home as your wife, because what is conceived in her is from the Holy Spirit. She will give birth to a son, and you are to give him the name Jesus, because he will save his people from their sins."

However, the Bible does not give a precise date for the birth of Jesus. It is also unclear when December 25 became associated with the birth of Jesus. The idea of turning this day into a celebration started in the early Middle Ages in Europe. During Reformation and up until the middle of the 1800s, Christmas was often not celebrated because partying and merry making was seen as unchristian. From about 1840, celebrating Christmas became more widespread. December 25 was declared a federal holiday in the U.S. in 1870. Since then Christmas Day has become a steadily more important holiday.

People in the U.S. celebrate Christmas Day in many ways. In the days before Christmas Day, many people decorate their homes and driveways with seasonal decorations. The centerpiece of the decorations is often a Christmas tree decorated with fairy lights, tinsel, angels, stars and other seasonal ornaments. Outdoor light sculptures are also becoming increasingly popular. These are many light bulbs or LEDs in the form of trees, sleighs, reindeer, Santa Claus, snowmen and other seasonal figures. Light sculptures may be placed on driveways, roofs or in gardens.

Santa Claus and the Reindeer

Christmas Eve is the day before Christmas Day. In the evening, often just before bedtime, many families, particularly those with children, will hang up stockings on the fireplace or the end of their bed. These Christmas stockings are often red with a white fluffy trim, although they may be of any design and are often much bigger than the socks that they represent. Children hope that Santa Claus, a mythical figure thought to represent an ancient European saint, will enter their home via the chimney and fill their stockings with gifts.

On Christmas Day, it is common to organize a special meal, often consisting of turkey and a lot of other festive foods, for family or friends and exchange gifts with them. Children, in particular, often receive a lot of gifts from their parents and other relatives. This has led to Christmas Day becoming an increasingly commercialized holiday, with a lot of families spending a large part of their income on gifts and food.

Government offices, organizations, businesses and schools are closed, almost without exception. Many people visit relatives or friends who are out of town. This may cause congestion on highways and at airports. Public transit systems do not run on their regular schedules. In general, public life closes down completely.

In the U.S., many holidays are uniquely their own and many have been borrowed from other countries. America is a country of many cultures and many holidays.

Section C   Holidays and Festivals in China

As China is a vast land and has many ethnic groups, different ethnic groups have different festivals in different places. Even on the same festival, they follow different customs. Characterized by diverse styles and themes, traditional Chinese festivals are an important part of the country's history and culture, both ancient and modern.

The formation of traditional festivals is a long process of historical and cultural accumulation in a nation or a state. Festival activities always reflect primitive sacrifice, superstitious taboo and earthly life, people's spirit and religious influence. Moreover, traditional Chinese festivals were often connected with ancient astronomy, calendars and mathematics. Most traditional festivals took shape during the Qin Dynasty. In the most prosperous Tang Dynasty, traditional festivals liberated themselves from primitive sacrifice, taboo and mystery, and became more entertaining. Gradually, festive occasions turned more brisk and exciting and more folk customs were developed. Some festivals and customs we still follow today, but others disappeared into the mists of time.

1. Spring Festival

The Spring Festival, also called Lunar New Year, falls on the first day of the first lunar month, often one month later than the Gregorian calendar, and the exact days are different in every year according to the lunar calendar. But in folk custom, this traditional holiday lasts from the twenty-third day of the twelfth month to the fifteenth day of the first month in the lunar calendar. Among these days, the Spring Festival Eve and the first three days of the New Year are the peak time. The Spring Festival is the most important one among the traditional festivals for the Chinese people. The Chinese government now stipulates that people have seven days off for the Chinese Lunar New Year. All people living away from home go back, and airports, railway stations and long-distance bus stations are crowded with home returnees.

The Spring Festival originated in the Shang Dynasty from people's sacrifice to gods and ancestors at the end of an old year and the beginning of a new one. Celebrating the Spring Festival came to be a widespread social custom in the Han Dynasty. The customs of worshipping deities and ancestors remain even though the ceremonies are not as grand as before. It is also the time that spring is coming, so people hold all kinds of ceremonies to welcome it.

There are many legends about Spring Festival in Chinese culture. A widely-accepted folklore depicts Nian as a strong monster

Monster Nian

moving faster than the wind and howling louder than the thunder. Since it had eaten and hurt numerous people and cattle, God chained it amid the remote mountains as a punishment and only allowed it to come out once a year. On the night of December 30, all the people hid at home and stayed all night to prepare for the sudden attack of Nian, since no one knew the exact time when the monster would break in. The way people spending the night was just like striving for a pass, and therefore, Nian was also called "Nian Guan" (literally means the pass of Nian). However, when Nian came out one year, it was suddenly frightened by the crack of burning bamboo, dazzled by a red coat hanging on the clothesline and got blinded by the shining lamp in a village. So after that, people made use of red color, loud sound and fire flash to scare it away. Traditionally, people pasted red paper onto doors and windows, set off fireworks or firecrackers, beat drums, stroke gongs, and lit lamps in the house.

Couplets

Red Paper-cuttings

The holiday season includes various traditional activities with strong ethnic flavors. The twenty-third day of the twelfth lunar month is called Preliminary Eve. At this time, people offer sacrifice to the kitchen god. Now however, most families make delicious food to enjoy by themselves. Before the New Year comes, people completely clean indoors and outdoors of their homes as well as their clothes, bedclothes and all their utensils. Then people begin decorating their clean rooms featuring an atmosphere of rejoicing and festivity. Red paper-cuttings can be seen on window glass and brightly colored New Year paintings with auspicious meanings may be put on the wall. All the door panels will be pasted with Spring Festival couplets. The content varies from house owners' wishes for a bright future to good luck for the New Year. The Chinese character "Fu" (meaning blessing or happiness) is a must. The character put on paper can be pasted normally or upside down, for in Chinese the "reversed Fu" is homophonic with "Fu comes". Also, pictures of the god of doors and wealth will be posted on front doors to ward off evil spirits and welcome peace and abundance. What's more, two big red lanterns can be raised on both sides of the front door.

People attach great importance to Spring Festival Eve. At that time, all family members eat dinner together. The meal is more luxurious than usual. Dishes such as chicken, fish and bean curd cannot be excluded, for in Chinese, their pronunciations, "ji", "yu" and "doufu", respectively mean auspiciousness, abundance and richness. After the dinner, the whole family will sit together, chatting and watching TV. In recent years, the Spring Festival Gala broadcast on China Central Television Station (CCTV) is an essential entertainment for the Chinese both at home and abroad. According to custom, each family will stay up to see the New Year in.

On the first morning of the Spring Festival, people greet with each other with lunar New

New Year Cake

Year wishes. Giving red packets or red envelopes is another famous tradition. Red packets, which are simply red envelopes with money inside to symbolize luck and wealth. Red packets are handed out to younger generations by parents, grandparents, relatives and friends, and the practice represents a desire for good fortune and wealth in the coming year. Besides, people in northern China will eat dumplings, as the shape of the dumpling is like gold ingot from ancient China, and people eat them and wish for money and treasure. Southern Chinese eat "niangao" (New Year cake made of glutinous rice flour) on this occasion, because as a homophone, "niangao" means "higher and higher, one year after another".

People have many taboos regarding the Spring Festival. Many bad words related to "death", "broken", "killing", "ghost" and "illness" are forbidden during conversations. In some places, there are more specific details. They consider it unlucky if the barrel of rice is empty, because they think they will have nothing to eat in the next year. Taking medicine is forbidden on this day; otherwise, people will be sick for the whole year and take medicine constantly. Sweeping floor was forbidden for fear of sweeping the good luck away. Although partly from superstitions, all those customs reflect people's good wishes for a safe and sound year.

Fireworks and Firecrackers

Burning fireworks was once the most typical custom during the Spring Festival. People thought the spluttering sound could help drive away evil spirits. However, in recent years, such an activity has been completely or partially forbidden in big cities as the government took security and pollution factors into consideration.

The lively atmosphere not only fills every household, but permeates to streets and lanes. A series of activities such as lion dancing, dragon lantern dancing, and temple fairs will be held for days. The Spring Festival then comes to an end when the Lantern Festival is finished.

2. Lantern Festival

The Lantern Festival falls on the fifteenth day of the first lunar month, usually in February or March in the Gregorian calendar. As the first festival after the Spring Festival and the first appearance of the full moon in the new year, the Lantern Festival was thought auspicious in ancient times. Since the first lunar month was also called "Yuan month" and the night was called "Xiao", thus came the name "Yuan Xiao" in Chinese.

The Lantern Festival has a history of more than 2,000 years. As early as in the Western

Han Dynasty, it had become a festival of great significance. After the death of Liu Bang, the first emperor of Han Dynasty, his wife Queen Lv seized the throne. After her death, Zhou Bo, a general, and Chen Ping, a prime minister, helped subdue the insurrection of Lv's relatives and supported Liu Heng, Liu Bang's son to the throne, who was titled Emperor Wen of the Han Dynasty in the history. Since the date of subduing the insurrection was the fifteenth day of the first lunar month, Emperor Wen went out of his palace on this night every year to celebrate it with common people. Therefore, "Yuan Xiao" Festival was established by the emperor.

The name "Lantern Festival" originated from the custom of decorating and appreciating the lanterns. In the East Han Dynasty, Buddhism was introduced to China. One emperor heard that Buddhist monks would watch "sarira" or remains from the cremation of Buddha's body, and light lanterns to worship Buddha on the fifteenth day of the first lunar month, so he ordered to light lanterns in the imperial palace and temples to show respect to Buddha on this day. Later, the Buddhist rite developed into a grand festival among common people and its influence expanded from the Central Plains to the whole China. Till today, the lantern

Red Lanterns

festival is still held each year around the country. When the festival comes, red lanterns can be seen in the street, and in each house. In the parks, lanterns of various shapes and types attract countless visitors. Children will hold self-made or buy lanterns to stroll on the streets.

"Guessing lantern riddles" is an essential part of the Festival. Lantern owners write riddles on a piece of paper and post them on the lanterns. If visitors have solutions to the riddles, they can pull the paper out and go to the lantern owners to check their answers. If they are right, they will get a small gift. The activity emerged during people's enjoyment of lanterns in the Song Dynasty. As riddle guessing is interesting and full of wisdom, it has become popular among all social strata.

The food Yuanxiao (glutinous rice ball), is an indispensable dish for every household on this day. It is the small dumpling ball made of glutinous rice flour, and it can be stuffed or not. The stuffing can either be sweet or salty, and the sweet ones include sugar, walnut, sesame, bean paste or jujube paste, while the salty ones include meat and vegetables. Yuanxiao can be boiled, fried or steamed, and it tastes delicious. What's more, Yuanxiao is round in shape, meaning reunion. Therefore, people eat them to denote union, harmony and happiness for the family.

In the daytime of the Festival, performances such as a dragon lantern dance, a lion dance, a land boat dance, a Yangge dance, walking on stilts and beating drums while dancing will be staged. On the night, besides magnificent lanterns, fireworks also form a beautiful scene. Most families spare some fireworks from the Spring Festival and set them off on the Lantern Festival. In the night, when the first full moon enters the New Year, people become really intoxicated by the imposing fireworks and bright moon in the sky.

For its rich and colorful activities, it is regarded as the most recreational among all the Chinese festivals and a day for appreciating the bright full moon and family reunion.

3. Qingming Festival

The Qingming Festival (also known as Tomb-sweeping Day) is one of the 24 seasonal division points in China, falling on either April 4th or 5th of the Gregorian calendar each year. After the festival, the temperature will rise up and rainfall increases. It is the high time for spring plowing and sowing. But the Qingming Festival is not only a seasonal point to guide farm work, it is more a festival of commemoration.

It is said that the Qingming Festival was originally held to commemorate a loyal man living in the Spring and Autumn Period, named Jie Zitui. Jie cut a piece of meat from his own leg in order to save his hungry lord who was forced to go into exile when the crown was in jeopardy. The lord came back to his position 19 years later and forgot Jie Zitui, but later felt ashamed and decided to reward him. However, Jie had blocked himself up in a mountain with his mother. In order to find Jie, the lord ordered

The Story of Jie Zitui

that the mountain should be set on fire. The fire lasted three whole days and nights, yet to the lord's disappointment, Jie never came out. In the end, Jie and his mother's burned bodies were found. The local people admired Jie Zitui for his moral integrity, and in order to commemorate Jie, they ate cold food and restrained from making fire on that day and the following two days. The Hanshi Festival was usually one day before the Qingming Festival. As our ancestors often extended the day to the Qingming, they were later combined.

Qingming Festival is a time of many different activities, among which the main ones are tomb sweeping, taking a spring outing and flying kites. Some other lost customs like wearing willow branches on the head and riding on swings have added infinite joy in past days. The Qingming Festival sees a combination of sadness and happiness.

Tomb sweeping is regarded as the most important custom in the Qingming Festival, so the Qingming Festival is also called Tomb-sweeping Day. Both the Han and minority ethnic groups at this time offer sacrifices to their ancestors and sweep the tombs of the deceased. Weeds around the tomb are cleared away and fresh soil is added to show care of the dead. The dead person's favorite food and wine are taken to sacrifice to them, along with incense and paper money. Kowtow before the memorial tablets set up for the dead are made. However, with cremation taking over from burying, today the customs have been greatly simplified in cities.

Tomb-sweeping

Only flowers are presented to show good prayers for the deceased.

In contrast to the sadness of the tomb sweepers, people also enjoy hope of spring on this day. Literally, "Qing" means purity and "Ming" means brightness. The Qingming Festival is a time when the sun shines brightly, the trees and grass become green and nature is again lively, which probably is the true meaning of "Qingming". Since ancient times, people have followed the custom of spring outings which were also called "Ta Qing" (tapping on the green grass) in Chinese. In old days, when people went spring outings, they either wore green willow wickers on their heads or hung them on the top of their sedan chairs to ward off evil spirits.

The Qingming Festival is also a time to plant trees, for the survival rate of saplings is high and trees grow fast later. In the past, the Qingming Festival was called "Arbor Day". But since 1979, "Arbor Day" was settled on March 12 according to the Gregorian calendar.

Besides, ancient people used to fly kites, play tug-of-war, and play the swings during the Qingming Festival. To fly a kite on a fine spring day is always a favorite game for many people. While flying a kite, one usually sets the kite free when it is high in the air in the hope that the whole family's adversities would be gone with it.

The Qingming Festival is an occasion of unique characteristics, integrating sorrowful tears to the dead with the continuous laughters from the spring outings.

4. Dragon Boat Festival

The Dragon Boat Festival, the fifth day of the fifth lunar month, has had a history of more than 2,000 years. It is usually in June in the Gregorian calendar. Actually, in Chinese the character "Duan" means beginning and the fifth day of the fifth lunar month was called "Duan Wu".

There are many legends about the evolution of the festival, the most popular of which is in commemoration of Qu Yuan. Qu Yuan was minister of the State of Chu and one of China's earliest poets. He advocated enriching the country and strengthening its military forces, and supported the decision to fight against the powerful State of Qin together with the State of Qi. However, he was slandered by the aristocrat Zi Lan and was subsequently exiled by the King Huai. In his exiled days, he still cared much for his country and people and composed immortal poems including Li Sao (The Lament), Tian Wen (Heavenly Questions) and Jiu Ge (Nine Songs), which had far-reaching influences. Later he heard the news that Qin troops had finally conquered Chu's capital, so he finished his last masterpiece Huai Sha (Embracing Sand) and plunged himself into the Miluo River, clasping his arms to a large stone. The day happened to be the

Qu Yuan

fifth day of the fifth month in the Chinese lunar calendar. On hearing of Qu Yuan's death, all the local people nearby were in great distress. The fishermen sailed their boats up and down the river to look for his body. People threw Zongzi and eggs into the water to divert possible fish or shrimp from attacking his body. An old doctor poured a jug of reaglar wine into the water, hoping to turn all aquatic beasts drunk. Later, many people imitated these acts to show their respect for the great patriot and the practice continues.

Dragon boat racing is an indispensable part of the festival. As the gun is fired, people will see racers in dragon-shaped canoes pulling the oars harmoniously and hurriedly, accompanied

Dragon Boat Racing

by rapid drums, speeding toward their destination. Folk tales say that the game originates from the activities of seeking Qu Yuan's body. Now dragon boat racing has developed into an aquatic sports item which features both Chinese tradition and modern sporting spirit.

Zongzi

It is a tradition to eat Zongzi on the Dragon Boat Festival. Suzhou in Jiangsu province and Ningbo and Jiaxing in Zhejiang province are known for their Zongzi with date and sweet bean paste, ham, or bacon fillings. Beijing is famous for date and preserved fruit fillings. They are made in various shapes, three-or-four-cornered, or in the shape of a pillow, ox horn and pagoda. Now the custom of eating Zongzi is also popular in North and South Korea, Japan and Southeast Asian nations.

On the Dragon Boat Festival, hanging Chinese mugwort and calamus is another folk custom. Mugwort is a perennial herb for medicine use. Traditional Chinese Medicine uses it to dispel phlegm and relieve inflammation, and repel mosquitoes by burning the dried mugwort. Calamus is also a perennial herb growing by water, the stems and roots of which can be made into spices. Traditional Chinese medicine uses it to strengthen the stomach and cure toothache and bleeding gums. Since the Dragon-boat Festival is in the beginning of summer, when moist weather breeds noxious insects and illness, hanging these two kinds of plants can help dissipate pathogenic influence and virus.

Mugwort and Calamus

Also, adults of a family drink realgar wine as a prevention against vermin and children, who are unfit to drink wine, have some of the wine applied to their noses and ears for the same purpose. People also like to sprinkle the wine over their floors for sterilization on that day. Besides, parents need to dress their children up with a perfume pouch.

Perfume Pouches

They first sew little bags with colorful silk cloth, then fill the bags with perfumes or herbal medicines, and finally string them with silk threads. The perfume pouch will be hung around the neck or tied to the front of a garment as an ornament. All these practices were created to repel evil spirits, but after long period of development, they have attained the meaning of blessing or the aesthetic function.

5. Double Seventh Festival

The Double Seventh Festival, on the seventh day of the seventh lunar month, is a traditional festival full of romance. It often goes into August in the Gregorian calendar. This festival is in mid-summer when the weather is warm and the grass and trees reveal their luxurious greens. At night when the sky is dotted with stars, people can see the Milky Way spanning from the north to the south. On each bank of it is a bright star, which sees each other from afar. They are the Cowherd and Weaver Maid, and there is a beautiful love story about them passed down from generation to generation.

Long long ago, there was an honest and kind-hearted fellow named Cowhand (Niu Lang), and his parents died when he was a child. Later he was driven out of his home by his sister-in-law, so he lived by himself herding cattle and farming. One day, his cow helped him get acquainted with Weaver Maid (Zhi Nv)— a fairy from the heaven. Soon they fell in love with each other and got married. The cowhand farmed in the field and the Weaver Maid wove at home. They lived a happy life and gave birth to a boy and a girl. Unfortunately, good times didn't last long because the God of Heaven found out the fact and ordered the Queen Mother of the Western Heavens to bring the Weaver Maid back. With the help of celestial cattle, the Cowhand flew to heaven with his son and daughter. At the time when he was about to catch up with his wife, the Queen Mother took off one of her gold hairpins and made a

Cowhand and Weaver Maid Meeting on the Magpie Bridge

stroke. One billowy river appeared in front of the Cowhand. The Cowhand and Weaver Maid were separated on the two banks forever and could only shed their tears. Their loyalty to love touched magpies, so tens of thousands of magpies came to build a bridge for the Cowhand and Weaver Maid to meet each other. The Queen Mother was eventually moved and allowed them to meet each year on the seventh day of the seventh lunar month. Hence their meeting date has been called "Qi Xi" (Double Seventh).

While the customs of this festival vary according to the different regions, the same hope is cherished by all. The most prevalent custom is that girls pray to Weaver Maid for skillful hands for sewing. Because Weaver Maid is regarded as a beautiful woman deft at weaving, in the evening of the festival, girls sew some articles to compete with each other and prepare some delicious fruits to worship Weaver Maid in order to be endowed with the masterly sewing skill. Not only hoping for this skill, they also pray to have a sweet love. As it is a day of great importance to girls, the event is also called Young Girls' Festival.

Today some traditional customs are still observed in rural areas of China, but have been weakened or diluted in urban cities. In Chinese cities, the Western Valentine's Day is more favored than the Double Seventh Festival by young people. Although some traditional customs have been changed or been lost, the legend of Cowhand and Weaver Maid is still passed down from generation to generation, and has taken root in the hearts of the people.

6. Mid-Autumn Festival

The Mid-Autumn Festival falls on the fifteenth day of the eighth lunar month, usually in October in Gregorian calendar, and it is the second grandest festival after the Spring Festival in China. It takes its name from the fact that it is always celebrated in the middle of the autumn season when crops and fruits are all ripe and weather pleasant. The day is also known as the Moon Festival, as at that time of the year the moon looks extremely round, big and bright.

Many beautiful folklores and legends relate to the origins of the Mid-Autumn Festival, and the most famous one is the story of "Chang E's Flight to the Moon".

Chang E's Flight to the Moon

In remote antiquity, there were ten suns rising in the sky, which scorched all crops and made people's lives very difficult. It was the hero Hou Yi who, owing to his great strength, drew his extraordinary bow and shot down nine of the ten suns one after another. He also ordered the last sun to rise and set according to time. For this reason, he was respected and loved by the people and lots of young people came to learn martial arts from him. Peng Meng was among these people. Hou Yi had a beautiful and kind-hearted wife named Chang E. One day on his way to the Kunlun Mountain to call on friends, he ran upon the Queen Mother of the Western Heavens who was passing by. The Queen Mother of the Western Heavens presented him an elixir which, if drunk, would cause him to ascend immediately to heaven and become an immortal. Hou Yi, however, hated to part with his wife. So he took it home and gave the elixir to Chang E to treasure for the time being. Unfortunately, Peng Meng secretly saw Hou Yi giving the elixir to his wife and three days later, while Hou Yi was out hunting, Peng Meng rushed into the inner chamber and forced Chang E to hand over the elixir. Knowing that she could not win, she took out the elixir and swallowed it immediately. As soon as she swallowed the elixir, her body floated off the ground, flew out of the window and up into the sky. Chang E's great love for her husband drew her towards the moon, which is the nearest heavenly body to the earth. When Hou Yi returned home at dark, he knew from the maidservants what had happened. Hou Yi was so grief-stricken that he shouted Chang E's name to the sky. He was amazed to see a figure which looked just like his wife appeared in the moon. Thinking of his wife day and night, Hou Yi took the food liked by Chang E to an altar and offered it as a sacrifice for her. His countrymen did the same for the kind-hearted Chang E and prayed her for good fortune and peace. From then on, the tradition has been passed down from generation to generation.

The Mid-Autumn Festival has been regarded as an occasion for family reunion, because the full moon symbolizes the reunion. Sometimes even though family members may be far away from each other, they could still gaze at the full moon, with a full heart of warm wishes for each other under the glorious moonlight. Today, sacrifice has been replaced by a simple appreciation of the moon. Members of a family usually sit around a table eating and talking and at the same time admiring the bright moon.

Like other Chinese festivals, the Mid-Autumn Festival has its own special food. People eat moon cakes for celebration. The moon cake is a kind of cookie with various fillings and different artistic patterns on the surface depicting the legends of the festival. People treated this kind of food as one of the sacrificial offerings to the moon in the old days. Today, it has become an indispensable food while people are appreciating the bright moon. The common fillings of moon cakes are nuts, sugar, sesame, ham and egg yolk. Nowadays, people present the moon cakes to relatives and friends to demonstrate that they wish them a long and happy life.

7. Double Ninth Festival

The ninth day of the ninth lunar month is the traditional Chongyang Festival, or Double Ninth Festival. It usually falls in October in the Gregorian calendar. In an ancient and mysterious book *Yi Jing*, or *The Book of Changes*, number "6" was thought to be of "Yin" character, meaning feminine or negative, while number "9" was thought to be "Yang", meaning masculine or positive. The ninth day of the ninth month is the day that has two Yang numbers, and "chong" in Chinese means double, which is how the name Chongyang was created.

Just as other Chinese festivals have their own unique story, so does the Chongyang Festival. It is said that, during the Eastern Han Dynasty, a devil inhabited the Nu River, which caused disease in the neighboring people. The parent of a young man, named Hengjing, died because of the devil's magic. In order to rid the people of the devil, Hengjing went through extraordinary lengths to find an immortal to teach him swordsmanship in order to expel the devil. On the eighth day of the ninth lunar month, the immortal told Hengjing that the next day the devil would appear and he was to go back to get rid of the devil and the disease. Taking a bag of dogwood and some chrysanthemum wine, Hengjing returned to his hometown. In the morning of the ninth day of the ninth lunar month, Hengjing led all the villagers who were each holding a piece of dogwood leaf and a cup of Chrysanthemum wine to the nearest mountain. At noon, when the devil came out from the Nu River, the devil suddenly stopped because of the fragrance emitted from the dogwood and the chrysanthemum wine. At that moment Hengjing used the sword to battle the devil for a few rounds and won. Since then the customs of climbing mountains, drinking chrysanthemum wine and holding onto dogwood on the ninth day of the ninth month have become popular.

On the Double Ninth Festival, people come to have fun at mountain areas with a chrysanthemum-ornamented hat on the head and dogwood-inserted bags in hands. Dogwood can be used in medicine and was said to have the power of exorcising evil spirits. As a matter of fact, it has a strong aroma which can drive away insects, remove dampness and relieve chill and fever. That's why mountain climbers often carry a bundle of the plant. Now, family relatives or good friends gather to climb mountains to enjoy the beautiful scenery and share happiness of the holiday with each other.

Double Ninth Cake

On this day, people will eat the Double Ninth cake (Gao). The Double Ninth cake is alsoknown as "chrysanthemum cake" or "flower cake". It dates back to the Zhou Dynasty. It is said that the cake was originally prepared after autumn harvests for farmers to have a taste of what was just in season, and it gradually grew into the present cake for people to eat on the Double Ninth Day. The cake was usually made of glutinous rice flour, millet flour or bean flour. The Chinese word "Gao" (cake) is the homonym of the word "height", suggesting progress and prosperity, and people eat the Double Ninth cakes just to hope progress in everything they are engaged in. The cakes are given to friends and relatives as gifts and taken when people are climbing mountains.

The Double Ninth Festival is also a time when chrysanthemum blooms. Chrysanthemums are regarded as a kind of flower having the function of an antitoxin and can drive the evil away. Women used to stick such a flower into their hair or hang its branches on windows or doors to avoid evilness. China boasts diversified species of chrysanthemum and people have loved them since ancient times. So enjoying the flourishing chrysanthemum also becomes a key activity on this festival. Every year grand chrysanthemum exhibitions are held in big parks, which attract numerous visitors. Also, drinking Chrysanthemum wine is an indispensable part of the festival. People often think that, all kinds of diseases and disasters can be cured and prevented by drinking chrysanthemum wine.

Diversified Species of Chrysanthemum

In recent years, the festival has been connected with Chinese traditional virtue of respecting the elderly. Maybe the reason is the "Jiujiu" (the ninth day of the ninth lunar month) sounds similar to the word longevity in Chinese. In the year of 1989, Chongyang Festival was designated as Senior's Day, which not only contains the original meaning of the festival, but also expresses the common respect for the aged people and good wishes for longevity.

　　Almost every festival has its own unique origins and customs which reflect the traditional practices and morality of the whole Chinese nation and its people.

Notes

1. **a "Watch Night" service**: A watch night service is a late-night Christian church service. In many different Christian traditions, a watchnight service is held late on New Year's Eve, and ends after midnight. This provides the opportunity for Christians to review the year that has passed and make confession, and then prepare for the year ahead by praying and resolving. The services often include singing, praying, exhorting and preaching.

2. **All Saints' Day**: All Saints' Day (also known as All Hallows, Solemnity of All Saints, or The Feast of All Saints) is a solemnity celebrated on November 1st by parts of Western Christianity, and on the first Sunday after Pentecost in Eastern Christianity, in honor of all the saints, known and unknown. All Saints' Day is the second day of Hallowmas, and begins at sunrise on the 1st of November and finishes at sundown on the 1st of November.

3. **Founding Fathers**: The Founding Fathers of the United States of America were political leaders and statesmen who participated in the American Revolution by signing the United States Declaration of Independence, taking part in the American Revolutionary War, and establishing the United States Constitution.

Glossary

Epiphany [i'pifəni] *n.* 主显节

Gregorian ['gri'gɔːriən] *adj.* 罗马教皇的(Gregorian calendar 阳历，西历)

Hogmanay [ˌhɔgmə'nei] *n.* (苏格兰的)除夕

punch [pʌntʃ] *n.* 潘趣酒(一种用葡萄酒或烈性酒掺水、果汁、香料等调成的饮料,尤指热饮料)

wassail ['wɔseil] *n.* (主显节前夕和圣诞节前夕祝酒时用的)加香料的淡啤酒;加糖和香料的温热葡萄酒

mouldy ['məuldi] *adj.* 发了霉的；霉烂的

saltire ['sæltaiə] *n.* X形十字；圣安得列(St.Andrew)十字

diagonal [dai'æɡənl] *adj.* 斜的；对角线的

tartan ['tɑːtən] *n.* 格子花呢(服)；格子织物

weft [weft] *n.* (纺织用语)纬线,纬纱

warp [wɔːp] *n.* (纺织用语)经纱

piper ['paipə] *n.* 吹笛人；[苏]风笛手

bagpipes [ˈbæɡpaips] n. 风笛

pagan [ˈpeiɡən] n. 异教徒，非基督教徒

Lupercalia [ljuːpəˈkeiliə] n. (古罗马)牧神节

fondue [ˈfɔnduː] n. 溶化奶油，干酪

Lent [lent] n. (基督教的)四旬斋，大斋期(指复活节前的40天为纪念耶稣在荒野禁食)

simnel [ˈsimnəl] n. (为圣诞节或复活节做的)重油水果蛋糕

marzipan [ˌmɑːziˈpæn] n. 杏仁蛋白软糖

bedlam [ˈbedləm] n. 喧闹的景象

Pasadena n. 帕萨迪娜(美国一城市名,位于加州洛杉矶的东面)

buggy [ˈbʌgi] n. 轻便马车

ecclesiastical [iˌkliːziˈæstikl] adj. 基督教会的

fervor [ˈfɜːvə] n. 热烈，热情

spook [spuːk] n. 鬼

deliverance [diˈlivərəns] n. 解救；释放

tinsel [ˈtinsəl] n. (装饰圣诞树，舞蹈服装的)(金属)箔，金属丝(片)，闪亮的装饰

howling [ˈhauliŋ] n. 啸声，嗥鸣

ingot [ˈiŋɡət] n. (常为砖形的)铸块，锭

seep [siːp] vi. 渗出；漏出，(观念等)渗入

permeate [ˈpəːmieit] vt. 渗入，透过；弥漫

subdue [sʌbˈdjuː] vt. 使屈服，驯服，征服；镇压

insurrection [ˌinsəˈrekʃən] n. 起义，叛乱

wicker [ˈwikə] n. 枝条；柳条(编制品)

arbor [ˈɑːbɔː] n. 树木 (Arbor Day 植树节)

tug-of-war [ˈtʌɡˌəvˌwɔː] n. 拔河

adversity [ədˈvəːsiti] n. 逆境，不幸，苦难

slander [ˈslɑːndə] n. 诽谤，诋毁

lament [ləˈment] n. 悲伤，哀悼，恸哭；挽歌

mugwort [ˈmʌɡwəːt] n. 艾属植物,篓蒿属植物

calamus [ˈkæləməs] n. (pl. -mi[-mai])菖蒲

perennial [pəˈrenjəl] adj. 四季不断的；长期的，持久不断的；多年生的

phlegm [flem] n. 痰

inflammation [ˌinfləˈmeiʃən] n. 着火；点燃；发光；起爆；愤怒；红肿，炎症

noxious [ˈnɔkʃəs] adj. 有害[毒]的，不卫生的

pathogenic [ˌpæθəˈdʒenik] adj. 引起疾病的

vermin [ˈvəːmin] n. 害虫；寄生虫；害兽，害鸟

sterilization [sterilaiˈzeiʃən] n. 消毒，灭菌

pouch [pautʃ] n. 小袋，小包，囊

garment [ˈɡɑːmənt] n. [pl.] 服装，衣服

celestial [siˈlestjəl] adj. 天上的；神圣的

billowy [ˈbiləui] *adj.* 巨浪似的，汹涌的

diluted [daiˈljuːtid] *adj.* 无力的；冲淡的

elixir [iˈliksə] *n.* 精药酒；万灵药，长生不老药

dogwood [ˈdɔgwud] *n.* 木属植物，山茱萸

chrysanthemum [kriˈsænθəməm] *n.* 菊(花)

exorcise [ˈeksɔːsaiz] *vt.* (用祈祷等)驱除(恶魔)

Further Reading

1) **Holidays and Festivals in Canada**

http://en.wikipedia.org/wiki/Public_holidays_in_Canada

http://www.ehow.com/list_6300480_holidays-festivals-canada.html

2) **Holidays and Festivals in Australia**

http://en.wikipedia.org/wiki/Public_holidays_in_Australia

3) **Holidays and Festivals in New Zealand**

http://en.wikipedia.org/wiki/Public_holidays_in_New_Zealand

Group Tasks

Your textbook relates some of the holiday and festival traditions of the U.K., China and the U.S.. Many of the traditions from all the three countries have ancient roots. Considerable details for the origin of the Chinese holiday rituals are given and you may like to research the deeper roots of the U.S. and U.K. festival traditions and some new ones, like the Notting Hill Carnival in London and the pan American tradition of the May Day Parade. Can you locate new festival traditions arising in China as the country changes rapidly?

Let us pause here to reflect more deeply on the meaning and nature of "holiday and festival". What purpose do they serve and are people right to regret the loss of traditions, and to resist the establishment of new ones, as appears to be the case in every country. Why is this? Think back to the earlier chapter on customs and courtesies, where we noted the phenomenon of ex-patriot communities and how national Diasporas may tend to retain and even elevate the status of traditions within their communities.

Take some time to speak with friends and family, as conduct your own informal research into attitudes to traditional holiday and festival forms. What is the consensus view about their value, why they should or should not be preserved and what they mean to everyday life.

With this background of enquiry, arrange to meet up with colleagues and consider either a formal discussion of the issues, or perhaps hold a formal debate with a proposal along the lines of, "this house believes that ancient customs and traditions must be allowed to disappear in their time without undue effort to preserve them as anachronistic reminders of a past that is no longer relevant." Ensure that you have speakers to support and oppose the statement. Hold a post debate discussion to clarify what you have learned as a group by questioning the concept of tradition and festival and what you each, as individuals, think of the relative importance of having a concept of "fluid and progressive identity" and "a firm respect for the traditions of the ancestors." Consider whether you are content with how your perspective actually affects your life.

References

1. 常耀信. 美国文学简史. 天津：南开大学出版社，2003.
2. 陈宏俊，张菅，李险峰. 英美文化体验. 北京：中国人民大学出版社，2008.
3. 大耳朵工作室. 新概念英语西方文化拾贝. 北京：中国水利水电出版社，2010.
4. 杜学增. 中英文化习俗比较. 北京：外语教学与研究出版社，1999.
5. 冯友兰. 中国哲学简史. 北京：北京大学出版社，2012.
6. 耿卫忠. 西方传统节日与文化. 太原：书海出版社，2006.
7. 顾卫星，叶建敏. 中国特色文化英语教程. 北京：高等教育出版社，2017.
8. 郭群英. 英国文学新编（上/下）. 北京：外语教学与研究出版社，2001.
9. 郝澎. 英美民间故事与民俗. 海口：南海出版公司，2004.
10. 胡荫桐. 美国文学新编. 北京：外语教学与研究出版社，2001.
11. 姜毓锋. 英美文化教程（下）. 北京：科学出版社，2009.
12. 焦英，钱清. 英美文化与习俗. 北京：北京大学出版社，2009.
13. 蒯大申，祁红著，彭颖译. 中国人的民俗世界. 合肥：安徽文艺出版社，2009.
14. 来安方. 英美概况. 郑州：河南人民出版社，2004.
15. 靳海林. 中国传统节日及传说. 重庆：重庆出版社，2001.
16. 李常磊. 英美文化博览. 上海：上海世界图书出版公司，2000.
17. 李颖. 中国文化英语听说教程. 上海：上海外语教育出版社，2018.
18. 刘炳善. 英国文学简史. 郑州：河南人民出版社，1993.
19. 刘泓，浩瀚. 风俗民情. 北京：科学技术文献出版社，2008.
20. 刘正. 英美文学实用教程. 北京：国防工业出版社，2007.
21. 龙毛忠，贾爱兵，颜静兰. 中国文化概览. 上海：华东理工大学出版社，2009.
22. 美国国务院国际信息局编，杨俊峰等译. 美国政府概况. 沈阳：辽宁教育出版社，2003.
23. 束定芳. 中国文化英语教程. 上海：上海外语教育出版社，2016.
24. 吴斐. 英国社会与文化. 武汉：武汉大学出版社，2003.
25. 谢福之. 英语国家概况. 北京：外语教学与研究出版社，2007.
26. 薛荣. 中国文化教程. 南京：南京大学出版社，2011.
27. 阎照祥. 英国政治制度史. 北京：人民出版社，1999.
28. 杨英杰. 中外民俗. 天津：南开大学出版社，2006.
29. 叶朗等著，章思英等译，张桂萍编. 中国文化英语教程. 北京：外语教学与研究出版社，2010.
30. 叶胜年. 中西文化比较教程. 上海：上海外语教育出版社，2010.

31. 余志远. 英语国家概况. 北京：外语教学与研究出版社，2000.

32. 云龙著，方云译绘. 漫画西方礼仪. 南昌：百花洲文艺出版社，2010.

33. 王惠. 中国社会与文化翻译教程. 北京：清华大学出版社，2016.

34. 王奇民. 英美社会与文化. 北京：科学出版社，2007.

35. 王焱等. 中西文化比较. 北京：清华大学出版社，2017.

36. 王佐良等. 欧洲文化入门. 北京：外语教学与研究出版社，1992.

37. 张亮平，李鹏. 英美文化精粹. 武汉：华中科技大学出版社，2010.

38. 张奎武. 英美概况（上/下）. 长春：吉林科学技术出版社，2008.

39. 周宝娣. 主要英语国家概况. 重庆：重庆大学出版社，2004.

40. 周叔麟等. 新编英美概况教程. 北京：北京大学出版社，2004.

41. 祝吉芳. 冲突、碰撞与趋同下的中西文化. 北京：外语教学与研究出版社，2016.

42. 朱永涛. 英美文化基础教程. 北京：外语教学与研究出版社，1991.

43. 朱永涛. 英语国家社会与文化入门（上/下）. 北京：高等教育出版社，1997.

44. Boyle, M 著，鄄玲玲译. 英国原来是这样 2：英国传统与习俗 50 主题. 北京：外文出版社，2010.

45. Rogers, P 著，徐欣吾改编. 西方文明史：问题与源头. 大连东北财经大学出版社，2009.

46. http://en.wikipedia.org/wiki/American_Cuisine

47. http://en.wikipedia.org/wiki/American_Government

48. https://en.wikipedia.org/wiki/British_philosophy

49. https://en.wikipedia.org/wiki/American_philosophy

50. http://en.wikipedia.org/wiki/British_cuisine

51. http://en.wikipedia.org/wiki/Chinese_art

52. http://en.wikipedia.org/wiki/Chinese_cuisine

53. http://en.wikipedia.org/wiki/Chinese_education

54. http://en.wikipedia.org/wiki/Chinese_Literature

55. http://en.wikipedia.org/wiki/Education_in_america

56. http://en.wikipedia.org/wiki/Education_in_Britain

57. http://en.wikipedia.org/wiki/English_art

58. http://en.wikipedia.org/wiki/English_literature

59. 国家地理信息公共服务平台. 标准地图服务：中国地图 1：3000 万［EB/OL］. http://bzdt.ch.mnr.gov.cn/jsp/browseMap.jsp？picId=%224o28b0625501ad13015501ad2bfc0123%22

60. http://en.wikipedia.org/wiki/Funeral_customs#Funerals_in_contemporary_North_America_and_Europe

61. http://en.wikipedia.org/wiki/Government_of_China

62. http://en.wikipedia.org/wiki/Government_of_U.K.

63. http://en.wikipedia.org/wiki/History_of_China

64. http://en.wikipedia.org/wiki/History_of_the_United_Kingdom

65. http://en.wikipedia.org/wiki/History_of_the_United_States

66. http://en.wikipedia.org/wiki/Literature_of_the_United_States

67. http://en.wikipedia.org/wiki/Society_of_the_United_States#Clothing

68. http://en.wikipedia.org/wiki/Visual_art_of_the_United_States

69. http://en.wikipedia.org/wiki/Wedding

70. https://www.iep.utm.edu/american/

71. https://www.thefamouspeople.com/briton-philosophers.php

72. http://oregonstate.edu/instruct/ed416/ae1.html

73. http://projectbritain.com/

74. http://resources.woodlands-junior.kent.sch.uk/customs/food.html

75. http://wwp.moms-day.com/

76. http://www.answers.com/topic/graveyard-poets

77. http://www.cctv.com/english/special/classicandimmortal/homepage/index.shtml

78. http://www.chinatraveldesigner.com/travel-wiki.aspx? id=801

79. http://www.churchofengland.org/weddings-baptisms-funerals/funerals/after-the-serv-ice.aspx

80. http://www.easytourchina.com/

81. http://www.timeanddate.com/holidays/

82. http://www.topchinatravel.com/china-guide/chinese-cuisine/

83. http://www.topchinatravel.com/chinese-history/people-republic-of-china/

84. http://www.travelchinaguide.com/

85. http://www.us-history.com/

86. http://zhidao.baidu.com/question/389162355.html

图书在版编目(CIP)数据

中西文化概况／孔文,颜榴红主编. —修订本.—
南京:南京大学出版社,2019.6(2021.8重印)
ISBN 978-7-305-21690-9

Ⅰ.①中… Ⅱ.①孔… ②颜… Ⅲ.①比较文化—中
国、西方国家—高等学校—教材 Ⅳ.①G04

中国版本图书馆 CIP 数据核字(2019)第 042081 号

出 版 者　南京大学出版社
社　　址　南京市汉口路 22 号　　邮　编　210093
出 版 人　金鑫荣

书　　名　**中西文化概况(修订版)**
主　　编　孔　文　颜榴红
责任编辑　董　颖　　　　编辑热线　025-83596997
照　　排　南京紫藤制版印务中心
印　　刷　南京玉河印刷厂
开　　本　787×1092　1/16　印张 16.25　字数 395 千
版　　次　2019 年 6 月第 1 版　2021 年 8 月第 3 次印刷
ISBN　978-7-305-21690-9
定　　价　50.00 元

网址:http://www.njupco.com
官方微博:http://weibo.com/njupco
官方微信号:njupress
销售咨询热线:(025)83594756